Clare Reilly

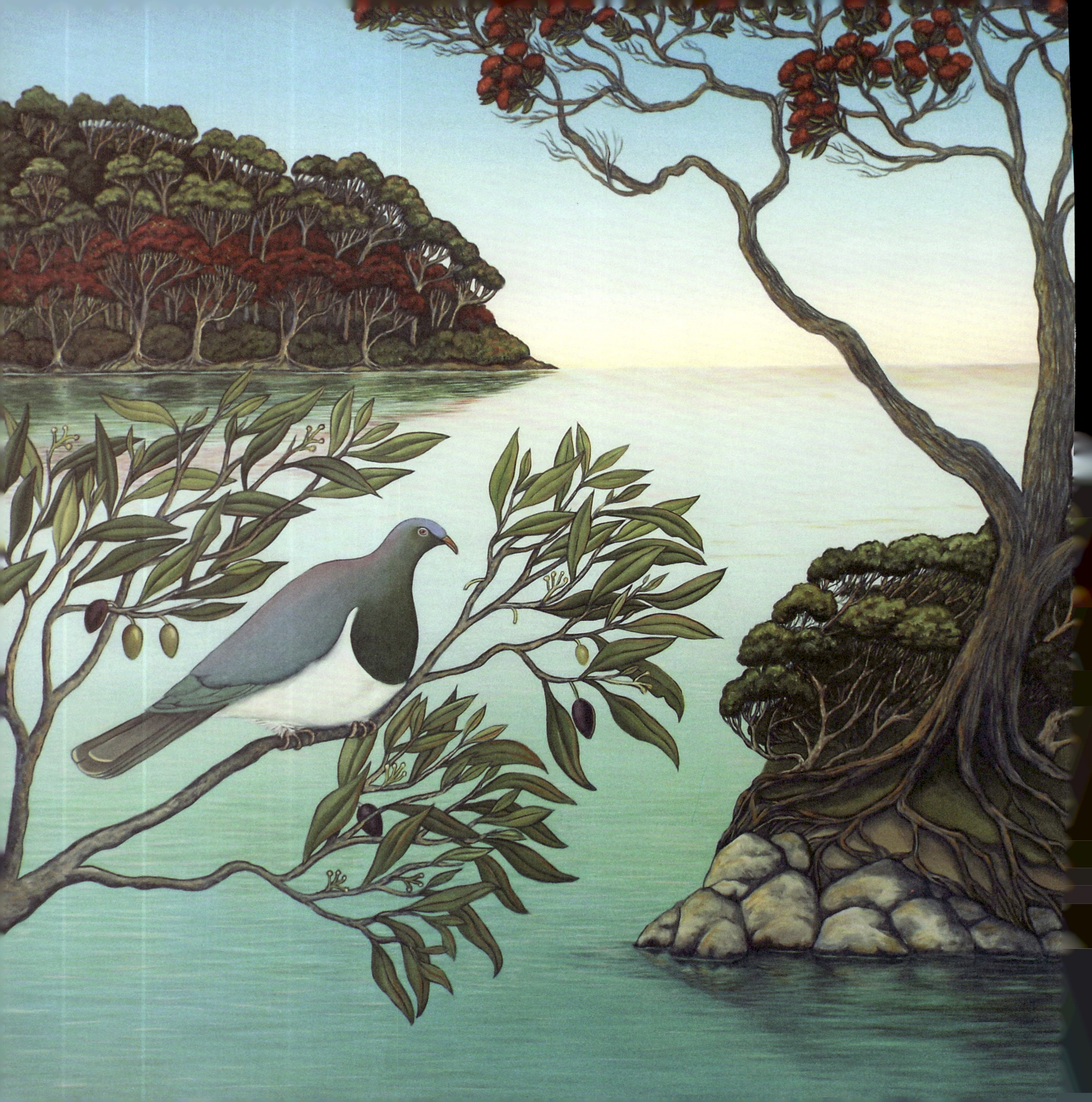

eye of the calm

Clare Reilly

First published 2021

Exisle Publishing Pty Ltd
226 High Street, Dunedin, 9016, New Zealand
PO Box 864, Chatswood, NSW 2057, Australia
www.exislepublishing.com

A CiP record for this book is available from the National Library of New Zealand.

ISBN 978-1-77559-429-1
ISBN 978-1-77559-430-7 (leatherbound edition)

Designed by Mark Thacker
Typset in Warnock Pro Light 10 on 17.25pt
Printed in China

This book uses paper sourced under ISO 14001 guidelines from well-managed forests and other controlled sources.

10 9 8 7 6 5 4 3 2 1

Previous page

Coastal Dreaming 2018
1000 x 1000 mm/39¼ x 39¼ in
Oil on board

Dedication

For my sons, Marcel and Kazimir, you have been the treasures of my life.

To my parents, Ian and Elizabeth Reilly, for providing me with an enriching childhood, and a loving home filled with music, art, literature, science.

To Max Podstolski, huge gratitude for sharing a life filled with love, passion and creativity with me, right until the end.

To Max's sisters, Jeannie Beauchamp and Julie Podstolski, for your creativity, ideas and continued support.

To Ran Turner, for showing me that our lives can continue to expand through love, by being open to new possibilities.

CONTENTS

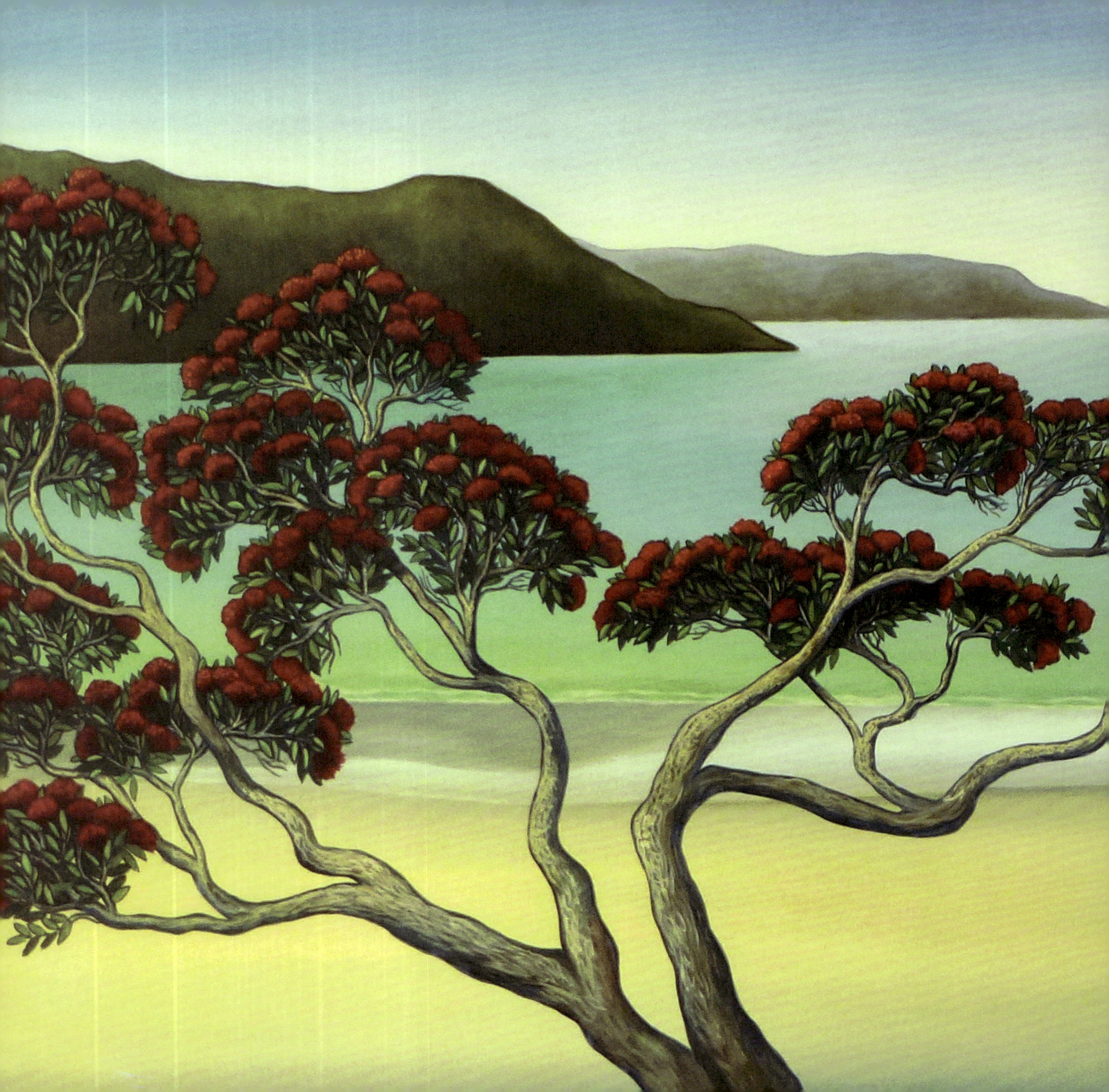

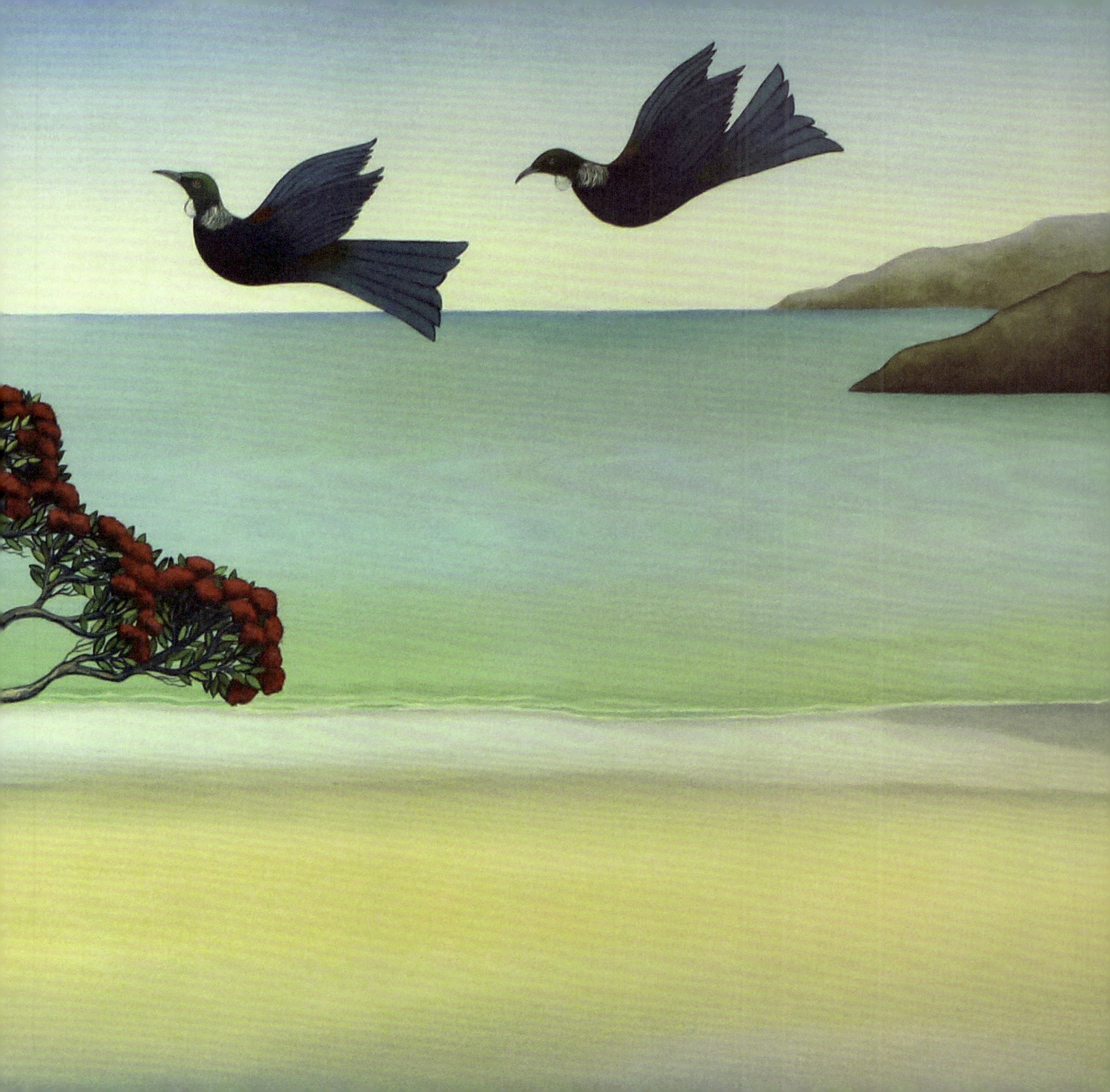

Elements of Inspiration

Previous page

Pōhutukawa Coast 2014
700 x 1220 mm/27½ x 48 in
Oil on board

Opposite

We Travel This Path 2016
1000 x 1000 mm/
39¼ x 39¼ in
Oil on board

It was a smooth grey wall, and in the middle, sat an old leaking garden tap. Over time, the water had created a bright rusty orange stain, while under the tap was a tiny colony of spongy iridescent-green moss.

As the morning sunlight slid across rooftops, there was a point where a shaft of light blazed across the wall, intensifying the colours. It was into this small patch of sunlight in a tiny courtyard that I was parked in my pram while my mother attended to morning chores, and for some odd reason this stain of rusty orange under the tap formed my earliest memory.

I feel I was drawn to art by a fascination for colour and pattern, permanently imprinted on me at such an early age.

I spent the first two years of my life in Tītahi Bay, north of Wellington. My parents rented a cramped one-bedroom flat attached to the back of the local store on a corner of the main street. Diagonally across from the store was the beach and this became our playground. As soon as I could crawl, I kept making a beeline for the waves, giving my parents no rest.

The visual pull of water has been a key element of my painting life.

A long wet week and the local grocer delivers a carton of groceries to our new house, high on the Paremata hills. At the top of the carton is a new box of crayons. The fire is going and I'm four years old, sitting in my favourite spot on the hearth, tracing a line with my finger on the creamy mortar between the bricks. I've traced this line many times before and it holds magical qualities for me. I choose a brown crayon from the new box and draw in my magic line, pleased to be revealing it to the world.

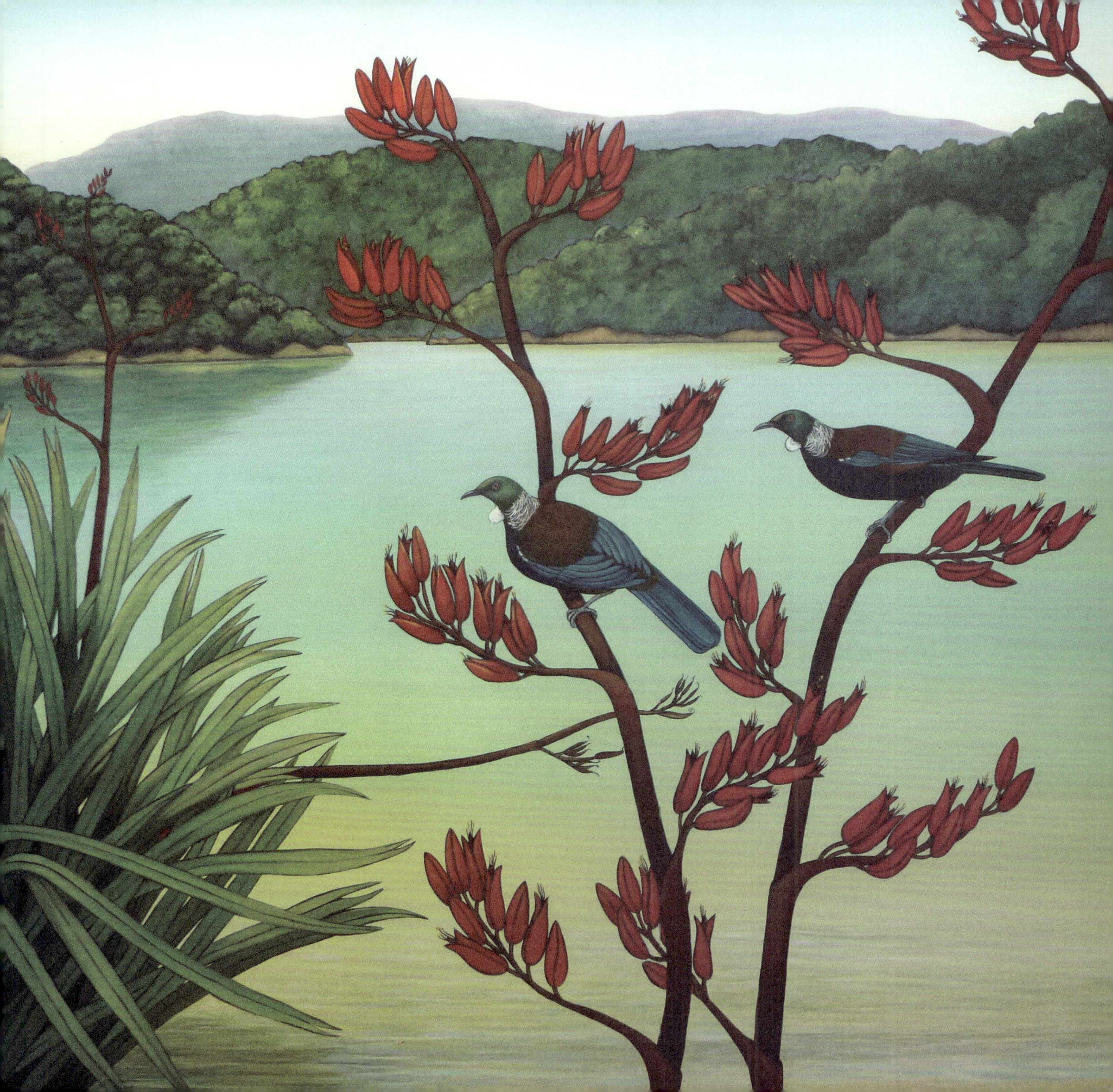

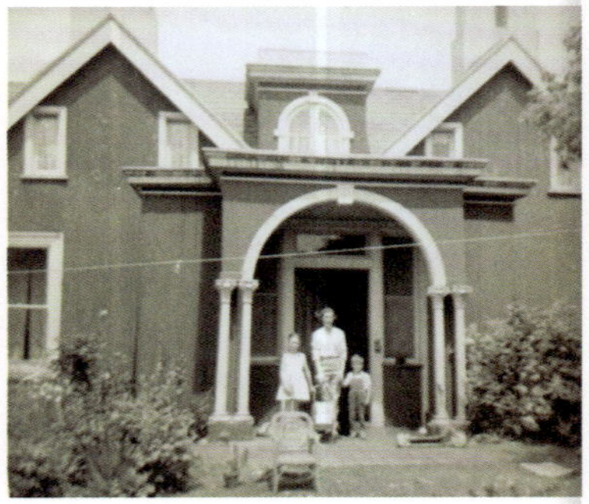
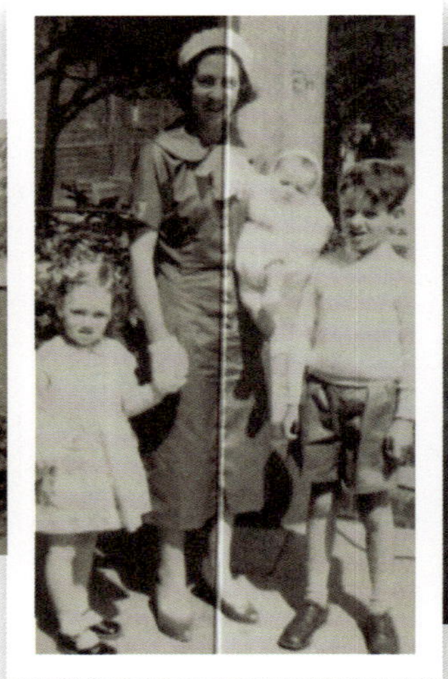
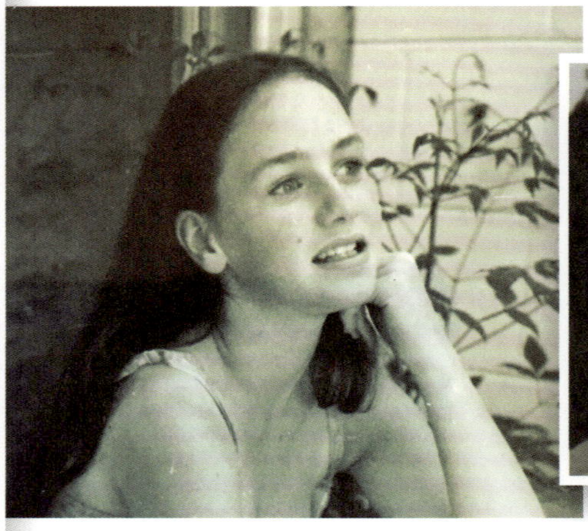
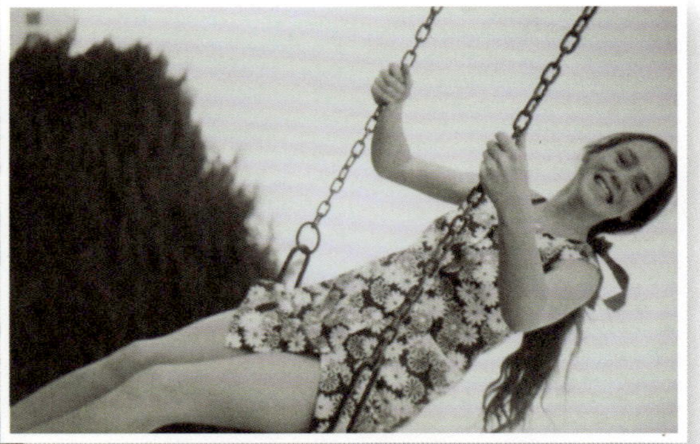

From left: Bellevue Street, Dunedin, 1962; Family group, Wellington, 1960; Clare, 1968; Clare, soaring high, 1969

My mother returns to the living room and sees what I have done. Angrily, she picks up the box of beautiful glistening crayons and hurls them into the fire, where they sizzle into a globby mess.

I'm horrified on two counts! Not because I'm also smacked for doing such a thing, but because I'm confused that she can't see the beauty I see in my line, and the potential of using the crayons has just been lost to me. Scrubbing as hard as she could, the line remained on the mortar, an indelible mark.

The artistic spirit, however, continued to burn within me.

My daily journey to school involved a long walk down a steep hill. From the top, there were expansive views of the surrounding terrain, rolling hills, open farmland, and looking down on the twin harbour inlets of Porirua and Pāuatahanui. In the distance, I could see Mana and Kapiti Islands, and on a clear day the alluring smudge of the South Island.

This landscape, shifting and falling away, or rising up during the descent and ascent of the hill, came to be of endless fascination to me, as the perspectives changed constantly.

Overlooking hills and sea continues in most of my work, even after so many years.

The knoll of the hill where my childhood home was built had great views in every direction, but it was also exposed to all the winds, which blew fiercely at times. I loved the strong warm northerly winds that came up over the cliffs, where seagulls would wheel and ride the air above me.

Birds in flight!

I wanted to be one of them, attempting many times to run into the headwind and lift off. Disappointed by my lack of success, I would resort

Dream 1976
780 x 690 mm/31 x 27 in
Acrylic on board

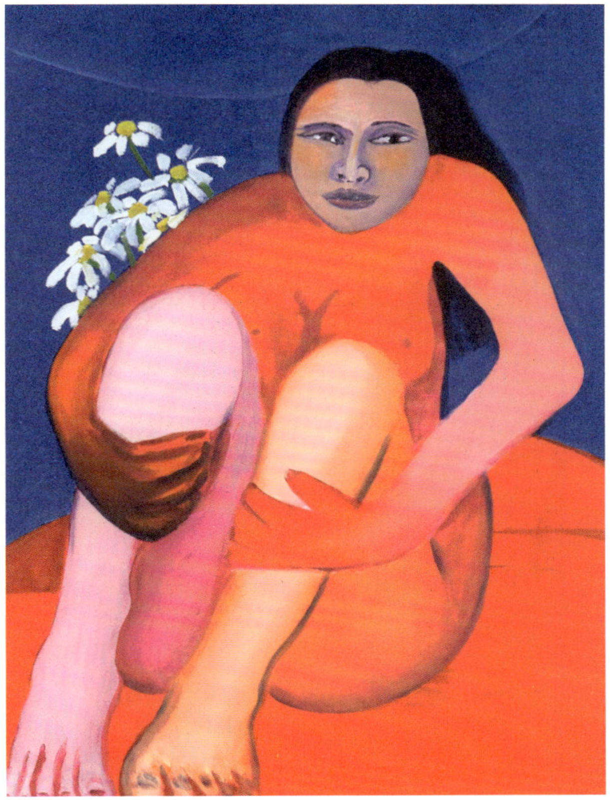

to endless hours of swinging high on my garden swing, dreaming I was a bird soaring.

As a family, we would travel every summer holiday by the overnight ferry from Wellington to Christchurch, then by train to Dunedin, to stay at my grandmother's beautiful old two-storey house in Belleknowes. It was surrounded by a lush garden and many old trees.

My first encounters with tūī, bellbirds and kereru happened here — all seemed exotic to me, and I loved their birdsong.

The lush damp of the Dunedin summer months spent exploring the surrounding suburbs, and into the city below, with the soft moody skies above, heavy with cloud, suited me and my fair skin.

The journey back home, seven weeks later, to the dry sunburnt hills of Paremata, bright harsh sunlight, stunted windswept trees and the screech of seagulls, always made my heart sink. I longed to be back south where I felt more at home.

It was to be six decades before I finally made that permanent move and achieved a sense of spiritual homecoming.

Almost as soon as I could walk, I started dancing. My father had a passion for classical music, and it was played every evening in our home. I danced freely and avidly, for as long as I could sustain the energy, before bedtime. By five, I was sent to ballet lessons, which continued until I reached a point of committing to a career or finishing. I chose to move on to modern dance in my senior years at high school and at university. Many decades later, I returned to a different form of movement called Nia. I loved to feel the sense of rhythm and movement once again be part of my expression of self and spirit.

I see the quality of dance and movement in my paintings. Within the calmness there also needs to be a dynamic of movement that dances the eye around the painting, compositionally, in the form of trees twisting or birds in flight.

Turning point: Wellington, October 1975

Everton Terrace rose steeply ahead, narrowing and winding upwards. A deep rumble announced the approach of passing cable cars, and moments later one clattered onto the overhead bridge, with a particular sound of steel cable grinding over cogs.

That sound had been an accompaniment to my early painting endeavours over the previous 18 months. I had missed it during my prior three months of travelling in Europe.

Rounding the bend, I could now see the roofline of the studio, a semi-derelict house that perched on a narrow ledge, right next to the mouth of the cable car tunnel. It was nearly smothered in wilding sycamore trees, a dank 'Rousseau's Jungle' of growth that tinged the interior light green.

We paid no rent for this space that I shared with two friends, Peter and Pru. We had found the abandoned house 18 months earlier and discovered it belonged to Victoria University. We boldly asked for permission to use it as a studio. Its location was ideal for us, three students, all studying various degrees full-time, who had an urge to also be creative in the downtime between lectures and at night.

We were informed that the house would be demolished sometime in the near future; however, we were granted permission to use it, providing no one lived there. It had no electricity, was dilapidated and filthy, but we felt like we had struck gold. It became a meeting place for other young artists. Peter, the sculptor, promptly moved in, not minding the squalor and the rats too much.

As I got closer to the studio, my heart sank, then an eddy of irritation arose within me.

'Not this idiot!' instantly came to my mind.

I had glimpsed the lean, tall figure of a young man sitting on the front doorstep, his wispy long fair hair bright within the shadows of the building.

Annoyed, I decided not to enter my studio as intended. Several days before I had encountered this person, Max, and his Scottish friend, Pete, in my

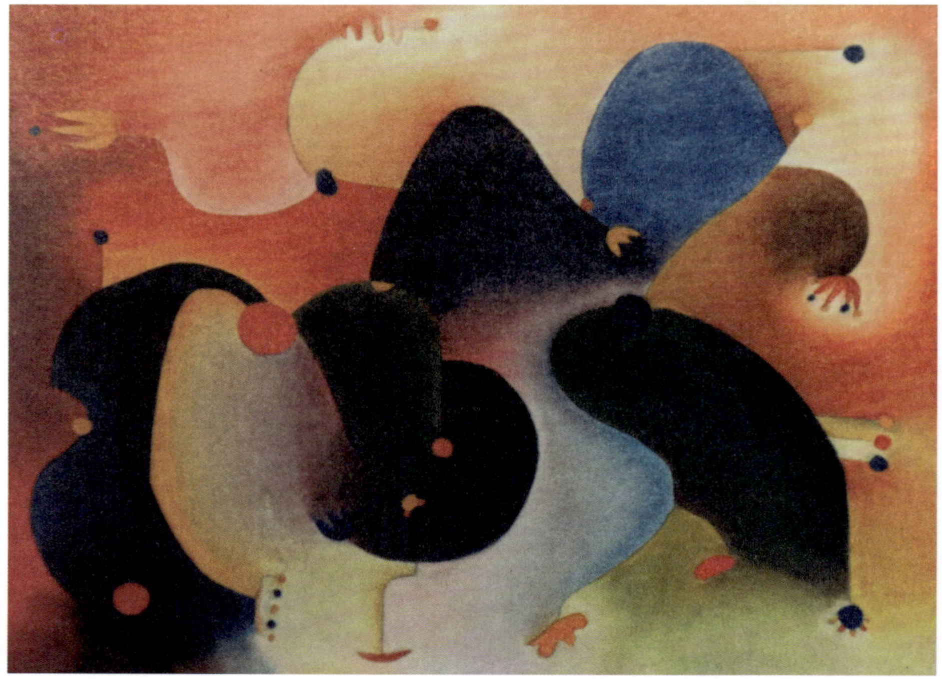

The Dance 1977
500 x 600 mm/19½ x 23½ in
Oil on canvas

studio space on my first return visit there after my trip away. They had been inside the house, strangers and, not having met me before, had teased me when I arrived. Indignant, I had left after a few minutes, in no mood for their playful banter.

The man on the step called out to me, 'Do you have a key for the front door?'

Of course I did, but I said I wasn't stopping, I was heading on up the hill.

He sprang up and started walking beside me, asking if he could come too.

I shrugged, trying to ignore his presence, and determined to walk fast and leave him behind. I didn't want to engage in conversation or even look at him. Out of my peripheral vision I could see he was easily striding, while I was soon out of breath. This strategy wasn't working!

At the crest of the hill we descended into the Botanic Gardens. It was a warm spring afternoon, we found an old log to sit on and, with increasing ease, began to talk about art and life.

I discovered that he, too, was a self-taught painter.

The afternoon slipped into dusk, then night. I felt lost in time, until we realised how late it had become and we retraced our steps to my studio.

Peter was at work in his room on a sculpture as we entered the dim candlelit main room, and I sat down at a table opposite Max and looked at him properly for the first time.

Rousseau's Jungle

Waking up alone,
mid-nowhere,
remember the night with you;
how every one away
isn't the same.

Rousseau's Jungle:
us plonked in morning light
filtered through fronds
of hanging exotic specimens and
greenish phosphorescent windows.

I want to lie in Rousseau's Jungle
forever with you.

A poem for Clare. Max Podstolski, 1975

Max at Everton Terrace studio, 1975

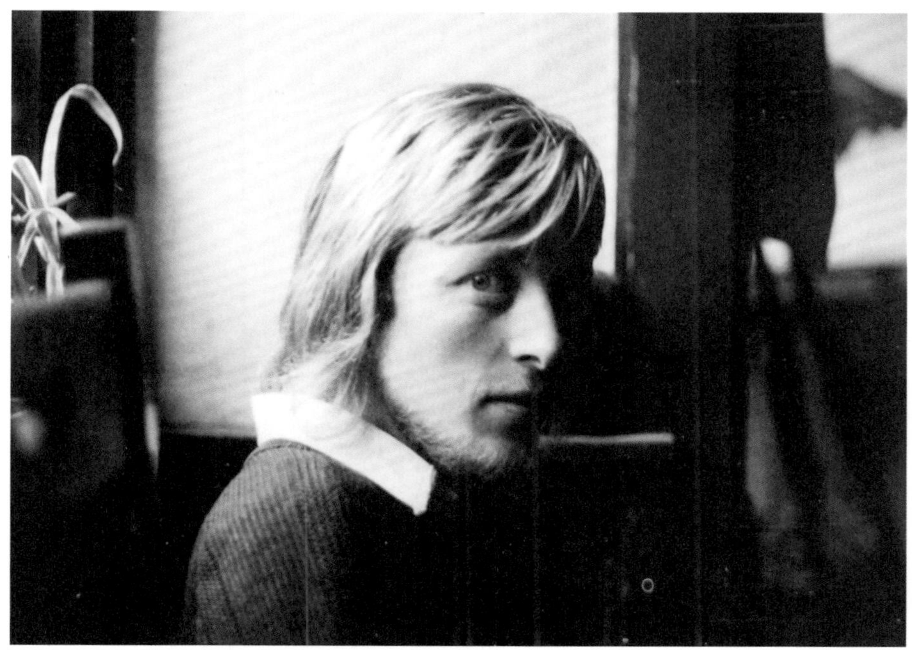

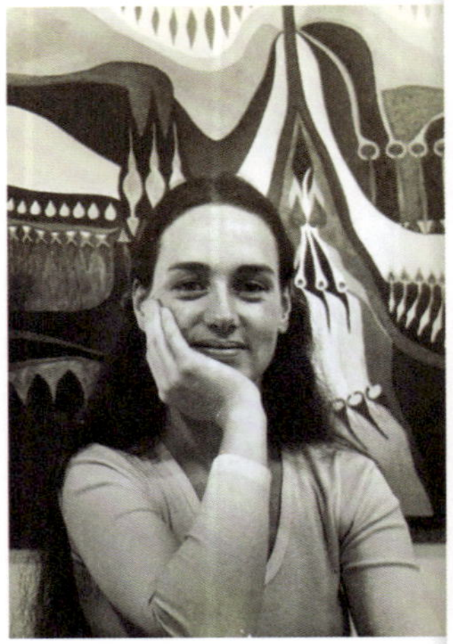

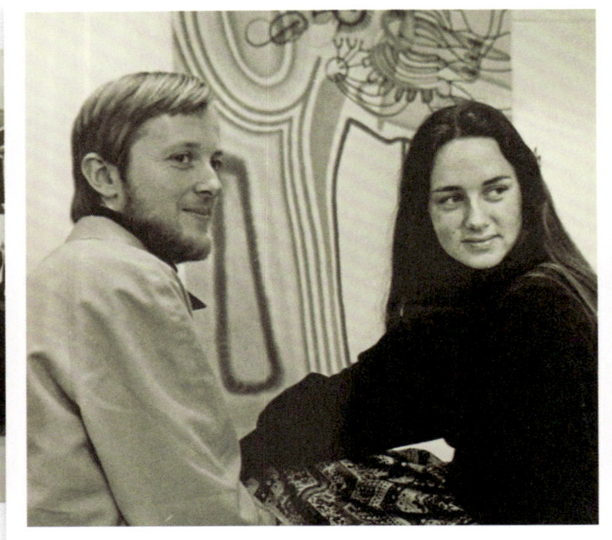

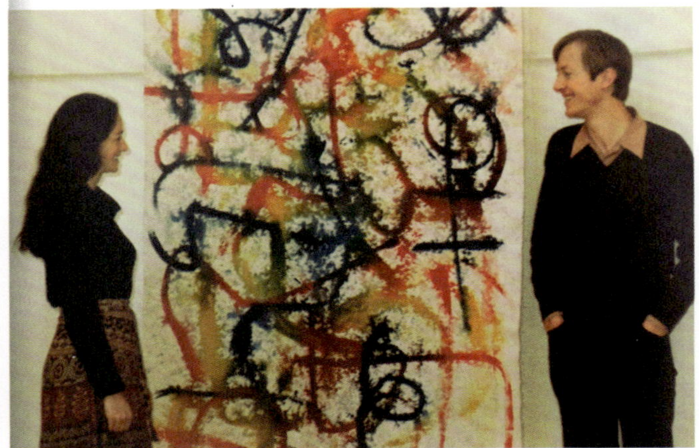

From left: Clare at C.S.A. Gallery Christchurch, 1980, *The Press*: Max and Clare C.S.A. Gallery, 1979: Clare and Max, C.S.A. Gallery, 1981

He had an intense gaze in his blue eyes, but also something deeper.

I was overtaken by a bolt of sensation that this was the man I was going to spend the rest of my life with!

I had no idea why I should have this thought. I had no young girl's romantic fantasies of marriage and children, so this bolt of recognition came as a complete shock to me. However, in all our years together, I never doubted or regretted this intuition.

In a matter of those few previous hours, the axis of my life tilted and shifted, casting me into an entirely new and unpredictable direction. Max Podstolski was to become my partner, my muse and the love of my life.

I was raised by a feminist father to be an independent young woman. I had been studying law and arts, following my parents' wise advice to get a good degree behind me. My father had suggested I could always paint later in my spare time. I used the studio space to continue my need for painting, in amongst my studies.

I had planned to travel more and blaze a career path into the male-dominated world of work.

I had used most of my teenage pocket money to buy beautiful art books on the work of many of my favourite artists: Chagall, Henri Rousseau, Picasso, Max Ernst, Klee, Miro, Francis Bacon, Monet, Gauguin and many others.

Growing up in Wellington, I was particularly inspired by the New Zealand artists Rita Angus, Michael Smither, Colin McCahon and Robin White.

After my trip, to visit major European art galleries, my head was filled with the images of many works of my favourite painters, and I felt inspired and daunted by what I had seen.

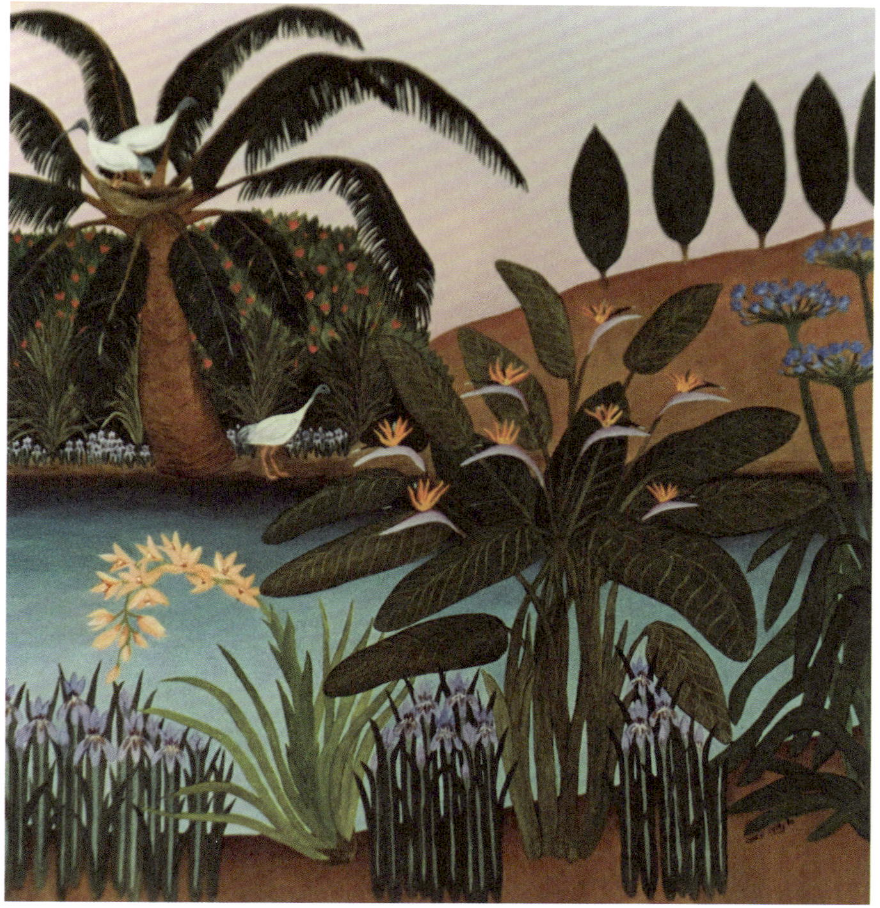

Ibises and Irises 1986
800 x 760 mm/31½ x 30 in
Oil on board

'There is an utter, utter joy and pleasure working with paint that fulfils me tremendously. I feel like I'm flying.'

Max encouraged me to be the painter I had longed to be. He asked me what I was waiting for and stated that I *should* be painting now! It was too tempting not to listen.

He had been painting, writing and playing guitar for a number of years, not quite sure which of these directions to follow, but the need to paint was strong in both of us.

Here began an intense dive into a passionate, sometimes volatile, existence of love and painting that was to sustain us over the next four decades.

Three weeks after we met, Max asked me if I would move with him to the South Island, where we might find a little place in the country, to start a simple existence and our true painting lives together.

I immediately said yes, having no idea how I would broach the subject with my parents. I delayed telling them until closer to our planned departure in March 1976. I left my studies and part-time work and set off with Max onto the precarious path of becoming an artist.

By now, I had a clear understanding that I needed to take this bold move forward for myself.

During my overseas absence, my friends had organised a group show at Wellington's Antipodes Gallery for February 1976. *Seven Young Wellington Artists* included my friends Peter and Pru and Max and me. We were a lively, diverse bunch of self-taught young artists, eager to take the first step on

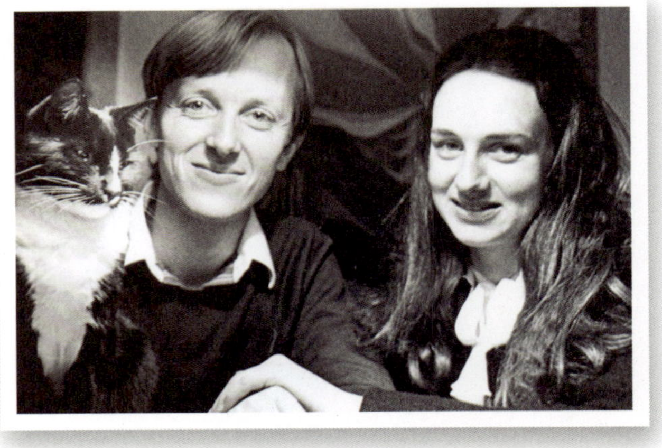

Max and Clare, Christchurch, *The Press*, Article 1982

our artistic ladders and go public. The opening was packed with friends, family and supporters, and it was a heady moment of excitement that we were having our first exhibition.

For the show, I had a collection of landscapes and portraits, and one large triptych that caused a bit of a stir. It was titled *The Artist and her Muse*. In the left-hand panel was a young woman, dressed in a painting smock, brushes clutched in her hand. She was sitting gazing quietly out at the viewer. Across the middle and right-hand panel was a reclining male nude, very recognisably Max.

I had wanted to make a feminist statement that women should be taken seriously as artists, and the male model in this case was the object of my observation and desire, and not the usual other way round.

My mother was horrified. She wanted me to explain the meaning of the painting to one of her closest friends, but I had also not told her much about Max, so her reaction was understandable.

Throughout her life, she (and my father) became extremely supportive of my work and gradually came to accept Max, although when I first revealed to her that I was moving to the South Island with him, she exclaimed that 'I would catch all sorts of diseases from such a man!'

Such was the reputation of artists in her mind. A seedy lot, indeed, entirely unsuitable for her only daughter.

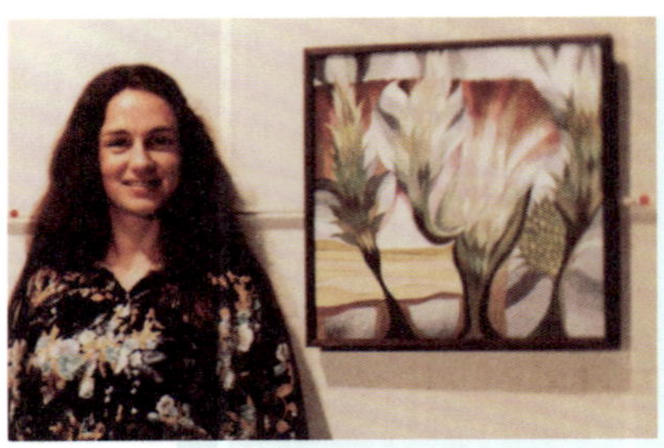

'Ms Reilly is clearly developing a unique style and evolving her own visual language. *Rusty Roofs with Whispering Trees*, for example, is a small painting blooming with glowing colours and subtle rhythm. The satisfying natural character of her imagery, the curving lines and pod-like accents that occur in all her works give strong unity to the exhibition but never appear to result from a formula. Each painting has its own logic and Ms Reilly's sense of colour is well developed enough for her to give each panel its individual set of hues.'

— Summer Colour at the CSA by John Coley, The Press, Christchurch, 22 August 1981

We went south soon after the exhibition, and standing on the rear deck of the ferry to Lyttelton I realised I was leaving behind all known safety and family support.

With our meagre possessions in two packs, totally naive, we believed we could find a small house to buy somewhere in the countryside. We had about $700 of savings between us and had heard that someone's friend had bought a rundown cottage in remote Central Otago for a similar sum. We headed to Dunedin to begin our search, but to our increasing despair, were unable to find such an elusive dwelling, although we really didn't have a clue how to find one.

Hitchhiking and bussing right round the South Island, we finally and despondently ended up in Christchurch, found a one-bedroom flat in an old house in Avonside and settled into the grand task of becoming 'real' painters, living and sleeping in one room and using the other as a studio.

One drizzly afternoon in August 1976, as Max went to open the front door, I stopped him, dashed away to get a pair of nail scissors and proceeded to trim the frayed edges on the cuffs of his shirt. Satisfied with this tiny act of domesticity, I headed out the door with him, into the rain, to walk the fifteen minutes into town and to the registry office. Arriving damp and bedraggled, we asked at the front desk how long it would take.

Our two witnesses, the only two people we

Kererū in the Plum Tree 1996
1220 x 800 mm/48 x 31½ in
Oil on board

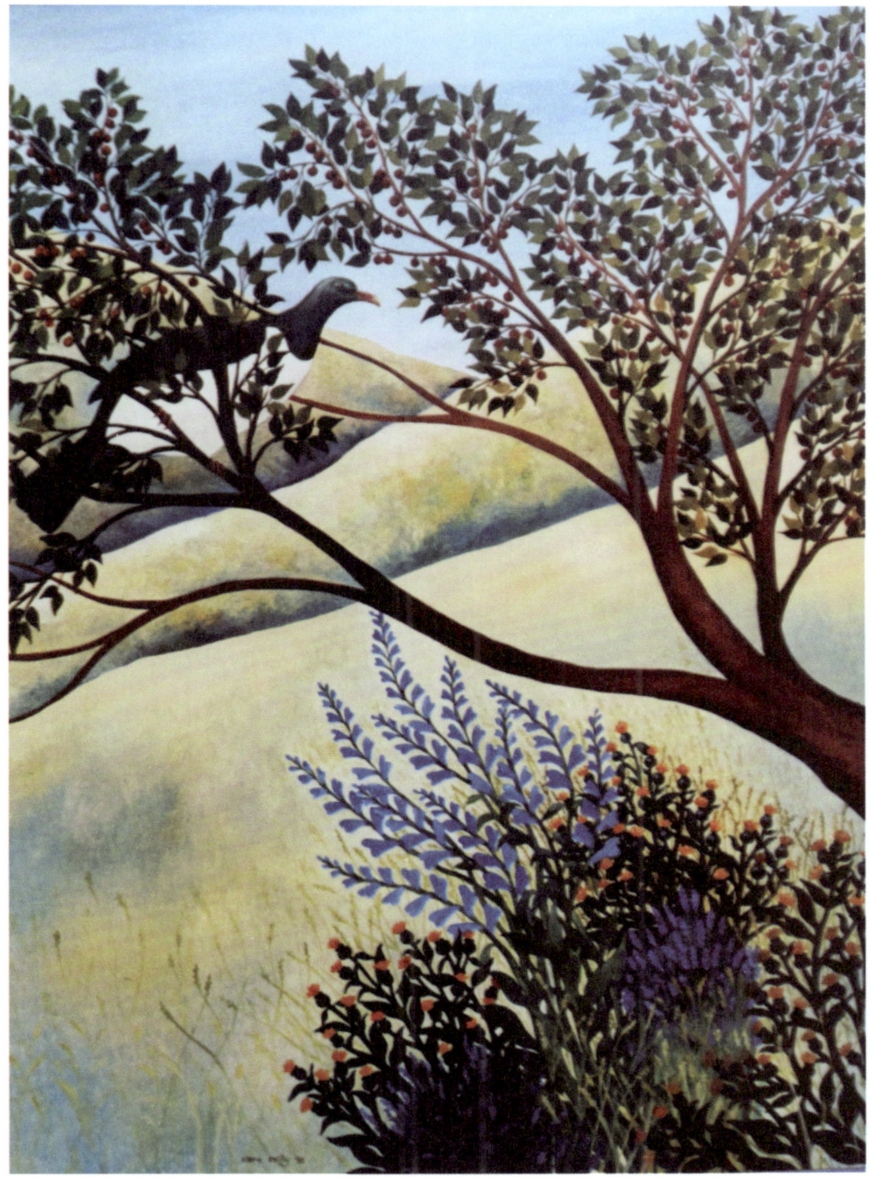

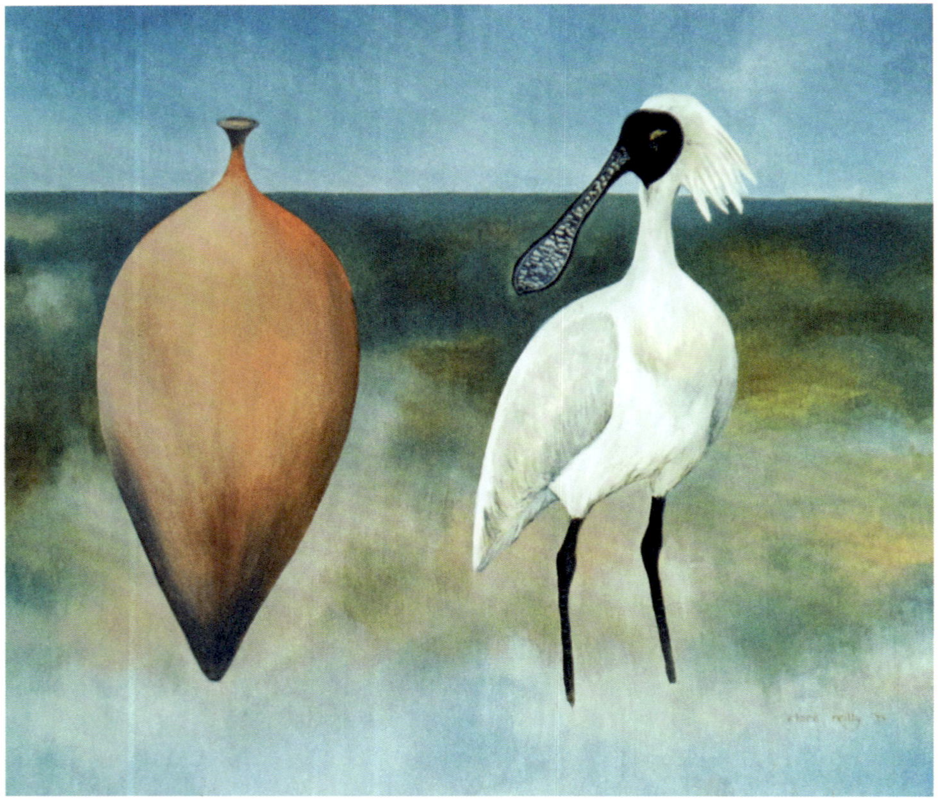

'Painting for me is like a life force, it bubbles up from a spring within, it occupies much of my daily thought, and often in the early hours of the morning, on sleepless nights, inspiration creeps in.'

Spoonbill with Amphora 1996
700 x 800 mm/27½ x 31½ in
Oil on board

knew in Christchurch, duly arrived and we were ushered into the main room, where we were formally married, then amazed when the registrar said, 'And now you may kiss the bride'! I didn't know they said that sort of thing in such an ordinary ceremony. We laughed and left quickly, going into Cathedral Square to find a café for coffee and a piece of cake together, before heading back home to paint for the rest of the afternoon.

It was the most casual of weddings, but our commitment to marriage was taken deeply, 'til death do us part'.

Several years of artistic exploration ensued, as I abandoned my realist beginnings in acrylics and experimented with painting techniques in oil, using bright abstract explosions of colour.

We were fortunate that the Antipodes Gallery was willing to continue showing our work and the two of us had joint exhibitions back in Wellington, which sold surprisingly well. Along with support from family and friends, it was enough encouragement for us to keep going.

We were exceedingly frugal, with very little money to live on, and our funds soon ran out.

We both had to find day jobs to be able to pay the rent. I worked part-time for several years until the job morphed into a full-time position, and Max would work a full-time job for a while to save up, then take months or a year off to get back into painting. We bought from an auction a bulk lot of framing lengths that had been scorched in a fire and did our own framing from the salvageable pieces. This saved us precious funds for quite a few years.

I toyed with the idea of going to art school at Ilam, Canterbury University, in 1978, but during my interview there with Bill Sutton, then acting Professor of Fine Arts, I was put off by a comment he made about one of the senior students. He remarked, during our tour of the working studios, that this student had thought he knew about painting when he arrived at art school, but they had successfully 'knocked the stuffing out of him'! Appalled, I departed, determined that no one was going to knock the stuffing out of me, and even though I knew it would take me far longer to figure things out on my own, I wanted to discover my own pathway, however long it took.

After one of my shows in 1980, I had sold sufficient paintings to accumulate just enough money for the deposit on a house, and as the real estate market in Christchurch had been in a trough for four years, we managed to arrange two mortgages to buy an old two-storey house in Gloucester Street, not for $700 but for $20,000.

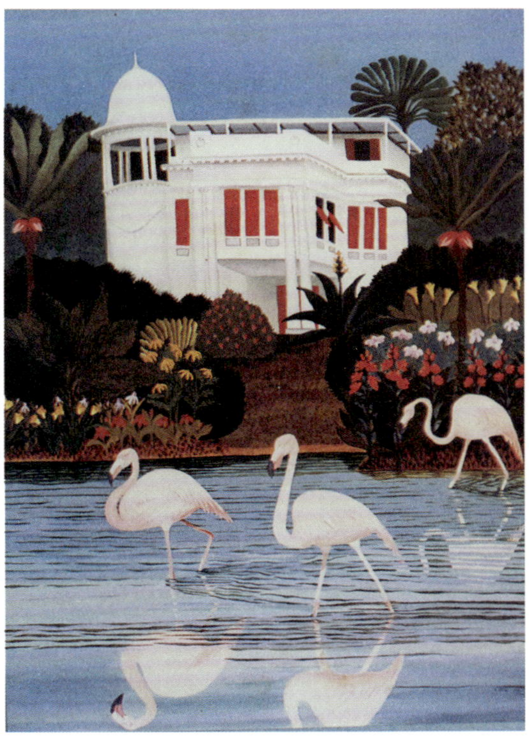

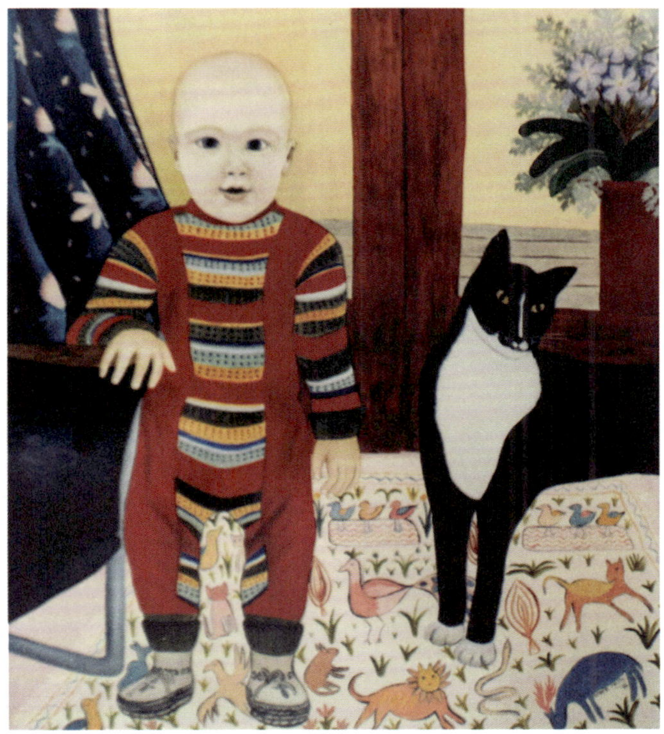

Left: **Flamingos** 1986
800 x 600 mm/31½ x 23½ in
Oil on board

Right: **Marcel and Pouffy the Cat** 1988
800 x 700 mm/31½ x 27½ in
Oil on board

Christchurch was to remain our home for 42 years, even though initially we loathed its flatness. It wasn't until we moved several decades later, onto the Port Hills, that our Wellington selves finally felt at ease.

Now that we had our large rambling house, we had plenty of room to have our own studios and a music room. I left behind the experimental abstract painting phase, and my work became filled with soft organic shapes of colour and more recognisable plant and landscape forms again.

Max began working on large canvases, continuously challenging himself to explore many different avenues of his self-expression, while my work developed in a slower way, gradually changing as the years went by. I found his dramatic use of colour both shocking and inspiring; he boldly put interesting colour combinations together, creating vibrant energy in his work and not adhering to any rules. I found his attitude to painting liberating, freeing me from the confines of my thoughts. He drew sustenance from what I was producing in my studio. We inspired each other.

It was an exciting, lively time, but also difficult as we settled into the unromantic reality and sometimes awkward and tense relationship of two different artists working and living together. We tried to find a balance in our work and home lives.

At no time did we seriously wish to give up painting or give up on each other. It wasn't a path

Paremata Boats 1992
900 x 600 mm/35½ x 23½ in
Oil on board

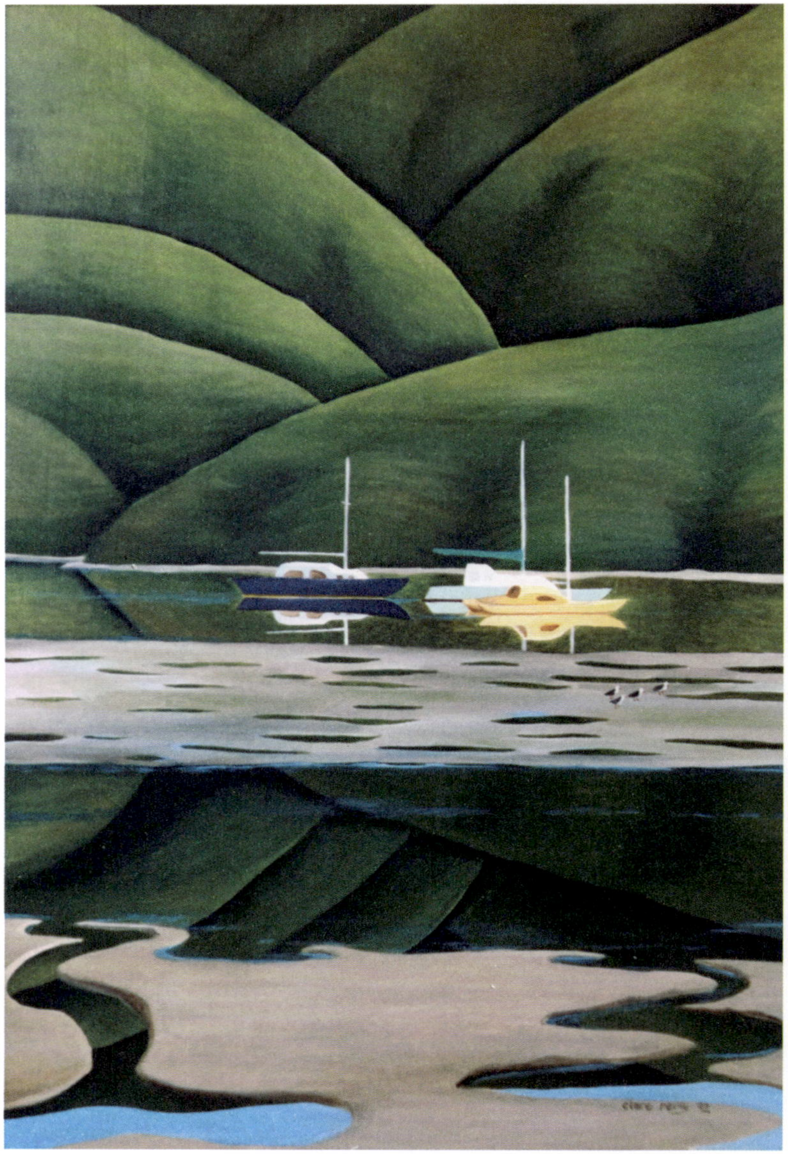

for the faint-hearted, but we had true passion. It took commitment to an ideal, rather than the reality of very little financial return for all our efforts.

As the necessity of paid work encroached into our days, we began the habit of waking around 5 am to paint before work and also painted late into the evenings. This pattern was to remain an important part of our lives as we juggled jobs and painting, then, later, family life with the birth of our two sons, Marcel in 1987 and Kazimir in 1990. Our boys quickly learnt the rules of the studios; they played happily nearby, and never put their fingers in wet paint on our easels.

We were determined not to use lack of time as an excuse not to paint, such was the strength of our inner conviction to be creative.

To be a painter can be a lonely and isolating pursuit; all progress needs to come from self-motivation. However, there was so much dialogue and energy between us that Max and I supported each other's creativity, and we pressed on, having regular joint and solo shows, first in Wellington and Christchurch and later also in Akaroa, Nelson, Auckland, Timaru, Greymouth, Dunedin, Little River and Mapua.

Max had introduced me to the seemingly wild discordant sound of jazz, initially with the exciting music of Herbie Hancock, Miles Davis and Thelonious Monk, and this music became an important energetic part of our painting process.

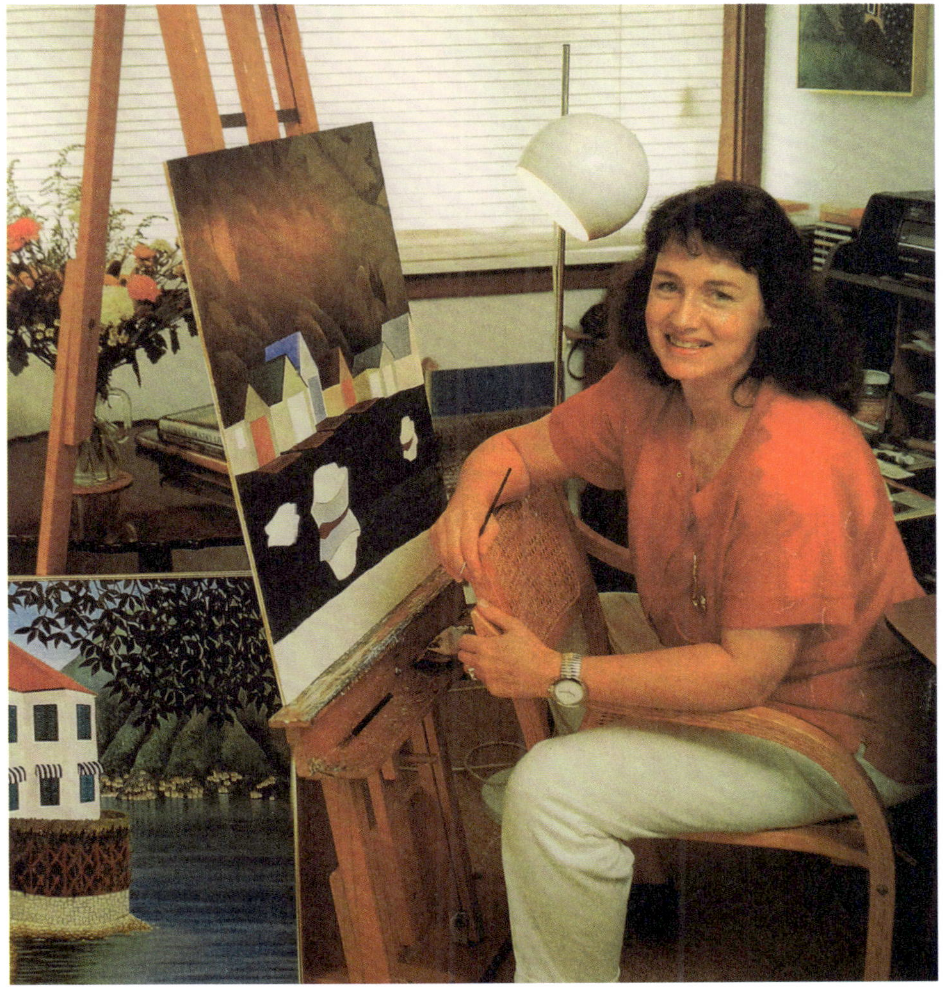

Clare in Gloucester Street studio, May 1992, *Next Magazine* article

We also played and composed our own music together. Over the years I bought a drum kit, a flute, a bass guitar and a vibraphone and experimented with sound textures, although I mastered none of these instruments.

I had always been drawn to birds and Max had been a keen birdwatcher from an early age, so this became a shared interest. I have become attuned to listening to birdsong and I notice their comings and goings throughout the day. We were enthusiastic about having birds in our environment and chose to live in places with nearby bush.

Over time, birds and bird motifs entered both our paintings in very different ways. Bird symbols were to become increasingly significant for us.

For me, birds in flight signified a soaring of spirit, an uplift and a sense of joy.

The presence of birds in my paintings became a vehicle of movement, small messengers of calm, peace and beauty, but they have also carried messages of threat to habitats and the importance of conservation efforts to halt the decline in native bird populations.

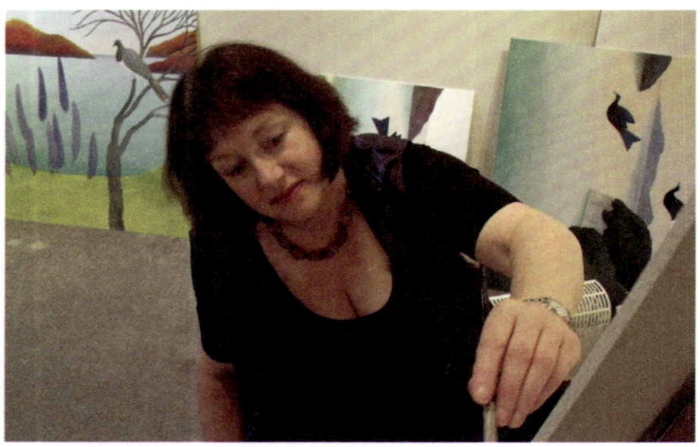

Clare in Cashmere studio, 2011

Throughout the middle years I maintained a small painting profile, as well as juggling the commitments of work and family life, with growing children and ageing parents to care for.

We moved to Wellington for a year in 1989, while Max did his postgraduate degree in librarianship. My energies were fractured in many different directions.

Then around the time of the new millennium, my painting again began to clarify in my mind, and I felt strengthened by a path forward. I received welcomed patronage from a couple who purchased a large number of my works and commissions came in from a range of people.

Max and I formed the Primitive Bird Group in 2001. We both felt like outsider artists and one day it occurred to us to bring our primitive/naive painting identities together and form this group. We launched a website under the group name (primitivebirdgroup.co.nz) and forged ahead in our exhibition schedules with renewed energy. A synergy arose from this decision that was to carry me forward into focused painting. We gathered more publicity for our joint and solo shows and felt empowered and supported openly by each other, in a way that hadn't quite been there before.

We shared the vision that we had strength as

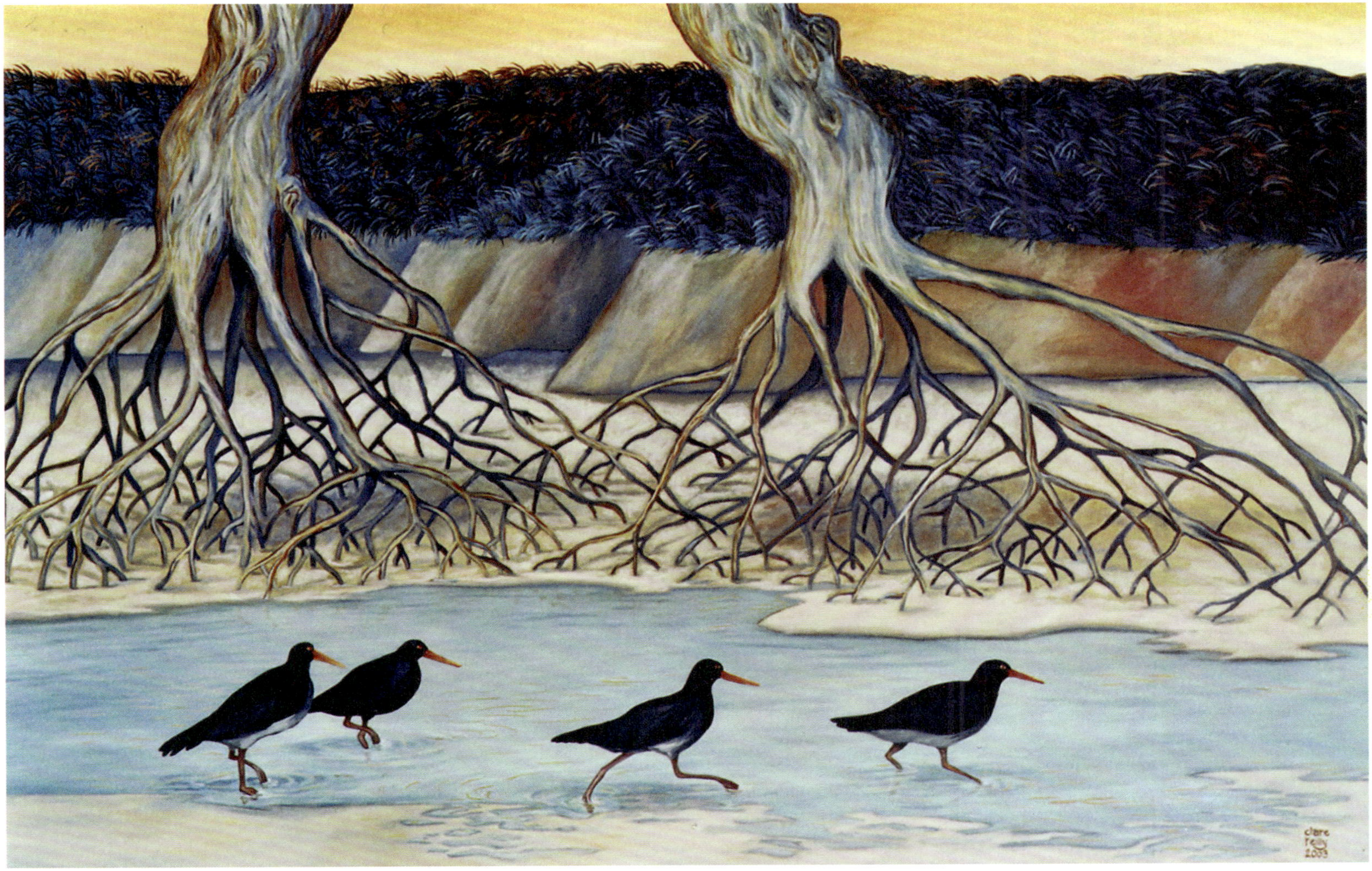

individual self-taught painters who hadn't needed grants or funding to keep being true about our work. It gave us a public voice.

We began making donations from our shows to various conservation projects. Birds being acknowledged as a source of our inspiration, it was important to us to give something back to help protect habitats and show our support for all the wonderful work provided by many volunteers in our local communities, who share the same conservation vision.

I became involved with the Banks Peninsula Conservation Trust's Tūī Restoration Project, and this enabled me to meet a wonderful new group of people and inspired a whole new series of paintings and exhibitions.

I had the opportunity to go, as part of the Tūī Capture team, to Maud Island in the Marlborough Sounds in 2010 and assist with capturing tūī for relocation to Hinewai Reserve behind Akaroa.

A marvellous ten days for me on the island

Oystercatchers 2003
900 x 1220 mm/35½ x 48 in
Oil on board

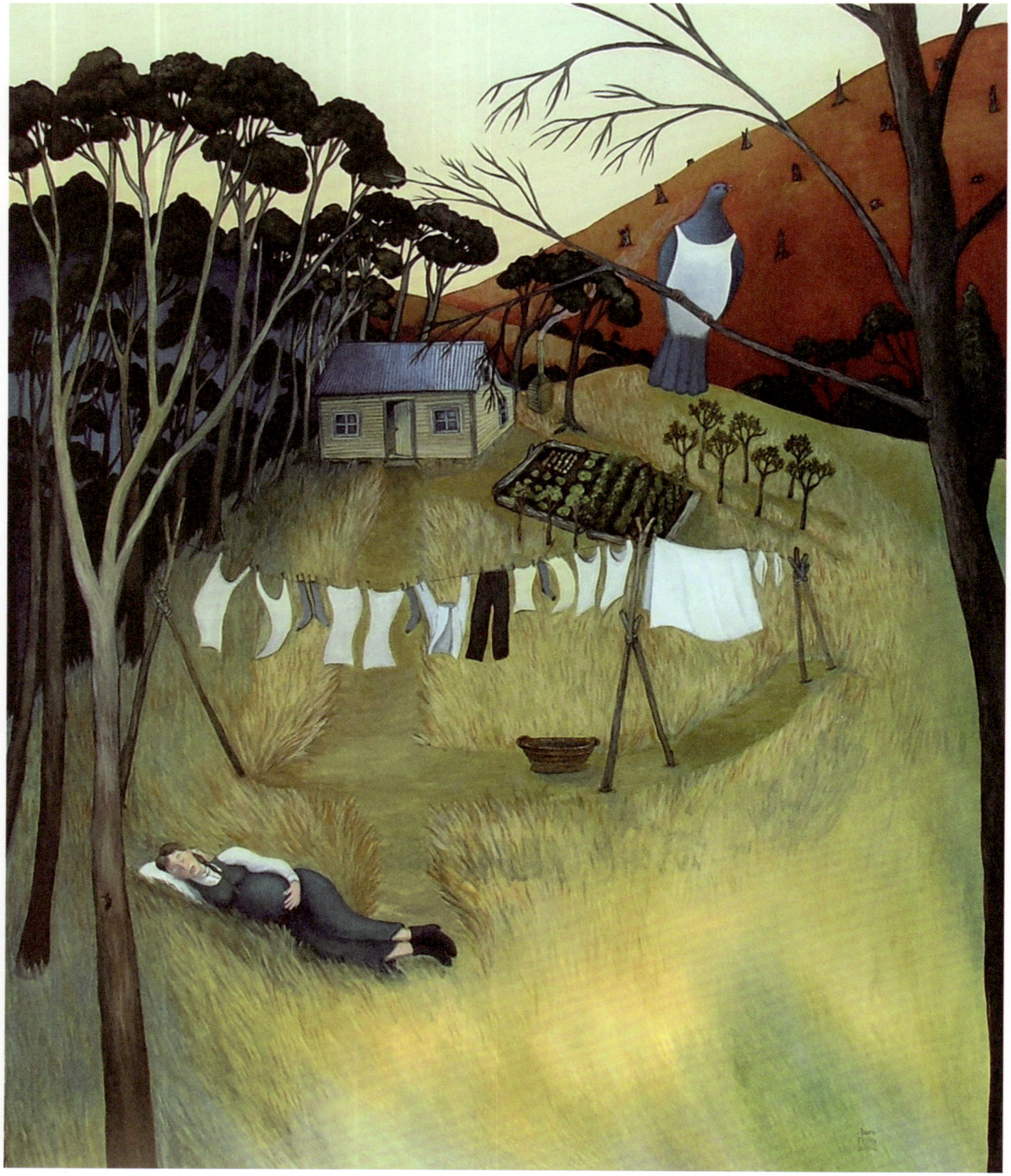

Opposite: Exhibition invitations

Guardian 2004
1000 x 800 mm/39¼ x 31½ in
Oil on board

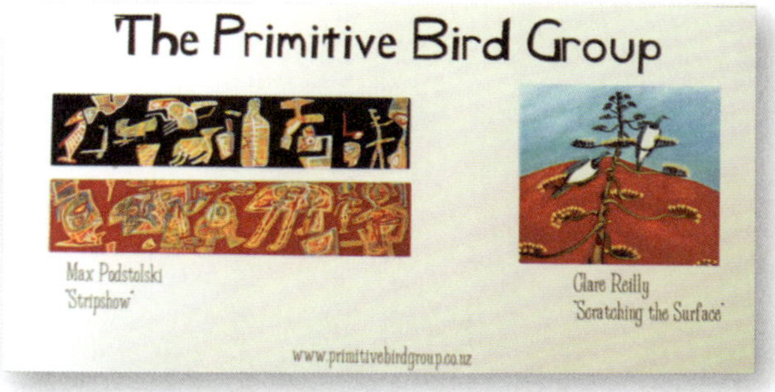

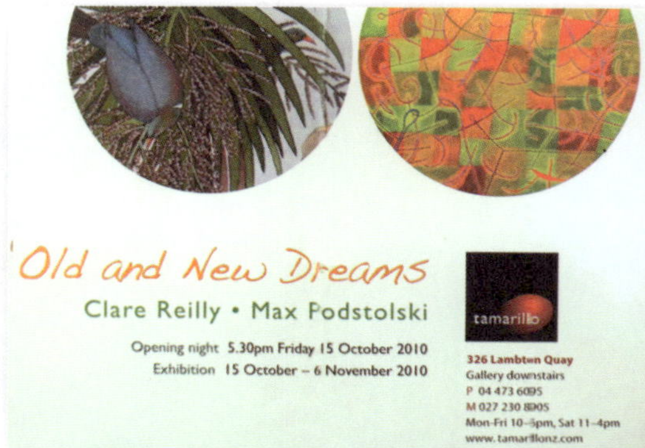

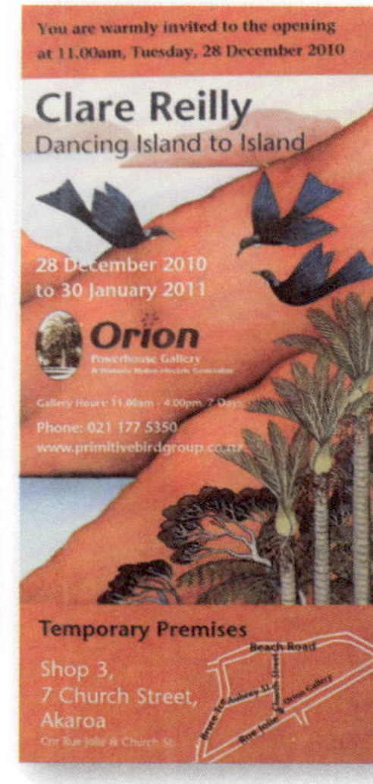

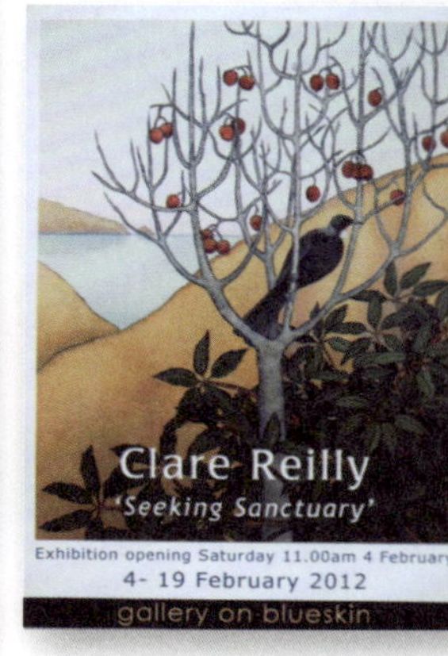

Clare framing at Doctors Point, 2020

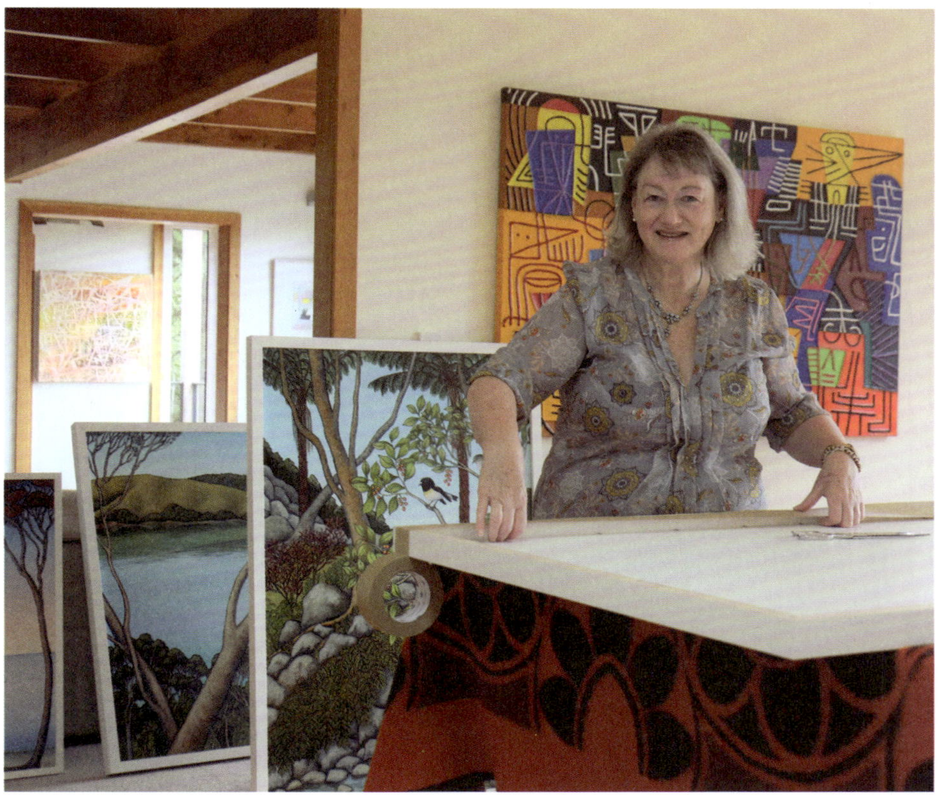

culminated in travelling in a float plane down the east coast of the South Island, with a cargo of 29 bouncing tūī in their cardboard boxes in my care, to Akaroa Harbour.

I exhibited at different galleries from Max, my work selling well in most shows, but we also enjoyed joint shows as the Primitive Bird Group, our diverse painting styles reaching different people.

We were two individuals and had fortunately always maintained our separate painting identities. It wouldn't have worked otherwise.

My work was used on three book covers and I was included in Potton's New Zealand Contemporary Landscape calendars for some years, then later, Live Wires New Zealand published annual Clare Reilly calendars and from 2004 they have reproduced my work on a number of greeting card series, so my work has reached a

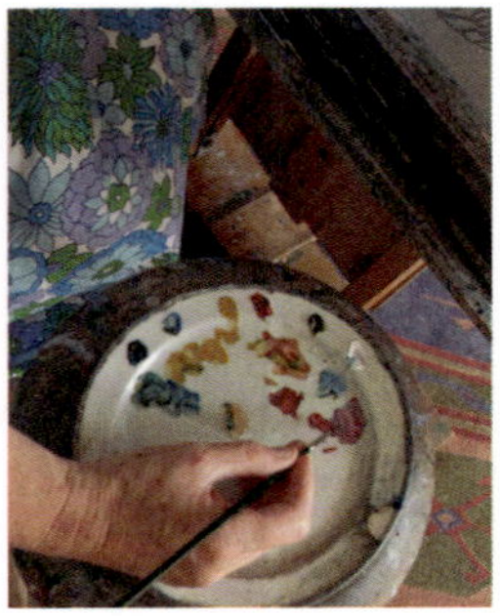

'I love the process of arriving in my studio in the morning, eager to start work at my easel, and in the evening, I always clean up my palette and survey the day's work, keenly planning what I might work on the next day. I can be very distracted into this internal/external world, which I would describe as a dreaming with eyes wide open.'

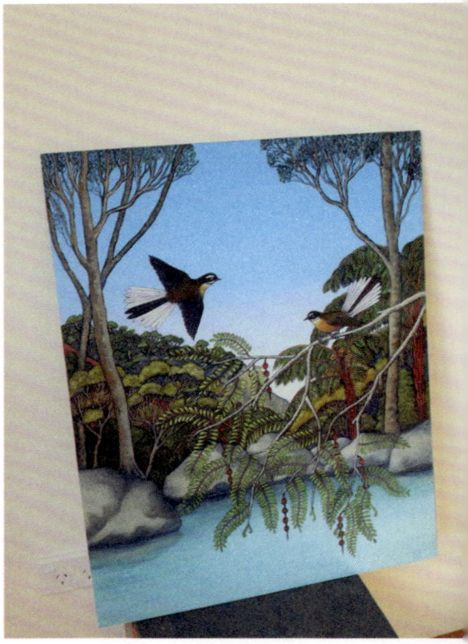

Clare at work in her Doctors Point studio, 2020

far wider audience in New Zealand and overseas.

It has been a pleasure to receive emails from all over the world from people who enjoy and follow my work from a distance.

In 2008 I finally returned to full-time painting, right in the middle of the global financial crisis, when galleries were struggling to survive and many had to close.

I had worked part-time as a Montessori preschool teacher for sixteen years, a job I had loved and found very rewarding, with painting and exhibiting continuing at a pace within the remaining time, but it was exhausting.

I found it increasingly difficult to juggle, back and forth, between these two work environments. I had reached a point where I needed to allow myself more time and focus to be fully immersed in painting again.

I knew I had a strong following, so although it seemed a precarious step to take, I leapt! And didn't look back with any regrets. I was rewarded by keen interest in my work and most paintings sold as soon as a show would open, with a stream of commissions as well.

Max continued to provide his steady financial support with his work full-time as the Humanities Librarian at the University of Canterbury Library, taking care of the gaps that occurred in my painter's income. His painting time was much more limited than mine and I have had huge gratitude for his

Opposite
The Arrival 2000
900 x 1200 mm/35½ x 47¼ in
Oil on board

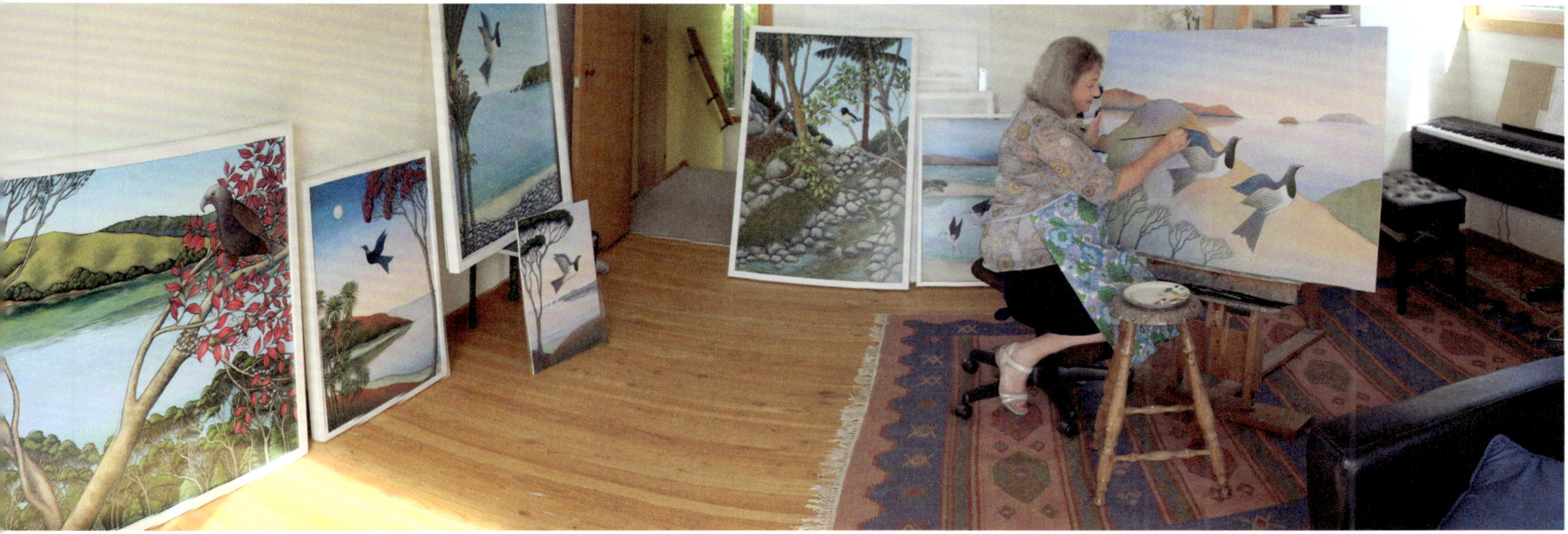

belief in, and encouragement of, me to be the one to finally paint full-time.

We still had the dream of living in the country and eventually decided to buy a house set in bush overlooking Blueskin Bay, north of Dunedin. Max would take early retirement from his job.

It was to be a fresh start, to paint and live the simple life — a vision we had held since our first days together. We planned to build a new studio for me and alter the house. However, just as building consent was granted, we were shocked to discover that Max had an aggressive brain tumour. Our world spun out of our control. We forged ahead with our plans, hoping to get some time together in our dream home.

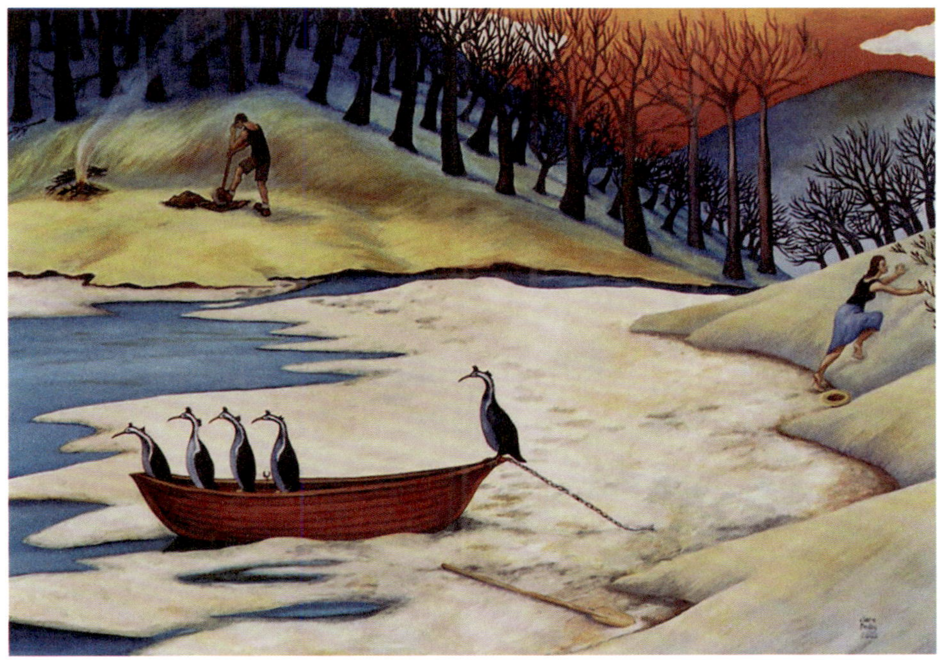

On moving day, ten months later, Max woke early, collapsed and had slipped into a coma by midday. He died peacefully seven days later. Our belongings had travelled on down to Dunedin, so three days after his memorial service, I headed south, leaving behind family and friends, to establish a new life in a new community, alone.

This wasn't the way the dream was supposed to go. Not only had I lost my life partner, but also my muse!

Our lives had been so closely intertwined that the gap felt enormous. I wasn't sure I could ever find my way back into feeling joy for life or painting. Max had kept telling me, during his illness, that I did have the strength to carry on and I would love working in my new studio.

It took time and a lot of patience to find my way back to that equilibrium.

I walked some of the Camino trail in Spain as a fundraiser for Leukaemia & Blood Cancer New Zealand. The opportunity to give something back to others facing similar cancer journeys became part of my self-healing process.

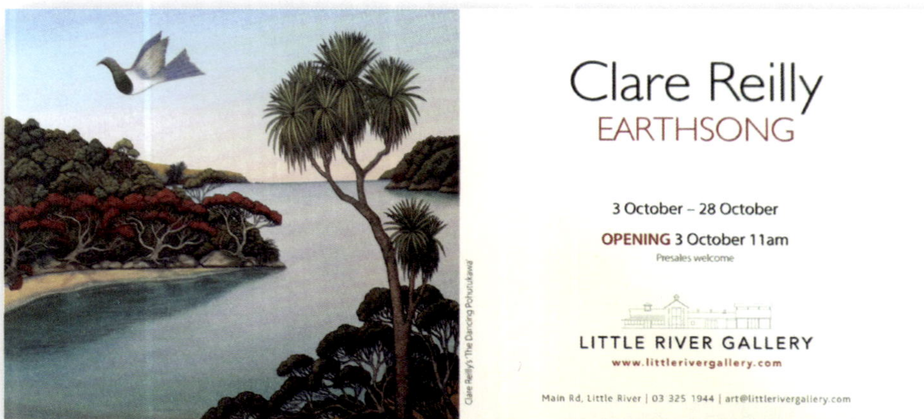

Eventually, a calm descended upon me. The beauty of the natural environment around my home sustained me in my solitude, and gradually I connected with my new community, stronger in my resolve to keep widening my horizons and value the life I had remaining. I still paint and exhibit.

Throughout my life, I have continued to express the dreamlike quality of calm and *joie de vivre,* in my paintings, my passion and lust for life.

Eye of the Calm was an exhibition title that I used in 2009 and a phrase that I created as an expression of my life's work.

In a world that is increasingly frenetic in activity, with visual imagery flashing on screens, transmitting the increasing woes of the planet, it is important to have moments to rest within a place of calm and meditation. My painting gives me that space.

I am grateful for daring to have stepped onto this artistic path so early on in my life, as it has sustained an important need within me.

I have received wonderful responses from my audience, and I still feel the frisson of excitement upon entering my studio each new day, a delightful surprise, after so many years and so many paintings.

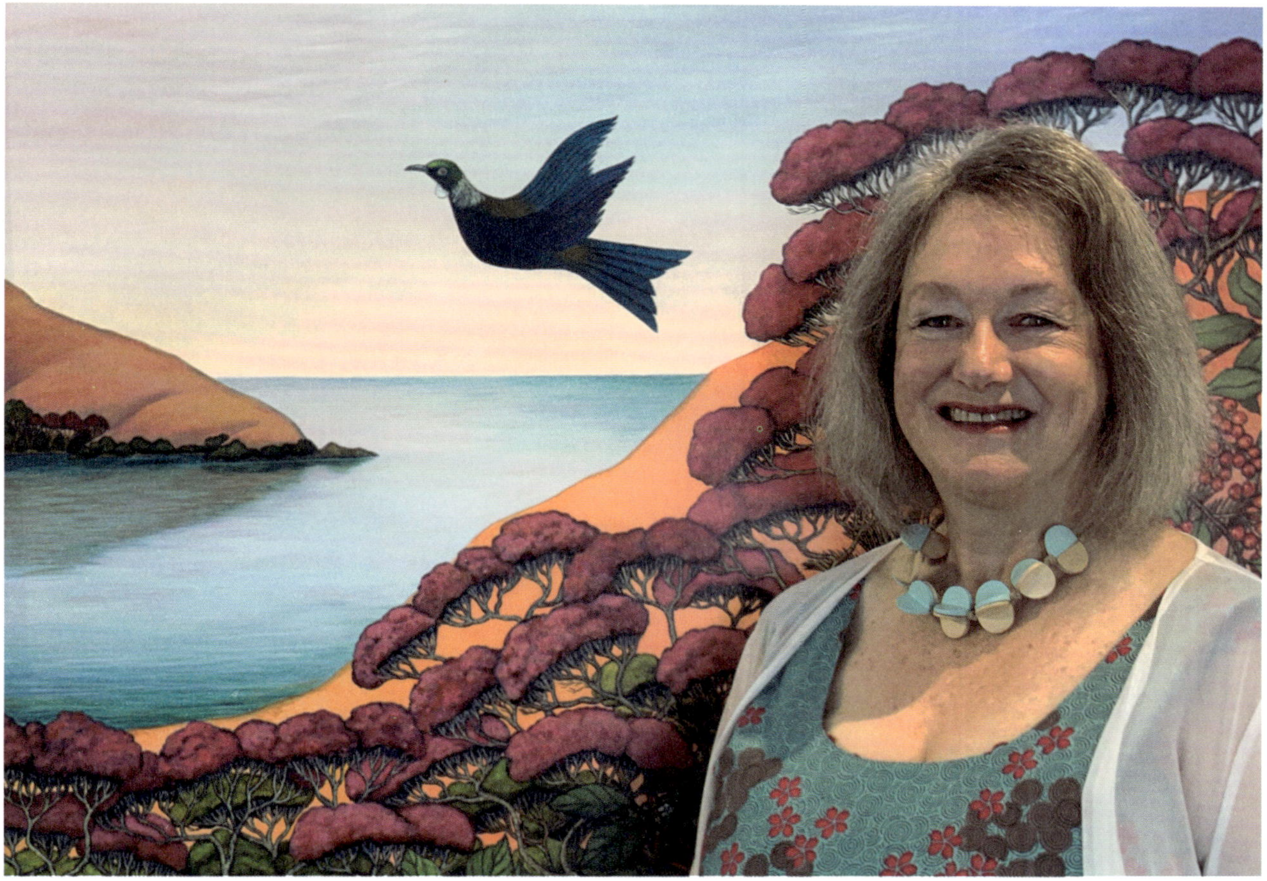

The Painting Process

Paintings come in from the dreamtime,
burbling up from an inner source, appearing
on the blank white spaces of new boards.
The pearls of ideas are stashed away over months
or years, till a glint of germination springs forth.
Not a sequential progress but a leaping out and
jumbling in with other paintings, in many stages
of completion. Each work begins with very little roadmap
as to where the end point may occur. Always an excitement.
An organic process that unfolds and reveals itself to me and
as the journey progresses, often the ending is a surprise
to any preconceived ideas I may have held at the start.

The heady smell of oil paint in the studio,
squeezing out fresh blobs of colours
and mixing subtle blends of different hues.
The pleasure of clean new brushes that
glide effortlessly, that dab and slide,
forming thousands of paint strokes which
settle onto the painted surface to dry slowly.
Paint being laid down in gossamer-thin layers,
the surface of the board gradually building up
a depth and luminosity, textures and forms.
All the while the dreaming, the looking, the pondering.
Being presented with obstacles, to be resolved.
Coming to an impasse, then the point when
the painting takes off, pulls together, a clear pathway
and vision forward to completion. A time for each work
to be sitting out of sight, face to the wall.
This can take weeks, months and occasionally years,
before being closely scrutinised again and accepted.

The gathering of works for an exhibition. New ways
of seeing the work framed and hanging on gallery walls.
Then the leave-taking as the work disappears
out into the world. I return to an empty studio,
ready to restart the cycle.
Living daily life, out and about, looking and seeing,
observing the detail, always noticing something new.
Open to new landscapes and birds and the emotions of being.
Word pictures noted down, feelings, senses recorded.
More seeds of ideas to be added to the storehouse of the inner eye.

A note on medium

All paintings in the Plates section are oil on board, with the exception of *The Observer at Dawn* on pages 32–33, which is oil on canvas.

More information about Clare and her work can be found at **www.clarereilly.co.nz**

THE PLATES

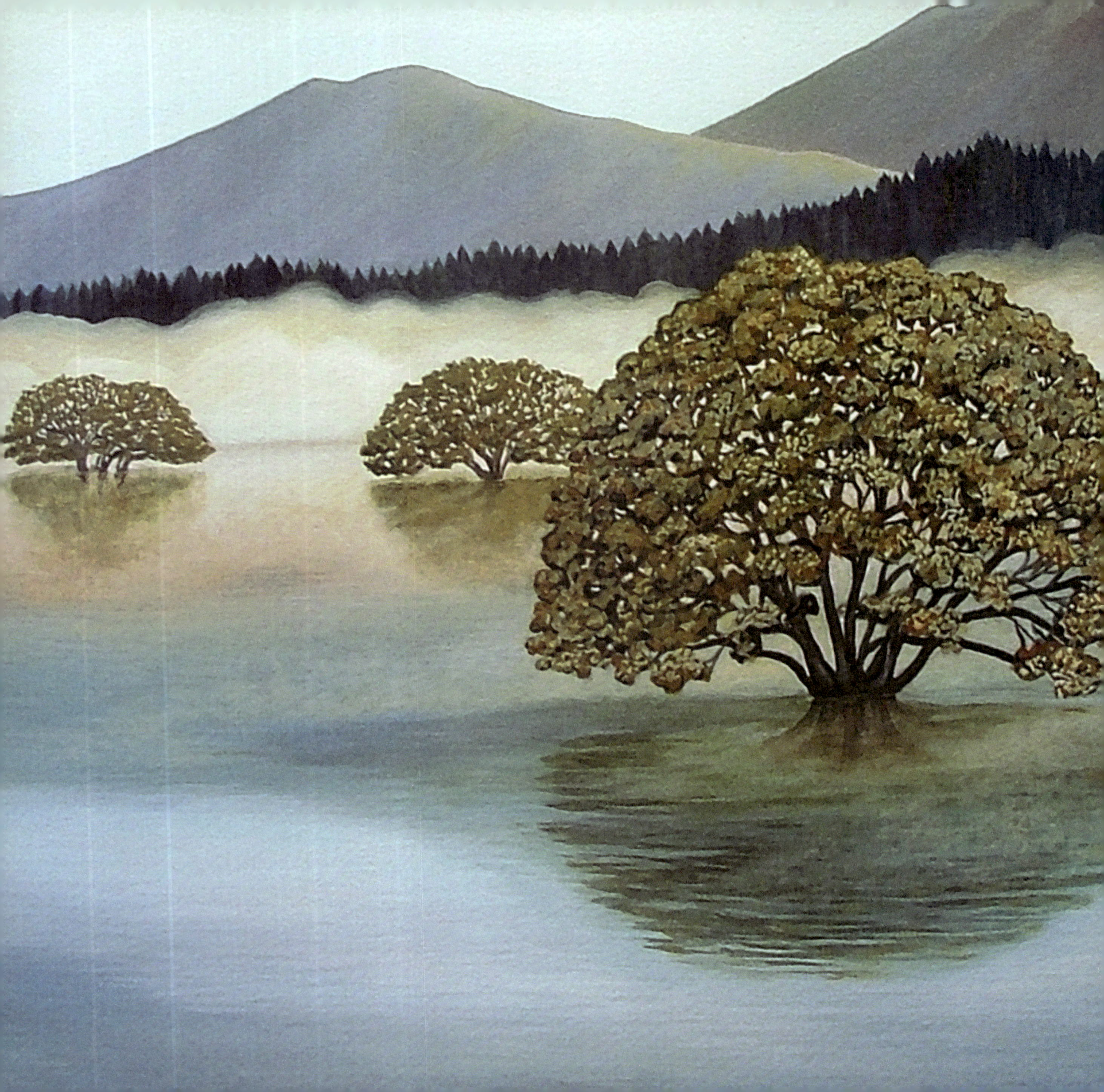

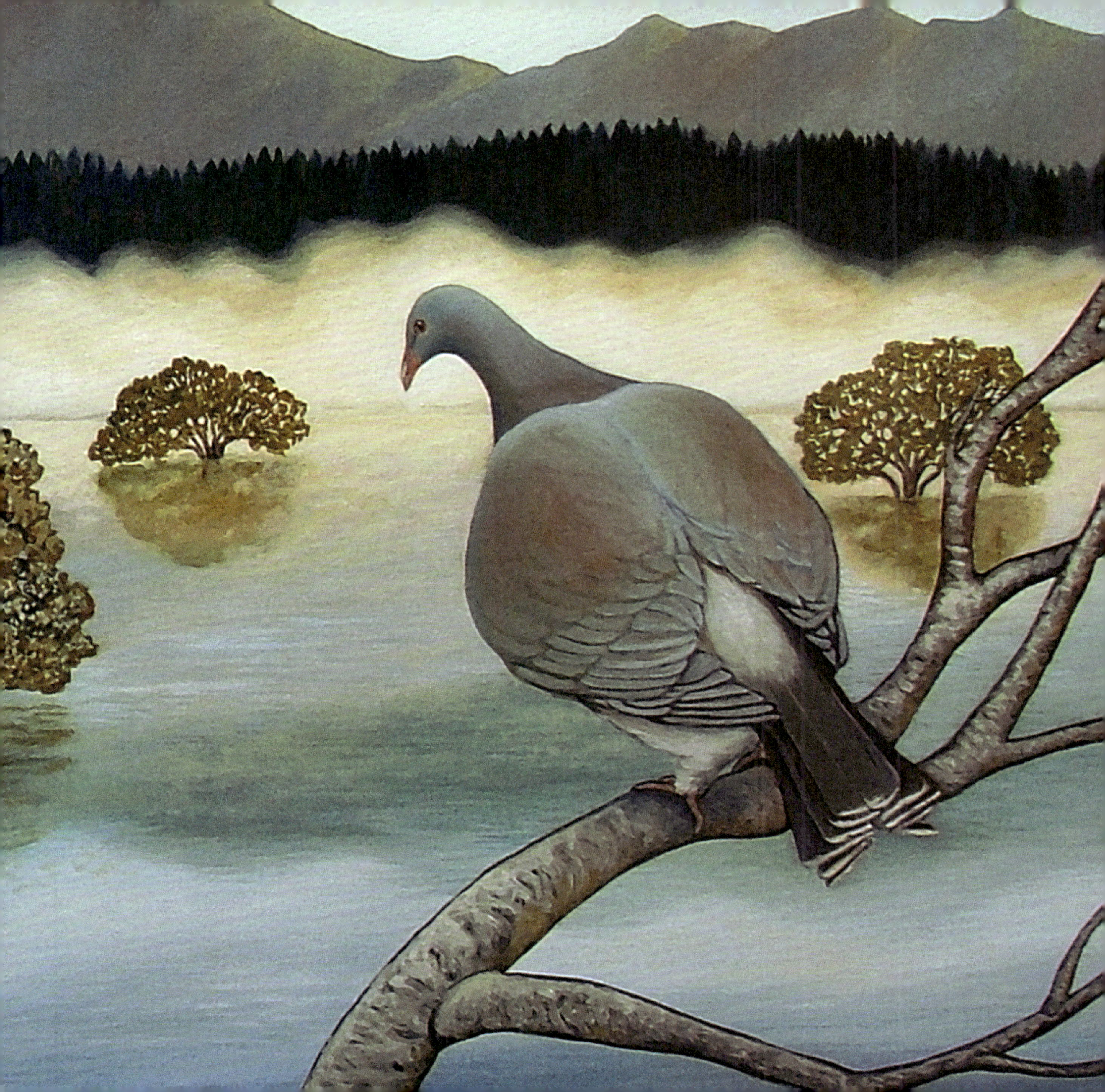

Dawn

Dawn, my favourite time of day, intrigues and beguiles me. It is full of the potential of the day and often gifts me with spectacular colour and mood.

It is the moment of calm before the day cranks up. The stillness and meditative quality that exists at dawn is where I am drawn to in my work. The soft fall of light, the blush in the sky, the magic of a dawn chorus given so freely to those willing to listen.

Opposite
A Sky Washed Clean 2015
1050 x 1050 mm/41¼ x 41¼ in

Previous page
Observer at Dawn 2006
460 x 915 mm/18 x 36 in

Daybreak, Doctors Point

The pied stilts are startled into a
graceful vertical rising, with a
Gaggle of delicate legs and wings
They wheel out over the water
Calling to each other

The sky hangs heavy and low
A tight drum of steely blue
Hugging the horizon, casting broody
Green light over a quiet sea

The channel is racing, a broiling
Pulsing thrust to the ocean,
As if the waters of the bay
Have been parted too long overnight
And now dash headlong to remingle
Into the warm body of the sea, like
Lovers distanced, now eagerly rejoining

Above, a circle of baby blue sky appears
Hints of dawn flushing pink on the rim of clouds
A small window of openness in the gloom

The spray of the waves leaves
A salty taste on my lips
I lick and draw the saline drops
Deep into the warmth of my mouth
As cold wind drags tears down my cheeks

Nearby in the channel a dark shape bobs
Maybe a tree trunk dragged in the current
Seagulls squawk and swirl above, agitated and annoyed

Not a log but the sleek dark body of a sea lion
His whiskers pricking the air as breath
Blasts out, nostrils wide open, after his dive

He and I pace our way up the channel
His graceful movements, a ballet of rippling dance
As he fishes the outgoing tide.

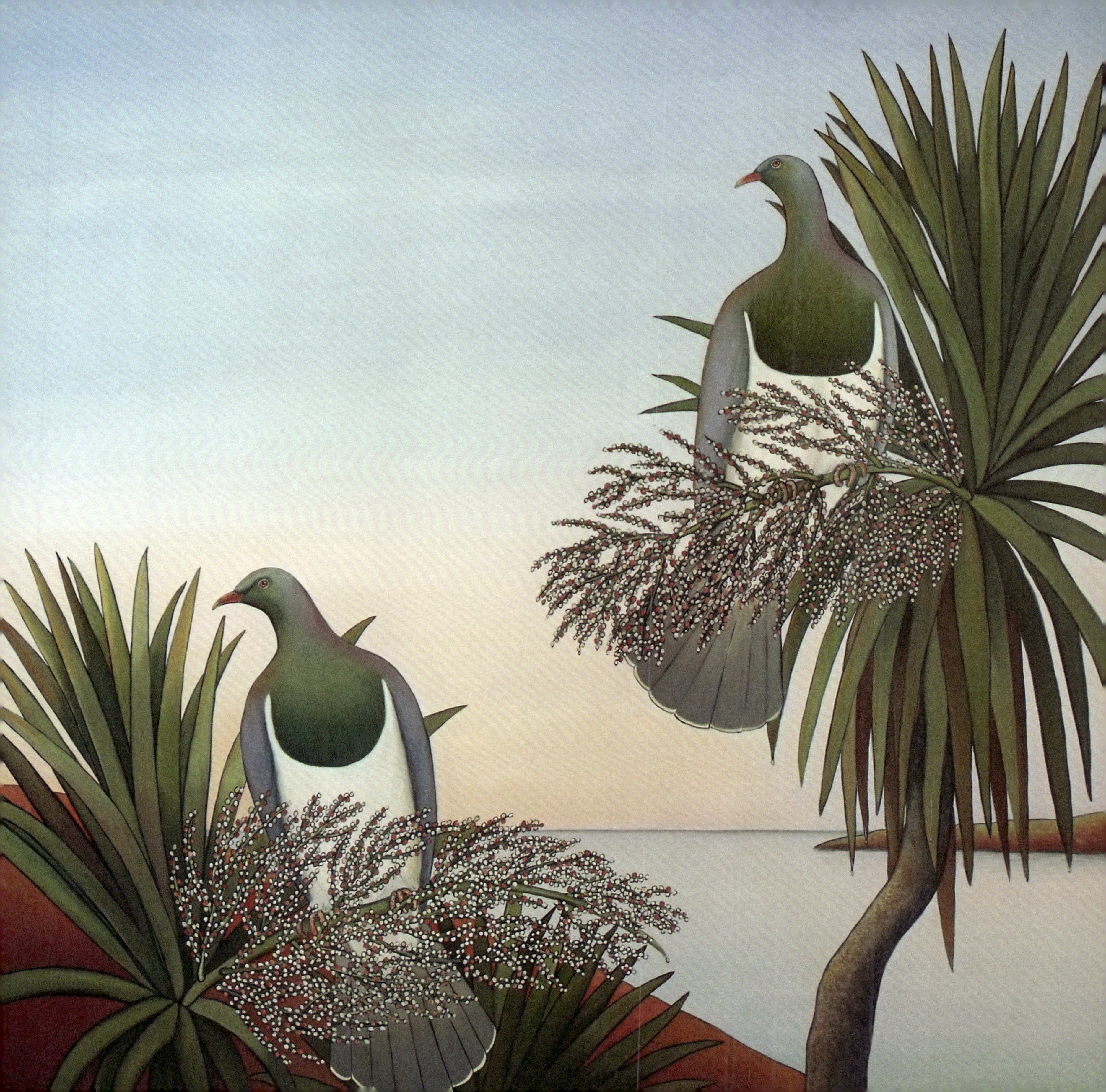

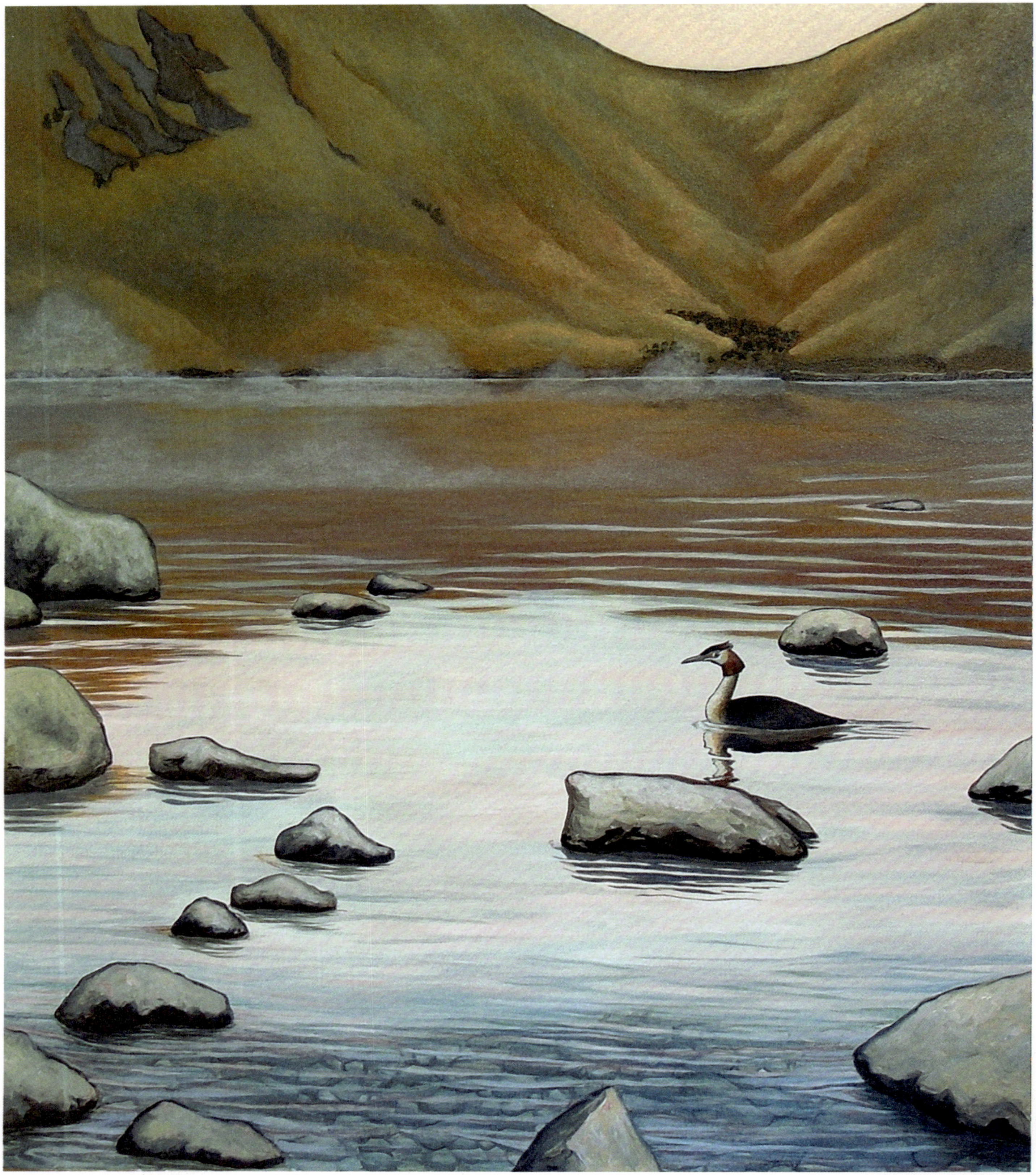

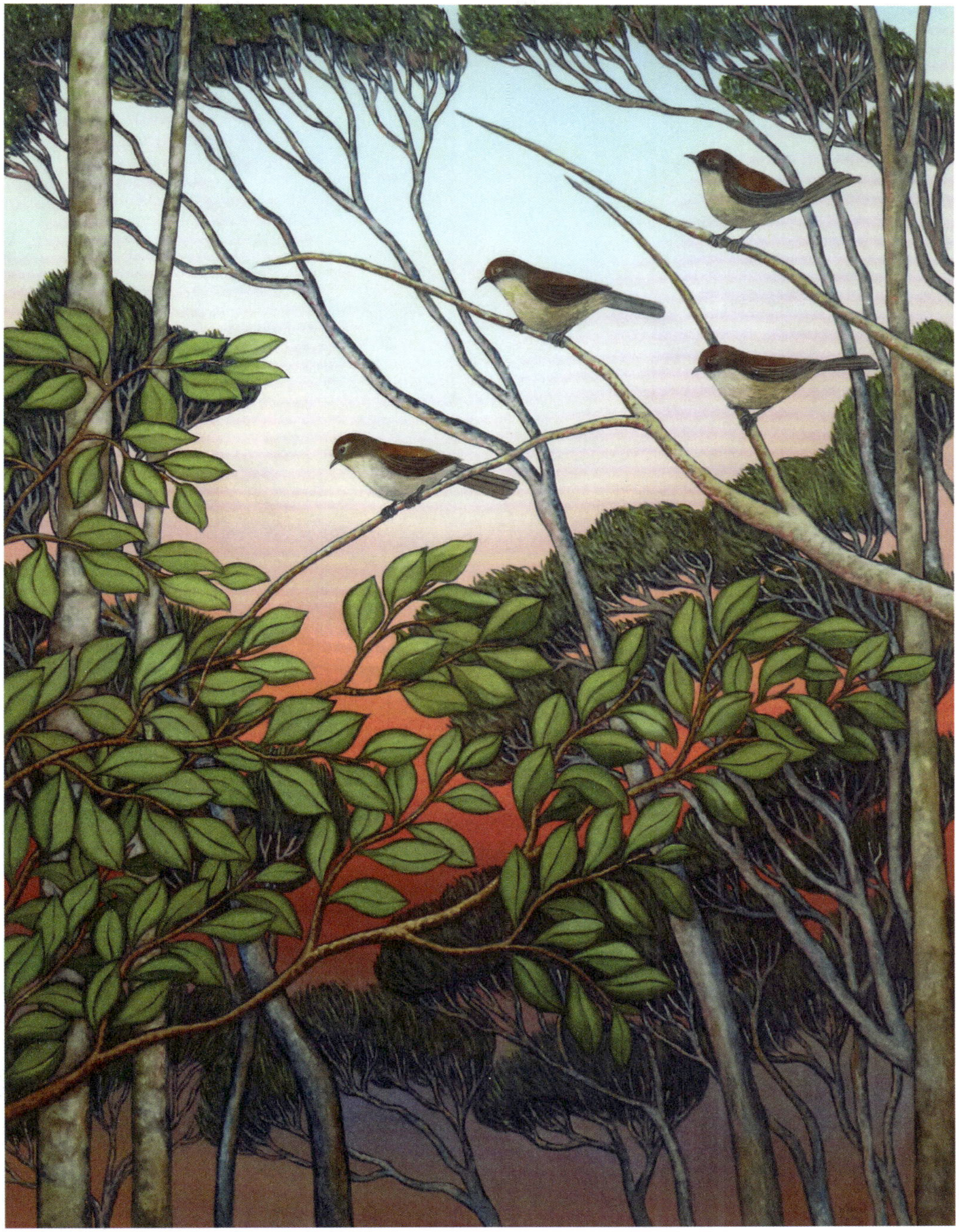

Pīpipi at Dawn 2015
800 x 600 mm/31½ x 23½ in

Opposite
Grebe at Dawn 2008
590 x 520 mm/23¼ x 20½ in

Tukurua Dawn

The dark velvety sky
is softened by
a luminous crescent
A silver sliver of moon
hanging in the east over
silhouetted nikau fronds

A tūī drops the first notes of dawn
into the inky blue-black bush
like ball bearings bouncing into the clearing

It is warm, the soft breeze brushing
dew from the verdant grass

Slow lazy waves unzip against the
jumble of quartz and greywacke stones
piled on the shore

The flat milkiness of the sea is
gradually blushing pink as the horizon
peels back revealing a wash of pale yellow

A second tūī drops notes from the bush behind
Two soloists, it is their time to savour
this Tukurua dawn
long before the chorus begins.

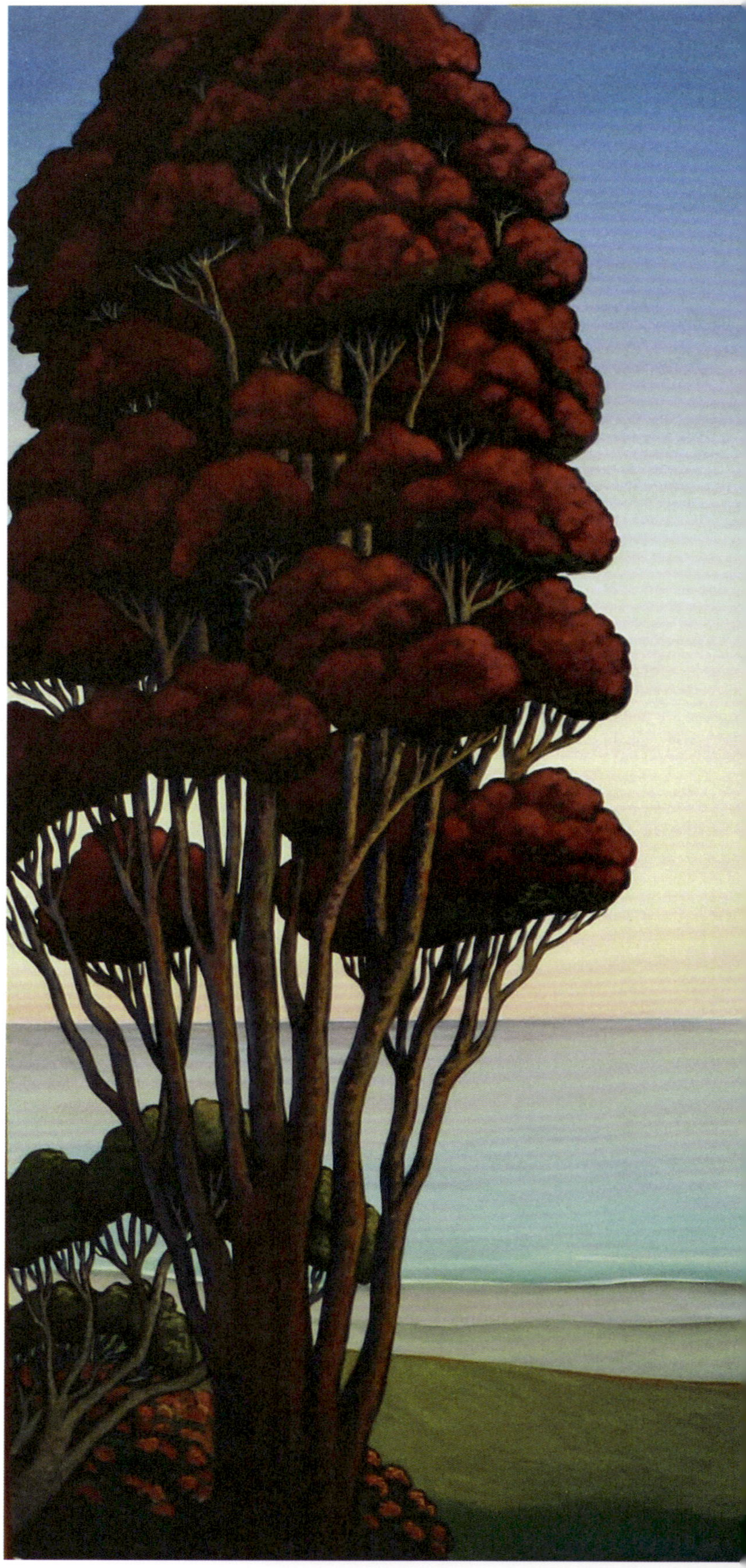

Tukurua Dawn 2015
800 x 1220 mm/31½ x 48 in

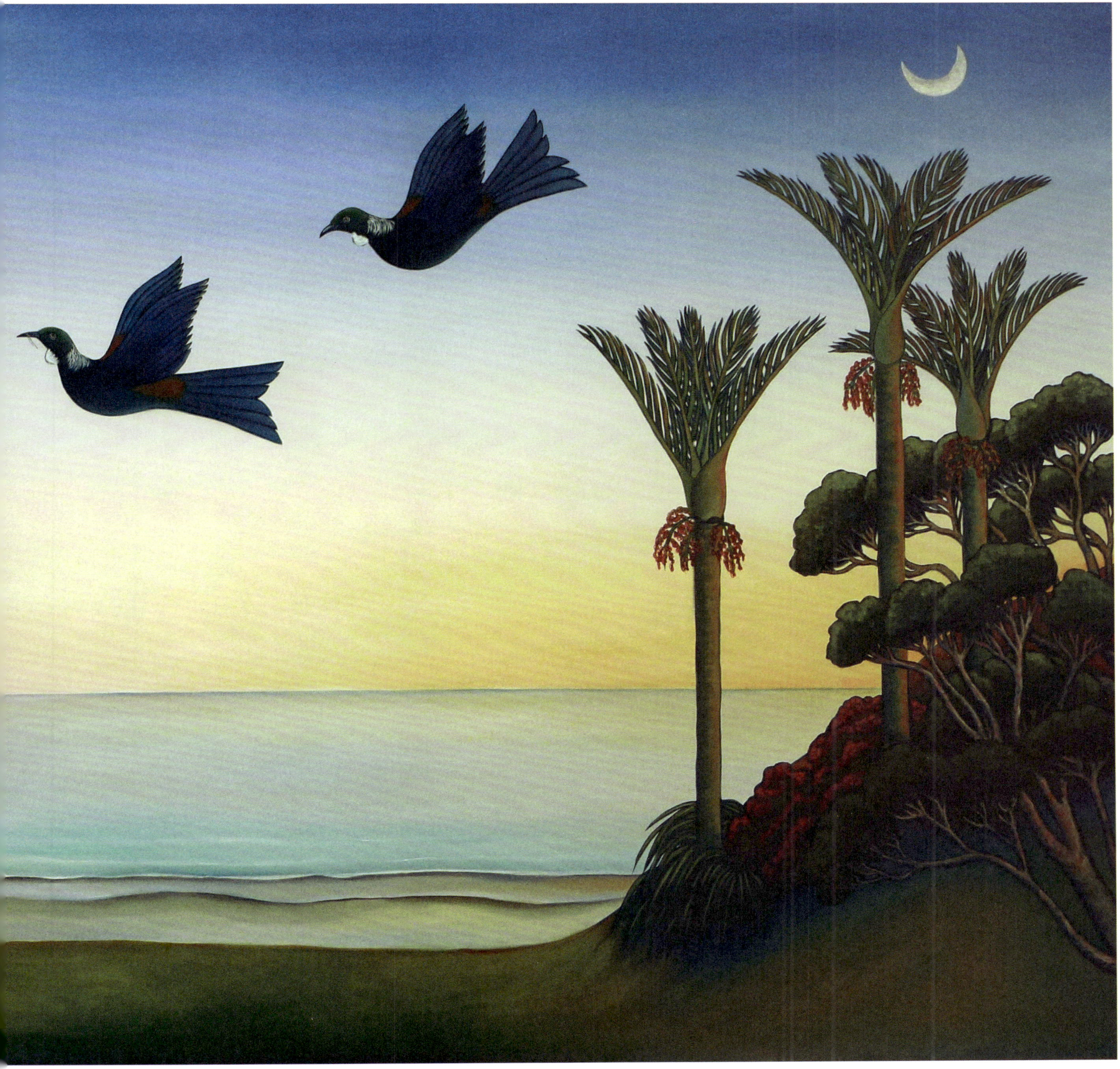

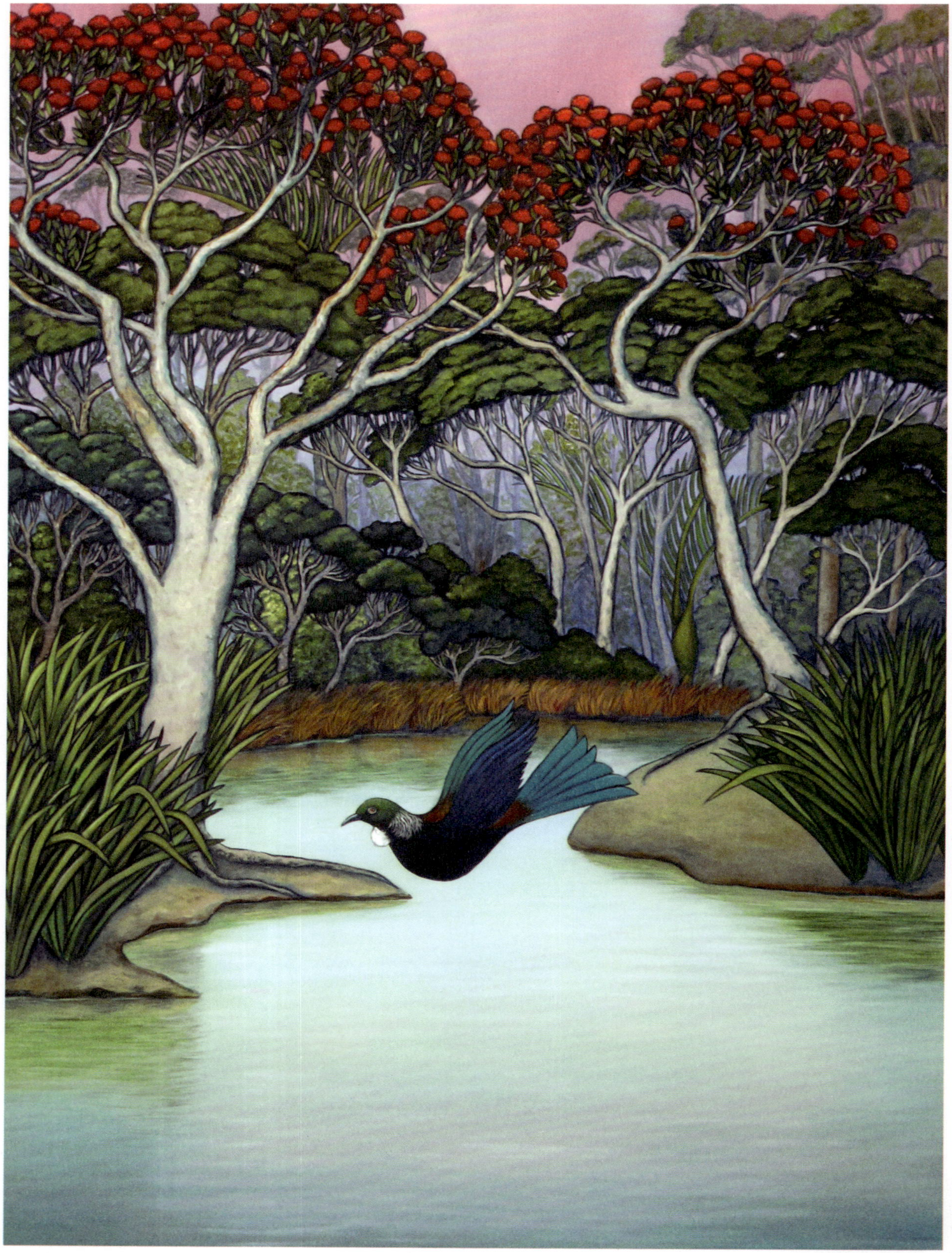

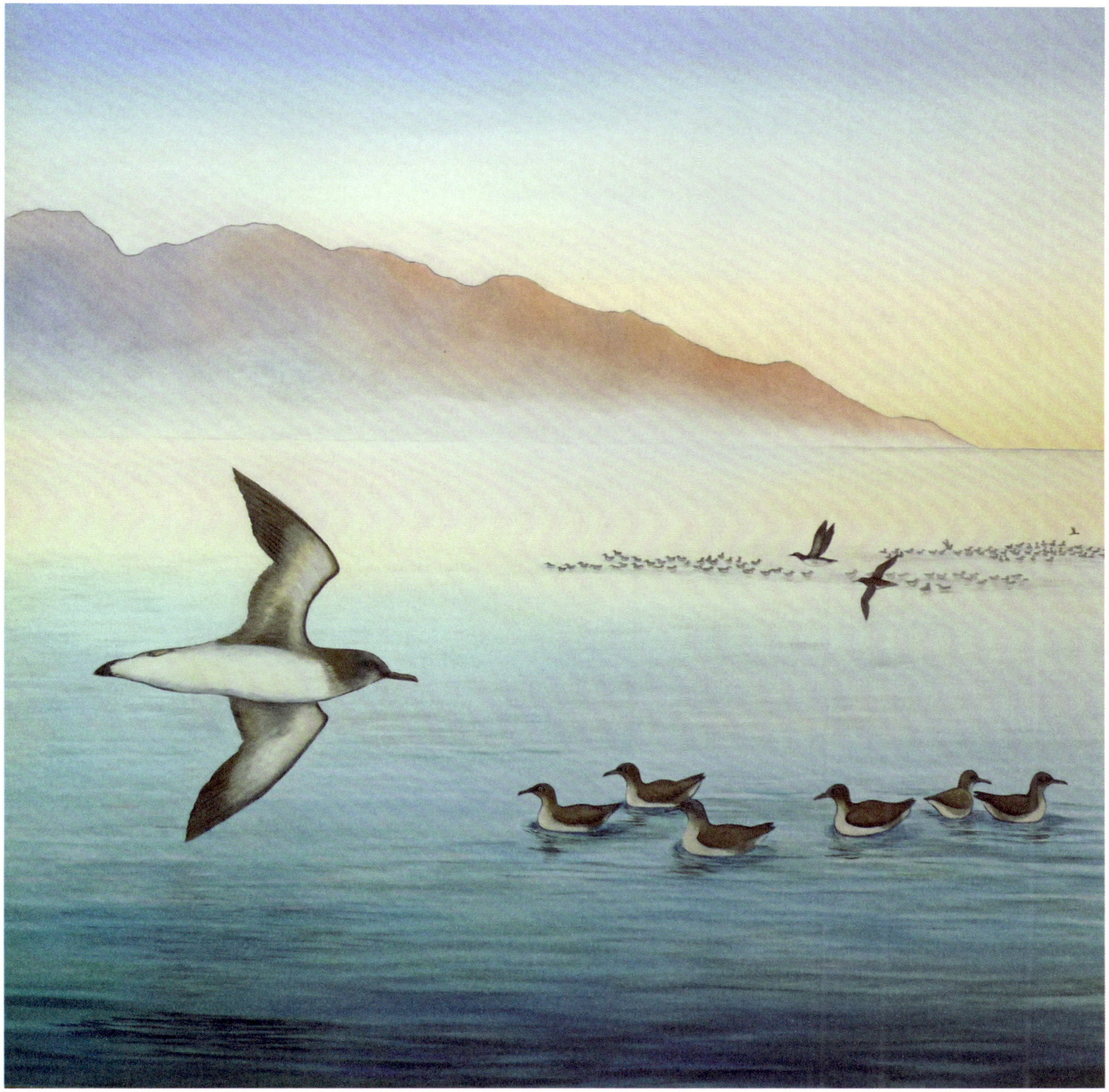

Joining the Raft 2016
900 x 900 mm/35½ x 35½ in

Opposite
The Rosy Blush of Dawn 2015
800 x 600 mm/31½ x 23½ in

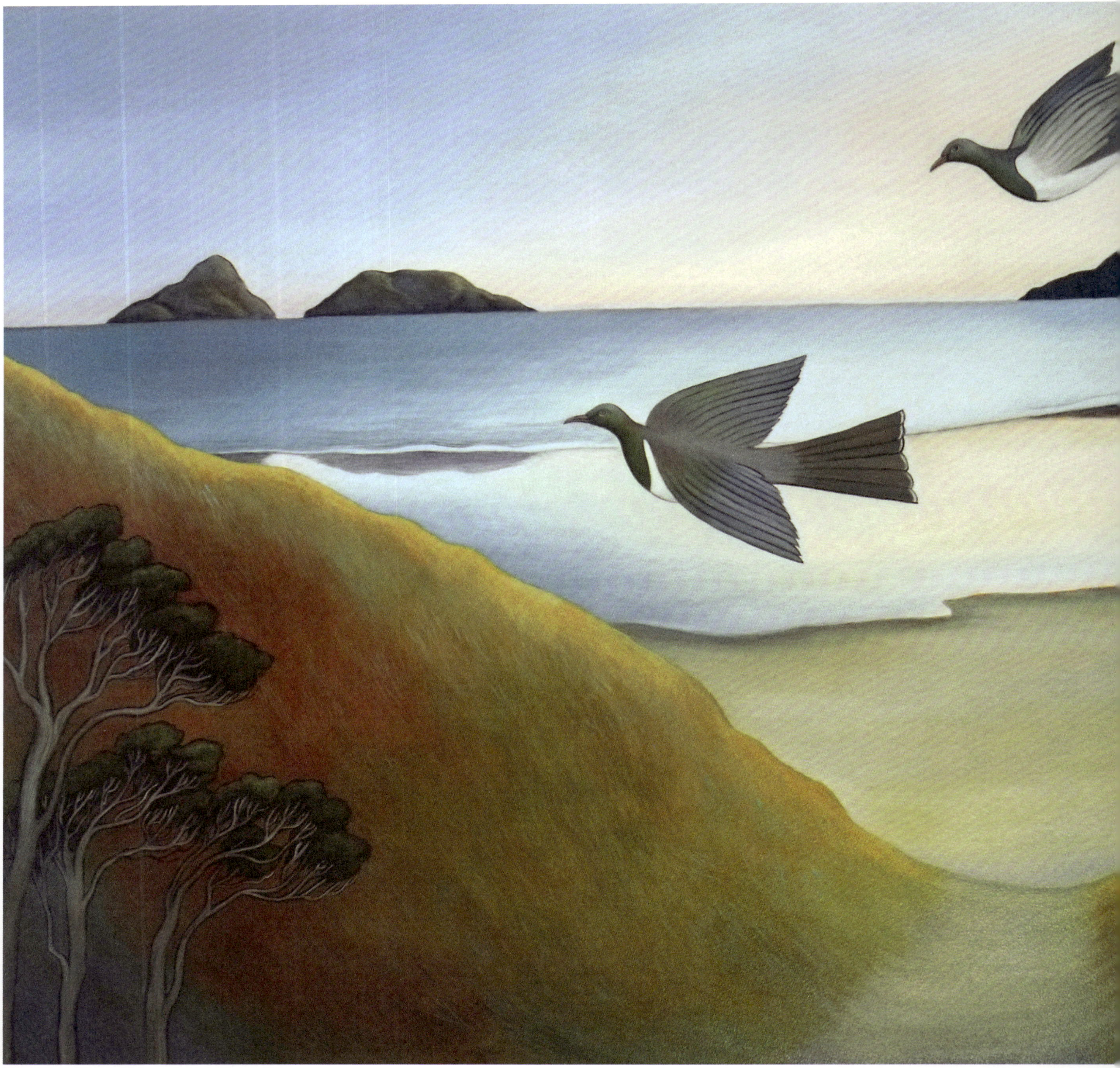

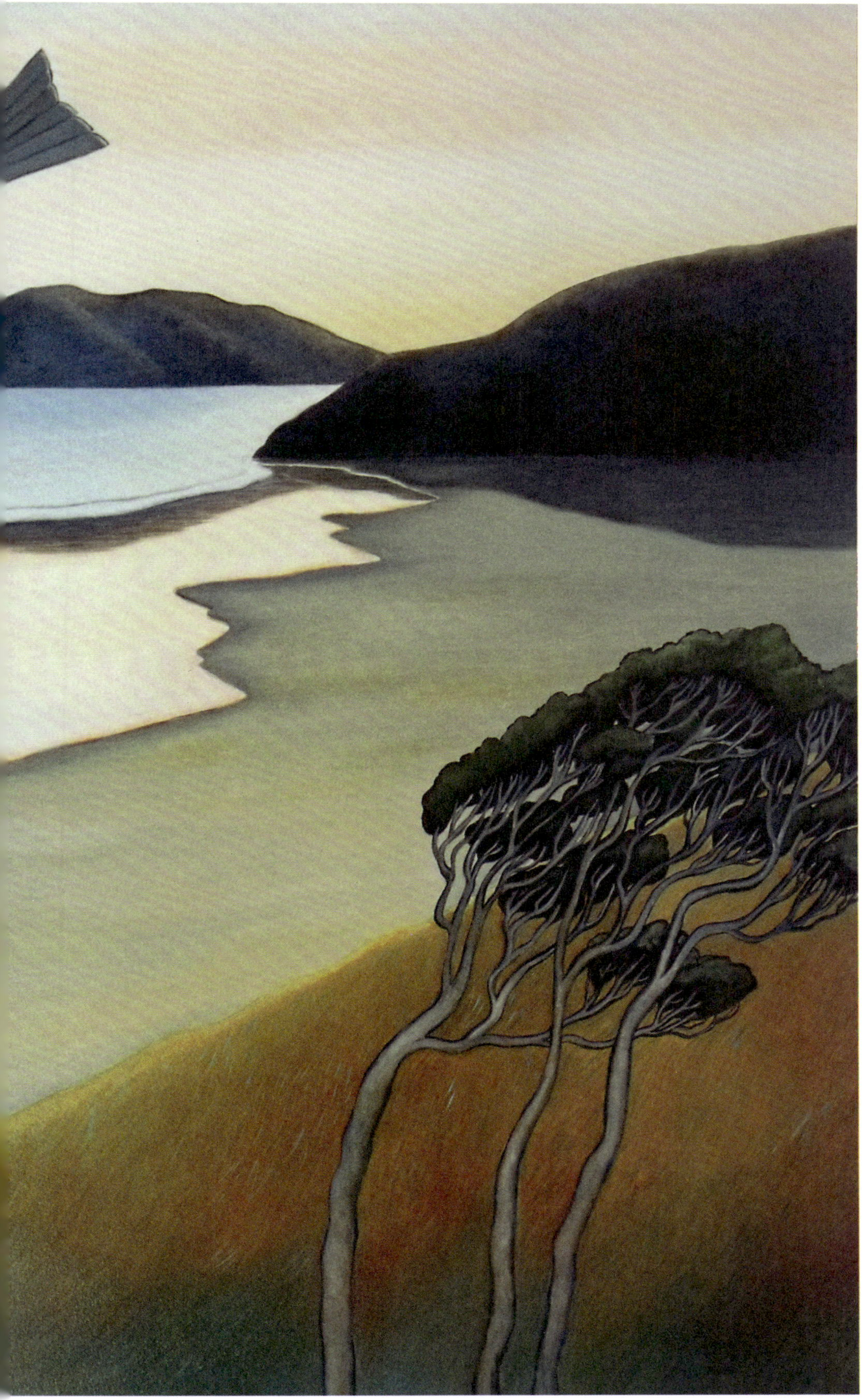

Sweeping the Bay 2010
740 x 1220 mm/29 x 48 in

'Serene and meditative, her paintings are sacred works for a secular age.'

— Gail Ross, *Eye of the Calm* catalogue, published 2009 by Primitive Bird Group

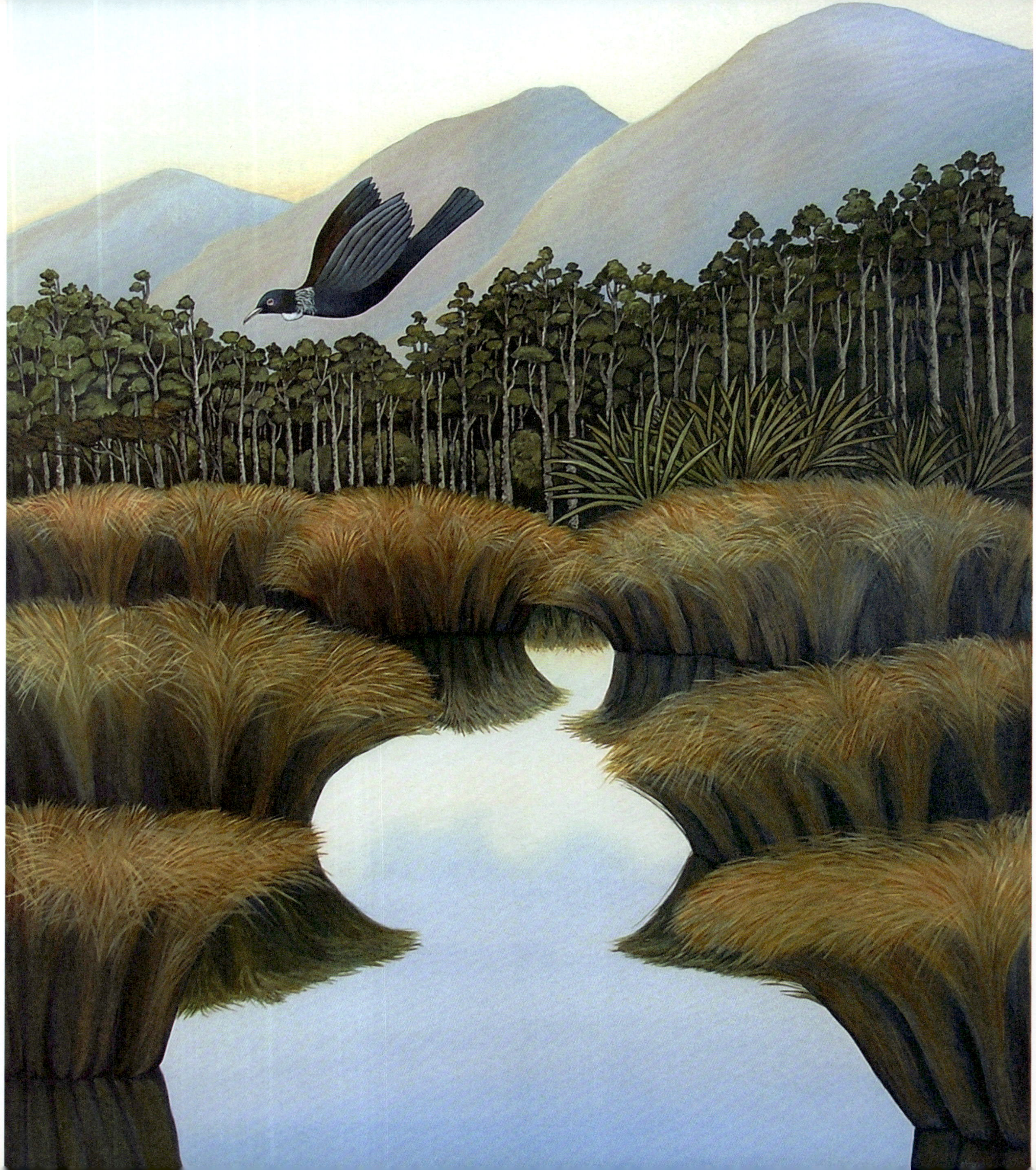

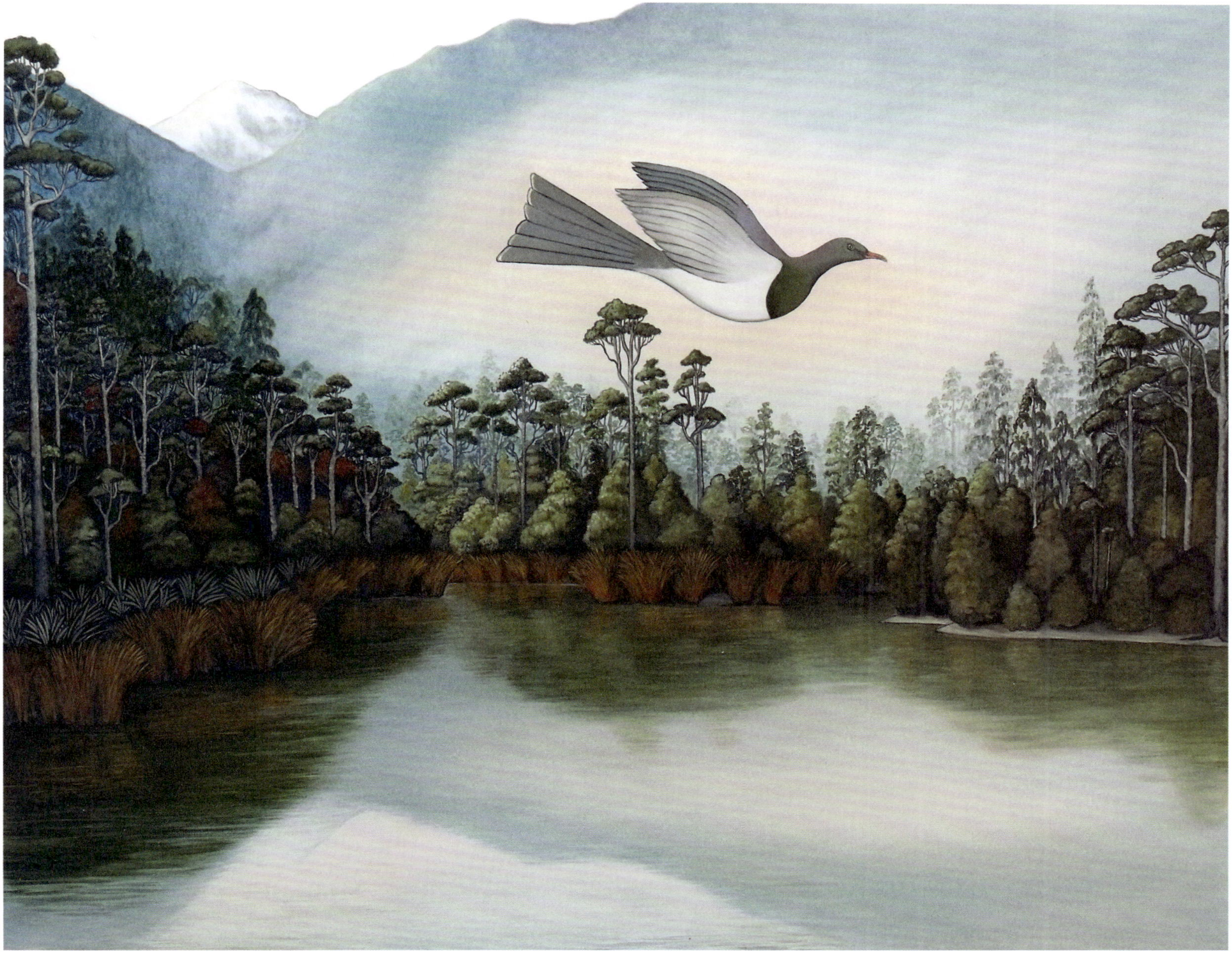

Opposite
Wetland Tūī, Westland 2008
1000 x 800 mm/39¼ x 31½ in

This Forest, Mine 2012
600 x 800 mm/23½ x 31½ in

Maud Island Magic

'When we step onto the Maud Island jetty, the lyrical wall of birdsong rises out of the underlying background silence, the sound of soft lapping waves on the shore and the warmth of the sun envelopes us.

'Once through the strict quarantine procedures, I find I have been allocated a little handmade slat bed, in the bunkroom. The bed looks flimsy and whimsical, but I find it surprisingly comfortable and am so tired each night that I experience my best nights of sleep in years. I am delighted by the two tiny windows by the bed. I gaze out at the numerous stars at night in the pitch-black sky.

'Our days become filled with early morning starts to get the mist nets in position at daybreak, and long days waiting in stillness for tūī to be distracted into the nets. Once a tūī is caught and untangled, one of my jobs is to quickly cross the hillsides with the tūī swinging wildly in a cloth bag, to be taken to the lodge lab, for checking and banding, before being released into one of the holding cages. Our day's work is not finished until late each evening. The 6 a.m. alarm always comes too quickly each following morning.'

My ten days on Maud became some of my most memorable experiences. The ease and rhythm of island life, fresh air and plenty of exercise, good company and excitement as we neared our goal provided a perfect antidote to endless hours spent at my easel in the confines of my studio and the normal stresses of everyday life.

A Chorus up the Valley 2013
1000 x 800 mm/39¼ x 31½ in

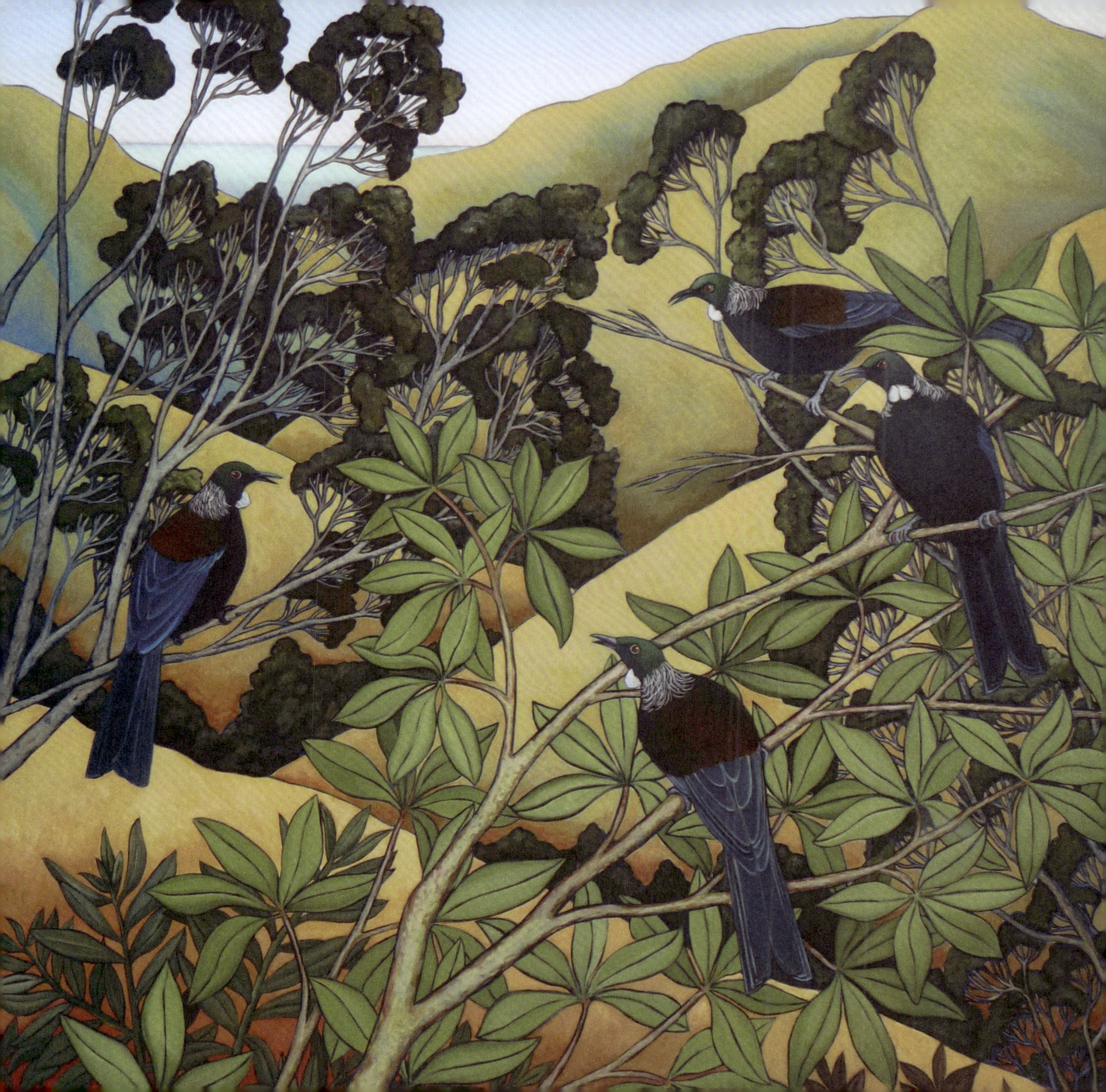

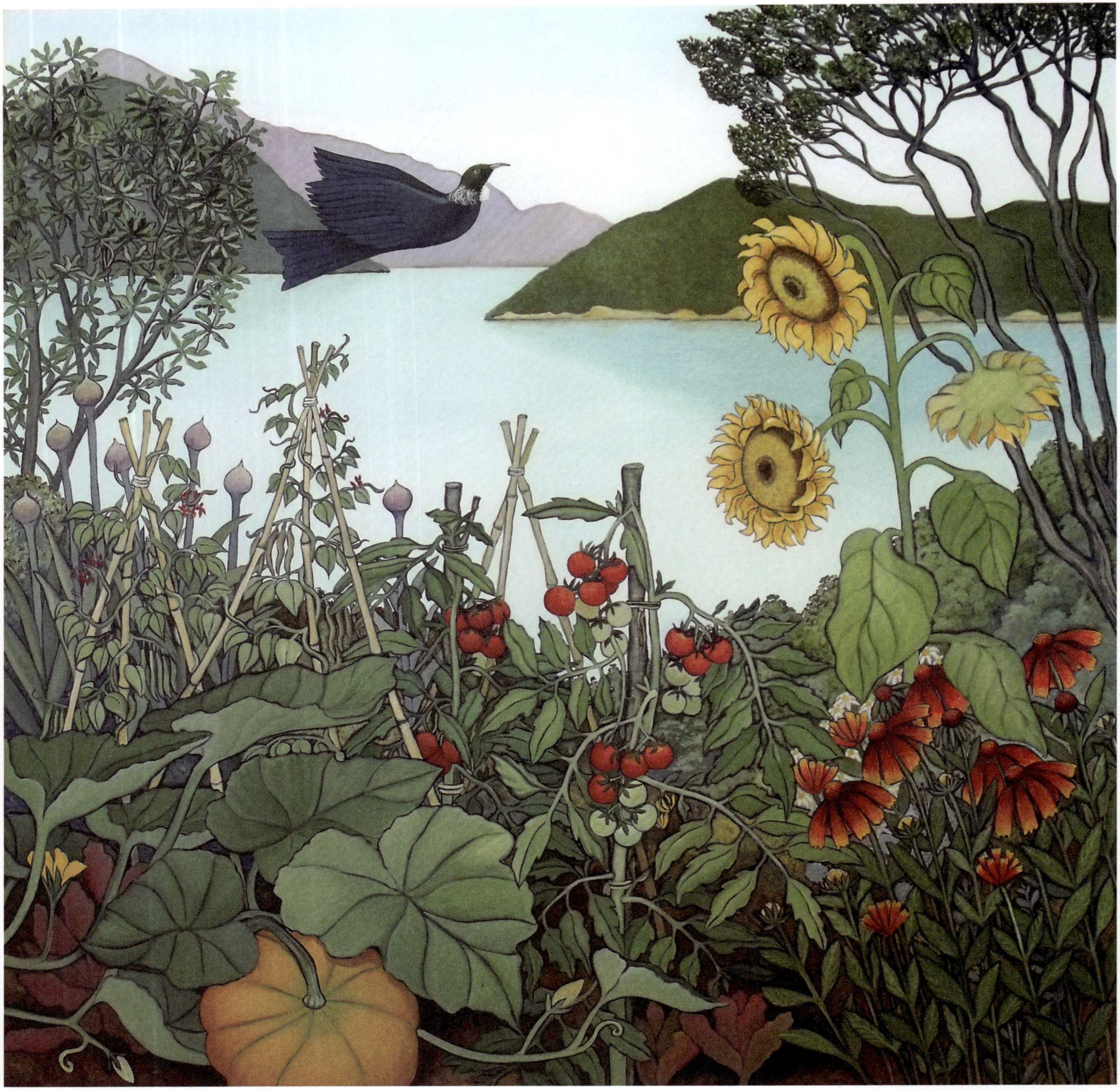

The Dance of the Juveniles 2010
1000 x 800 mm/39¼ x 31½ in

Opposite

Darting through the Kitchen Garden 2010
1000 x 1000 mm/39¼ x 39¼ in

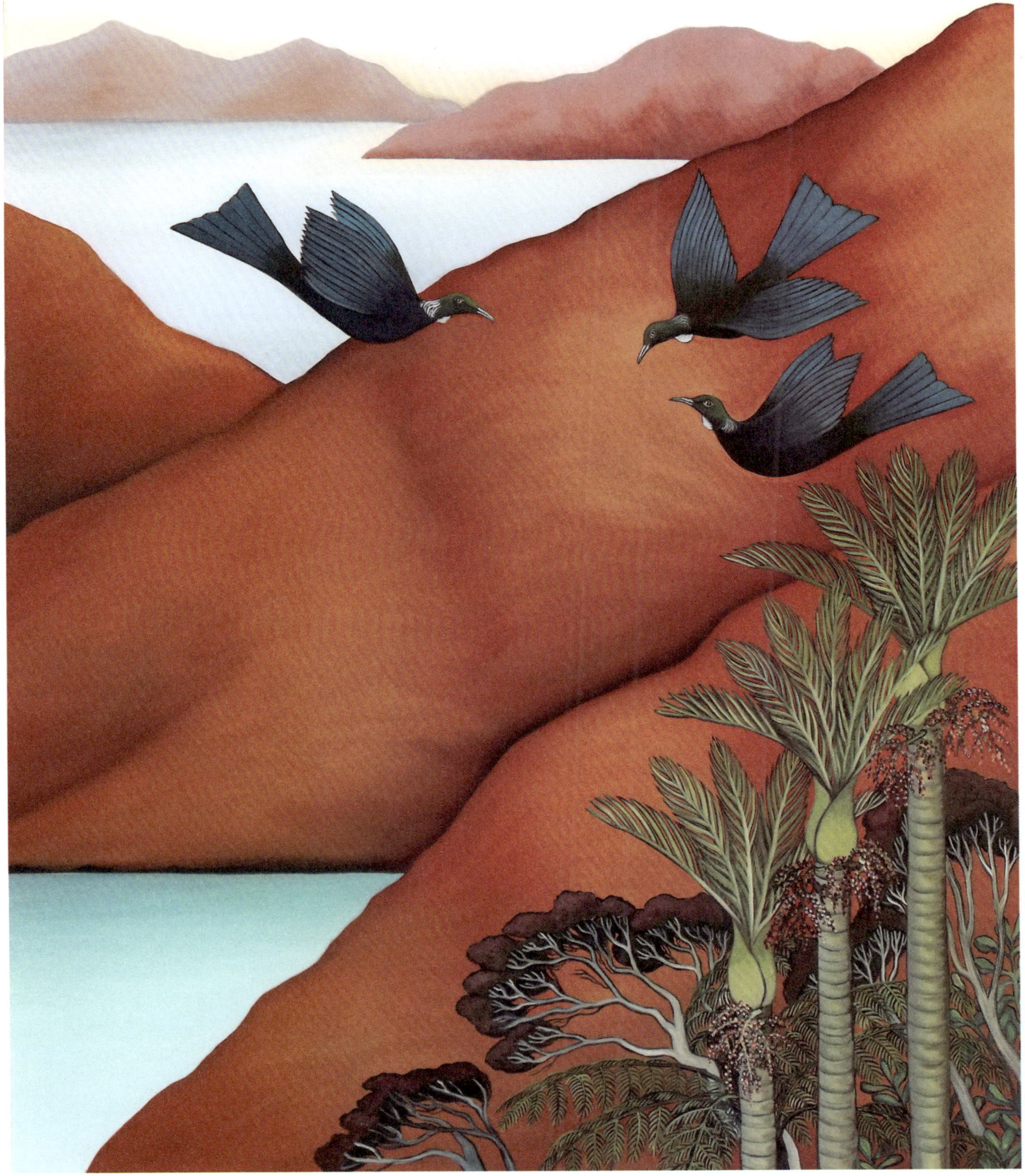

Drawing the Veil of Night

As the moon rises slowly over the horizon, three tūī sweep across the sky, drawing a veil of darkness behind them. It is the moment between dusk and dark, which holds the promise of night. Below them, the waters of the Marlborough Sounds shimmer in the changing light. Far from settlements, the stillness of the bay is stirred only by the flurry of their wing-beats, that special oily thrum of tūī-flight.

The water glistens in the moonlight, but also holds the inner sparkle of phosphorescence, tiny swirls of which explode in a cascade of brilliant sparks with the movement of the waves, as they reach the shore.

The heat of the day has passed and the potential for life and death, hope and renewal, is mirrored in the thrusting branch, offering up its nest from some submarine depth.

Behind the sparkle of the shoreline, the island is heaving into a new phase of existence, where the creatures of the night are stirring from their holes and crevasses. Some species have remained in an unchanged form for hundreds of thousands of years on this tiny scrap of land, called Maud Island.

The giant wētās form a highway on the clay path that rises up the hill. Their hard and shiny carapaces softly glow in the moonlight. The large female, (stretching the length of an adult's hand), signals to the males, who are half her size, to attend to her needs. Glow worms blink their light from damp fern-fronded banks. The ancient Maud Island frogs creep out from the fissures in the ground to roam the land. With their voices silent, they communicate through chemical signals, carrying their young froglets on their backs.

It is time for the invertebrates of the night to dance their way into the island evening.

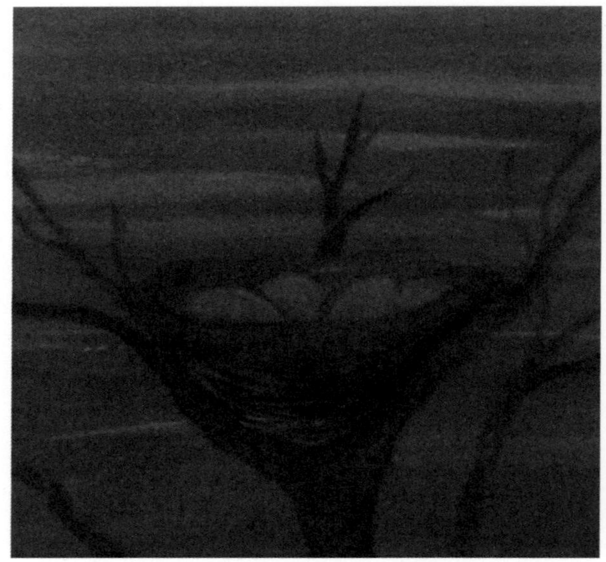

Detail
Drawing the Veil of Night

Opposite
Drawing the Veil of Night 2012
1000 x 800 mm/39¼ x 31½ in

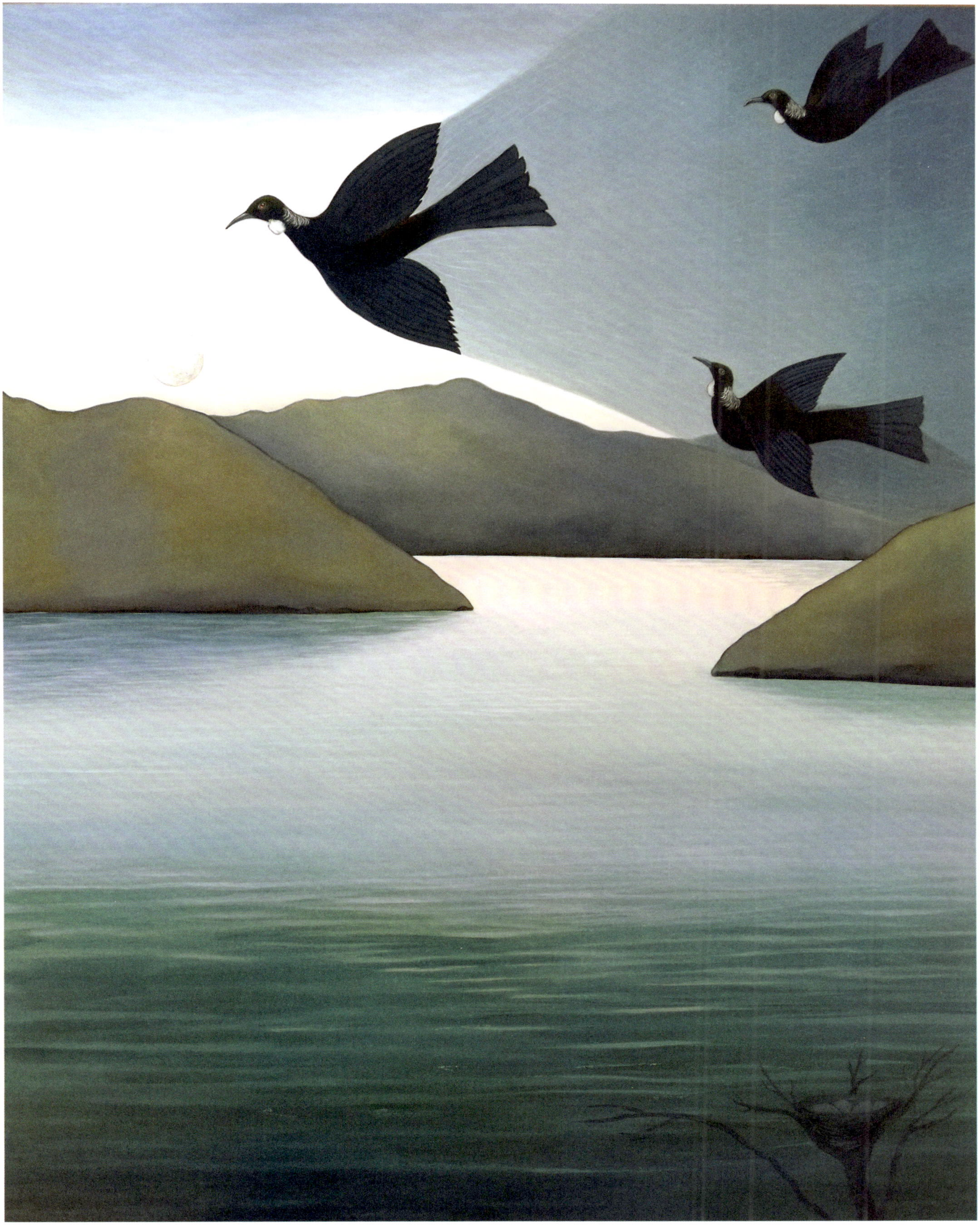

Eye of the Calm

As a young person, cycling round Pāuatahanui Inlet on a still morning always sent me into a deep sense of the sublime. That sense of freedom to roam in a beautiful peaceful setting has haunted me. Reflective water echoing sky and hills, maybe broken by the ripples of a wading bird. I was lucky enough to experience this nearby location at a time before major subdivisions filled the area with houses and traffic. There were few passing cars when I sojourned there in the 1960s and early 70s.

That pursuit of peaceful meditative water has stayed with me for many decades, and my most memorable days have always been linked to being on or by still water. A state of ecstasy and uplift, constantly being sought in my paintings, has driven my work.

I describe it as the Eye of the Calm, and in my days and my travels I seek out those moments of calm on inlets, estuaries and tidal harbours, wetlands and rivers.

Kohukohu Morning

A heron creaks a raspy call
And circles down from the
Old totara tree
Bulky neck and wide wing flap
He scoops the air forward to land
Down amongst the mangroves

Here at the water's edge
The thick gloop of mud
Glistens silver and sparkles in the
Soft moody light of morning

There is mist drifting in the hills
Across the stretch of water and
Luminous rising clouds are
Puffing into the pale washed sky
Reflecting blue/grey/white in the
Metallic sheen of this still harbour,
Hokianga

Late Afternoon Abundance 2014
1000 x 1000 mm/39¼ x 39¼ in

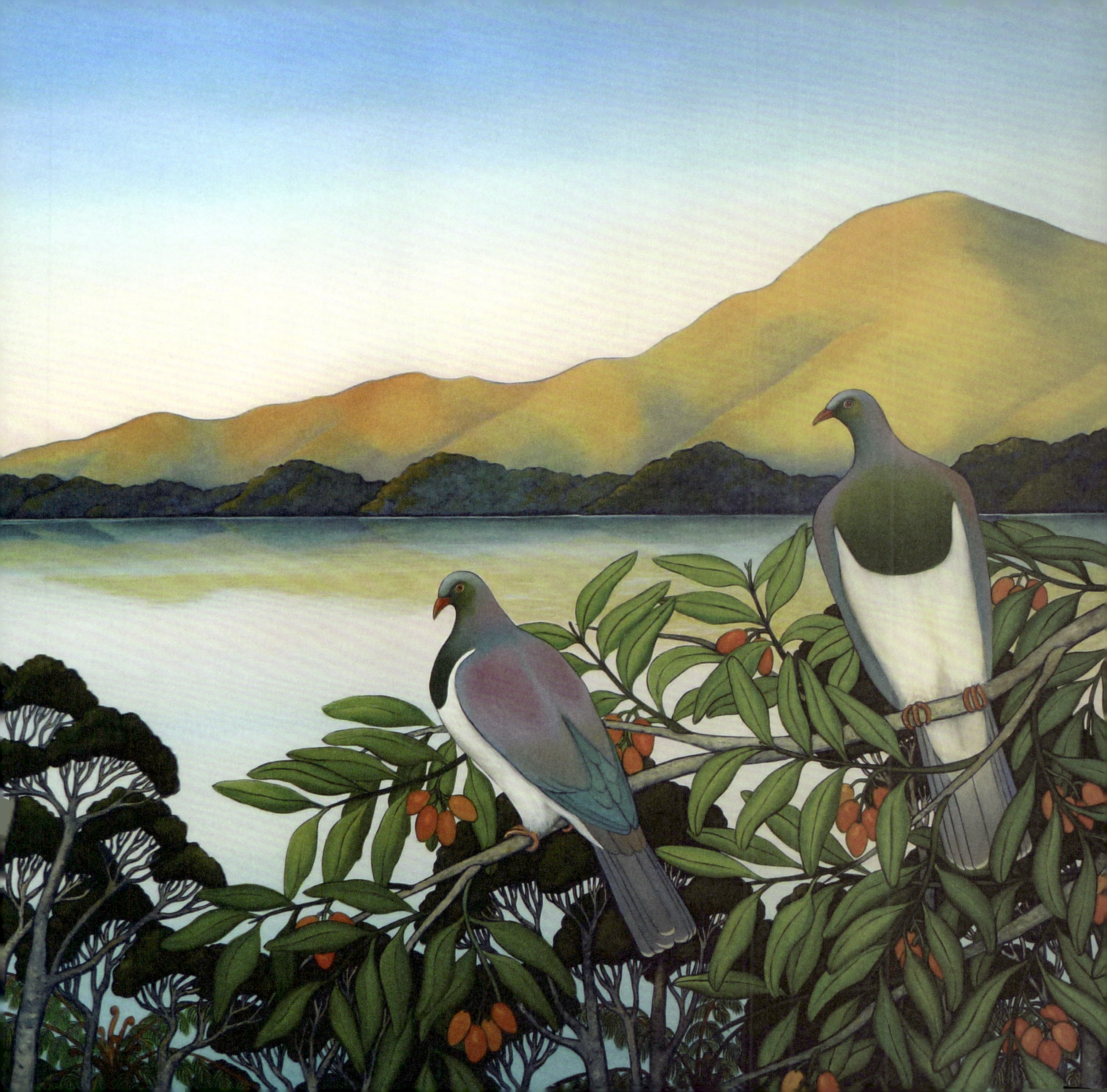

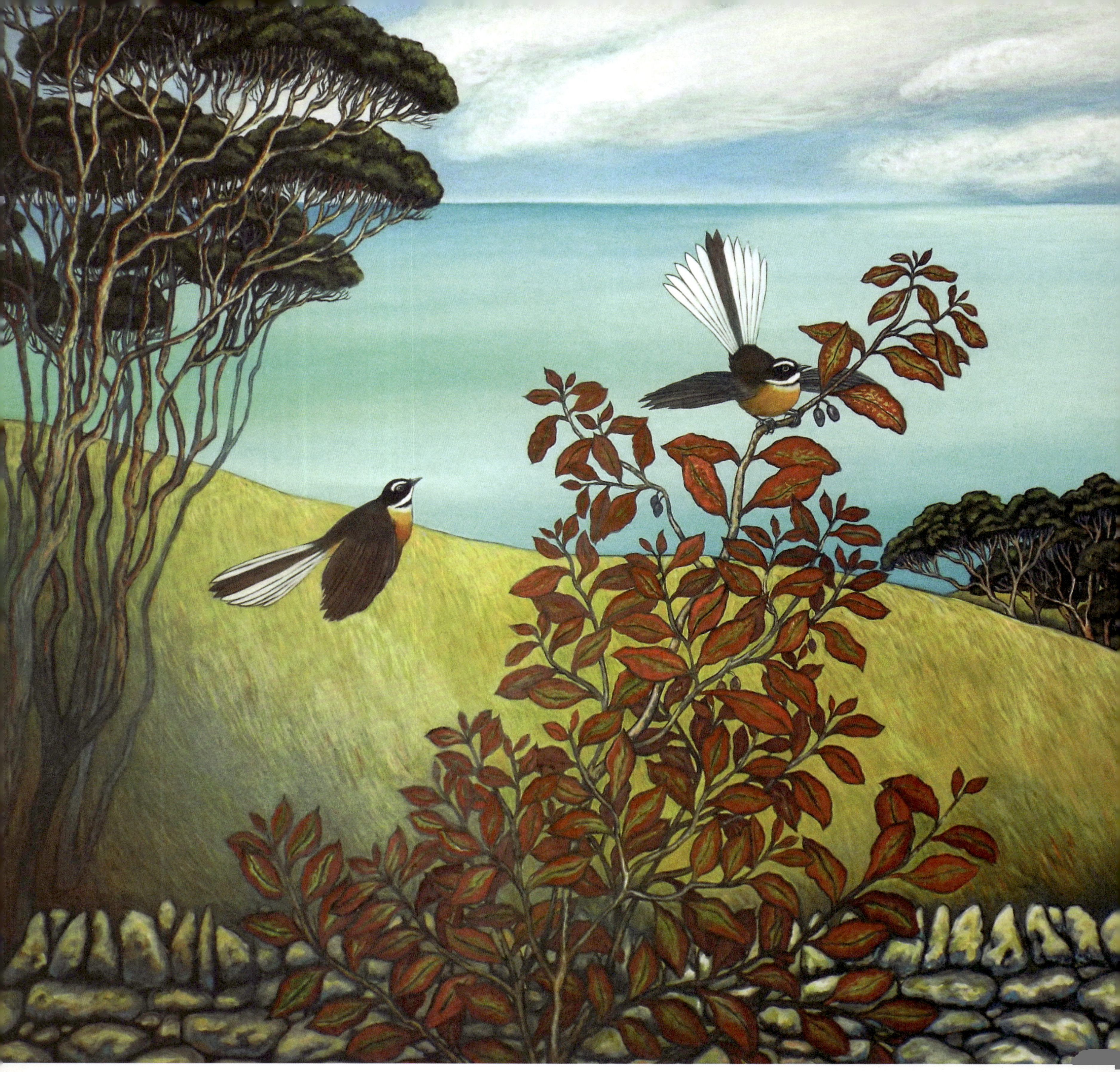

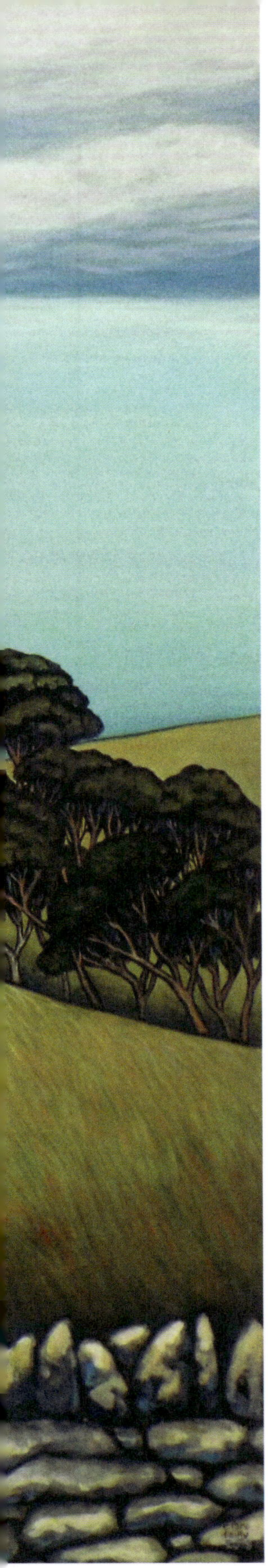

‘Reilly’s images of the natural world are alive with feeling. She confesses that she spends her life forever looking at what’s around her, very intensely, and by combining colour, form and line in her own particular and identifiable way, she succeeds in carrying us, enchanted, into the landscape of her artistic vision.’

— Zoe Reeves, *West to East*, paintings by Clare Reilly 2003

The Old Stone Wall 2019
840 x 1000 mm/33 x 39¼ in

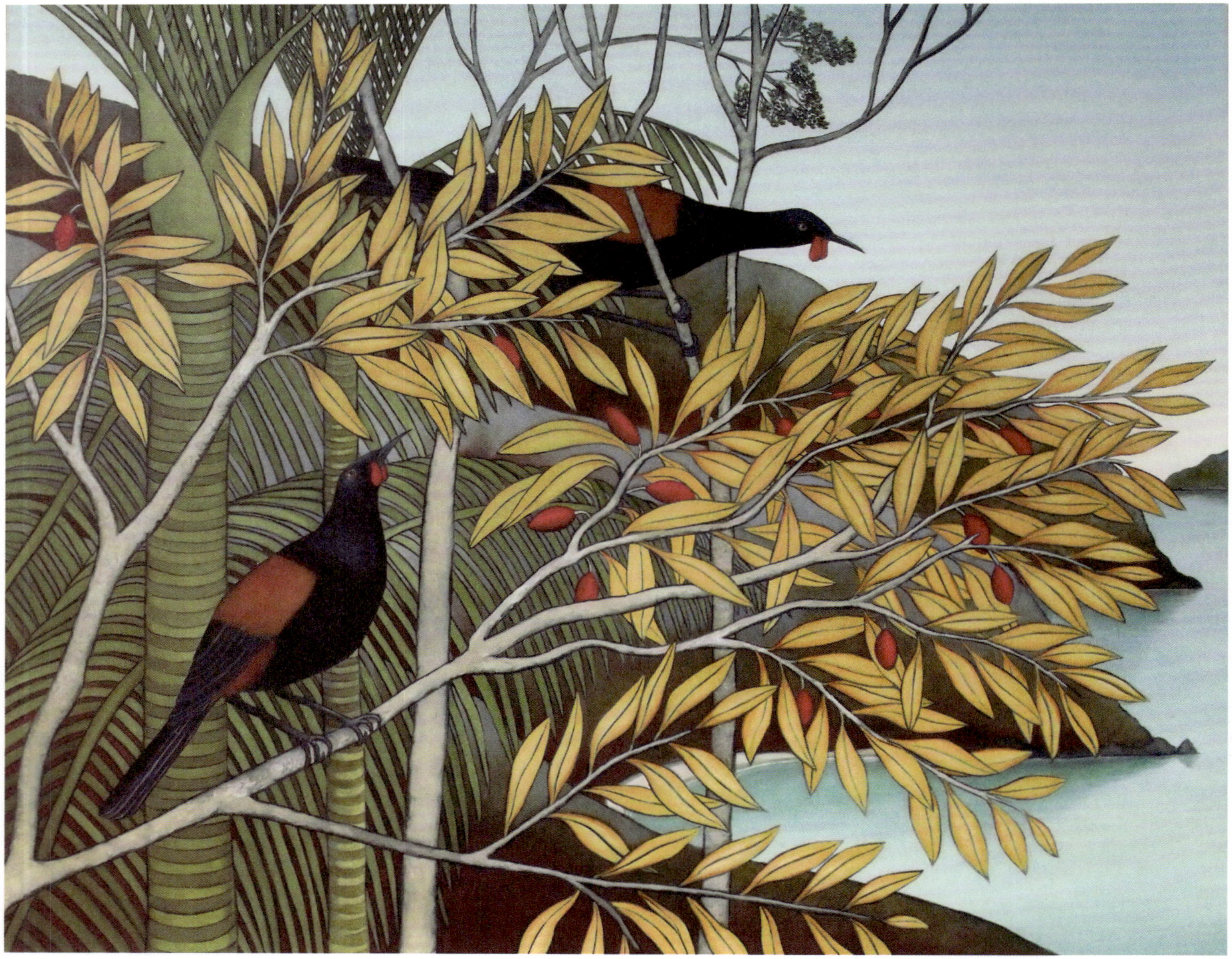

Saddlebacks Chant in the Land Before Time 2011
800 x 1000 mm/31½ x 39¼ in

Opposite

Arrival of the Shining Cuckoos 2016
800 x 600 mm/31½ x 23½ in

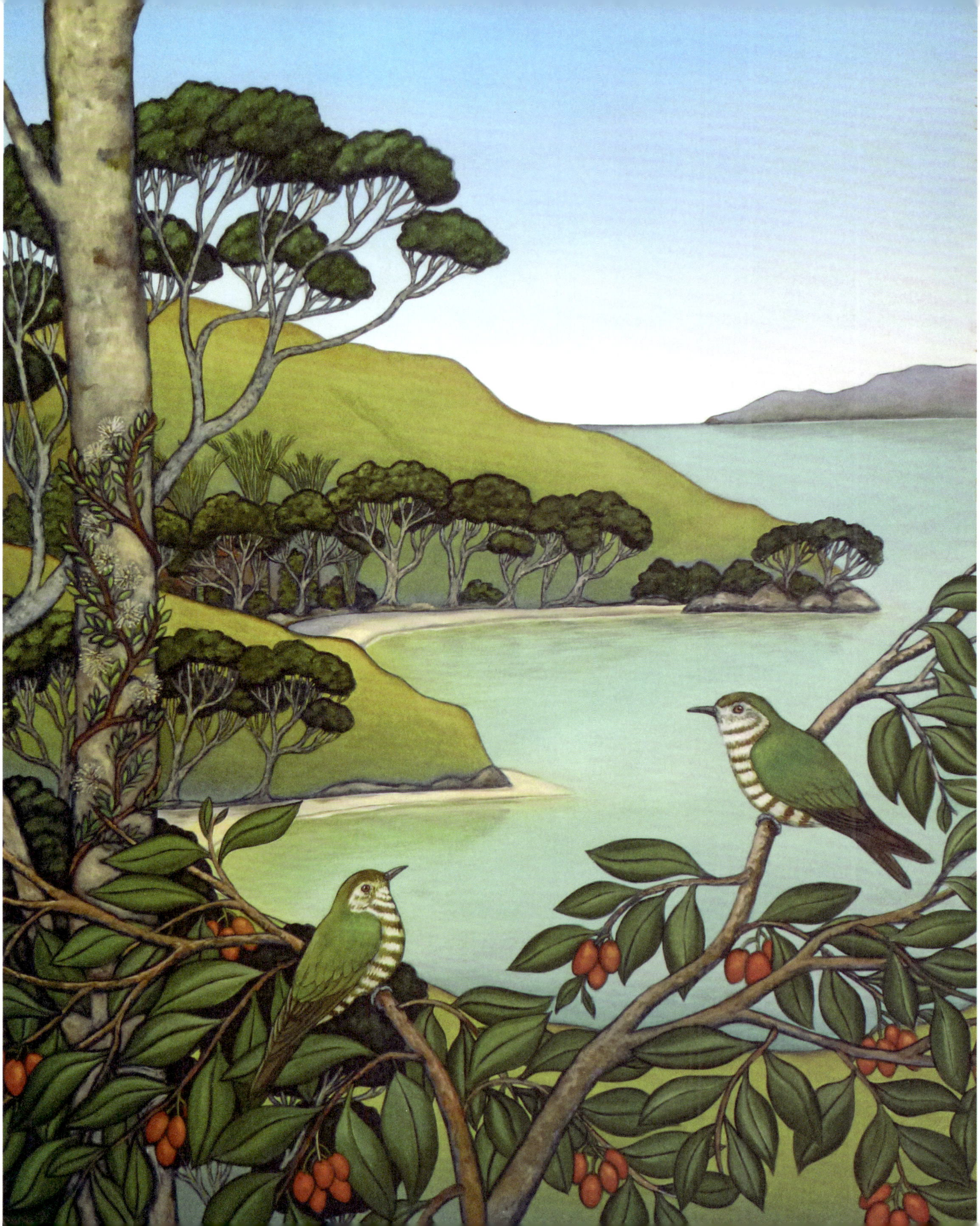

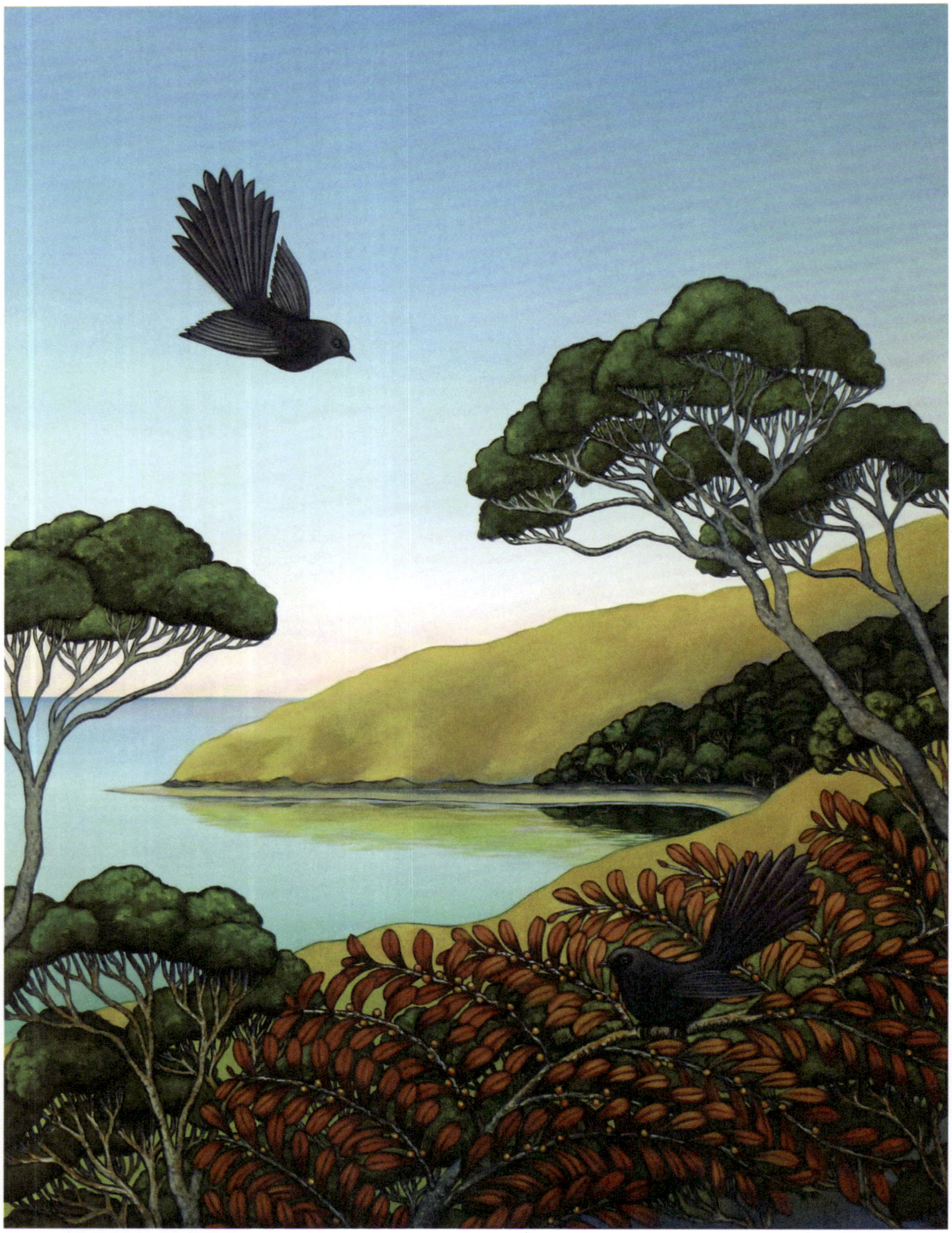

Black Fantails 2015
800 x 600 mm/31½ x 23½ in

Opposite
Across This Blazing Land 2010
1000 x 1000 mm/39¼ x 39¼ in

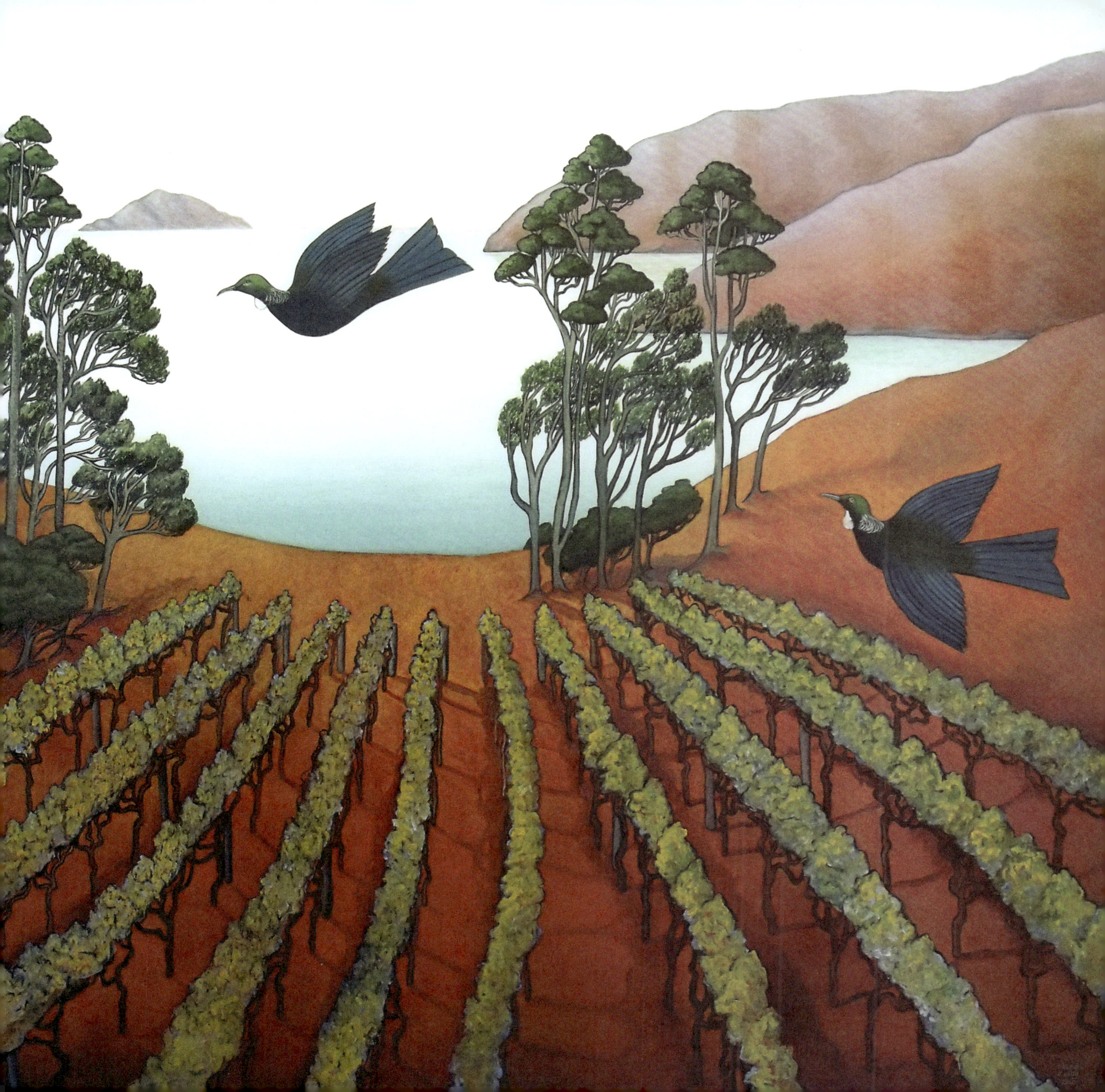

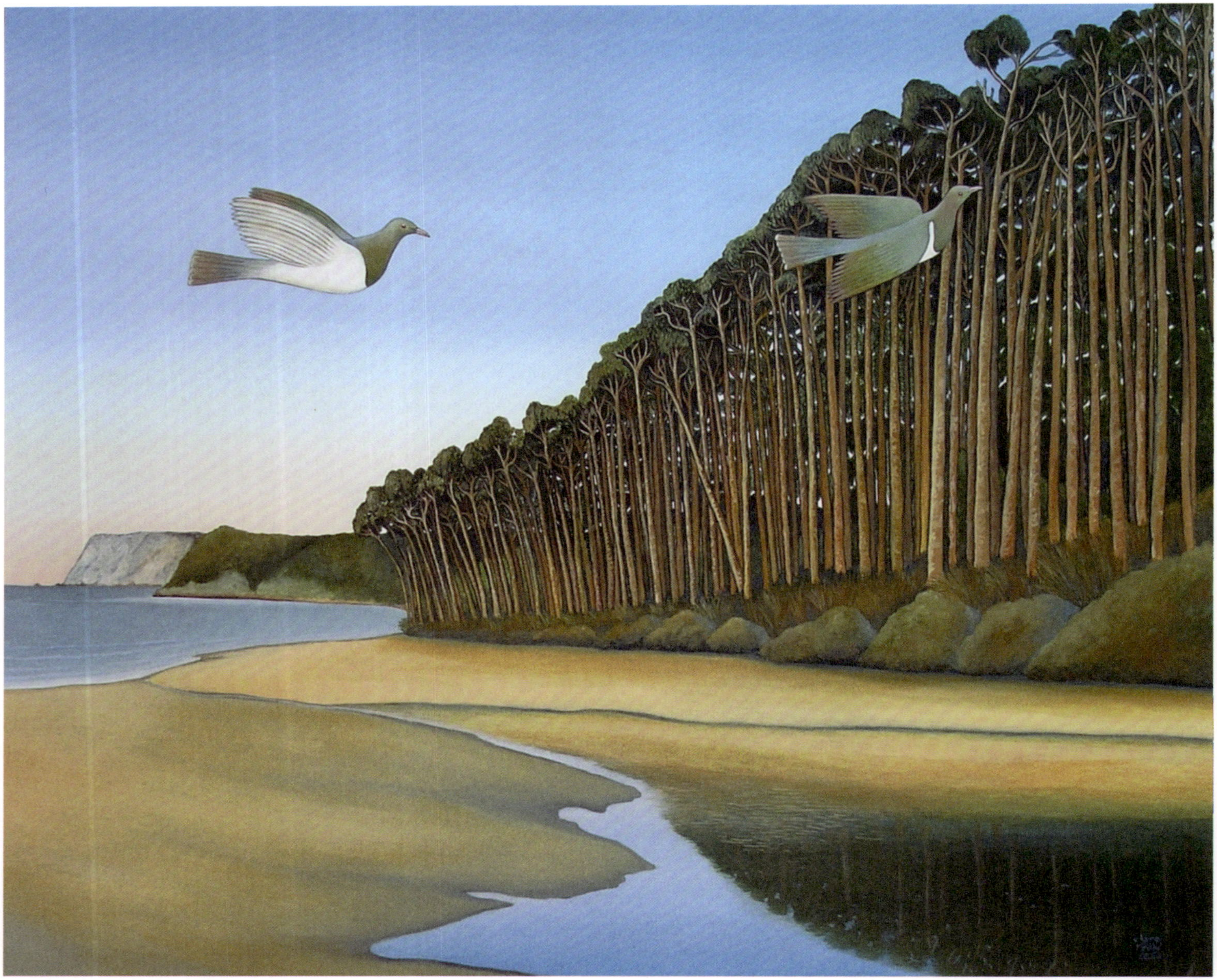

Coasting 2008
830 x 1000 mm/32½ x 39¼ in

Opposite
Mountain Kākā 2007
1000 x 800 mm/39¼ x 31½ in

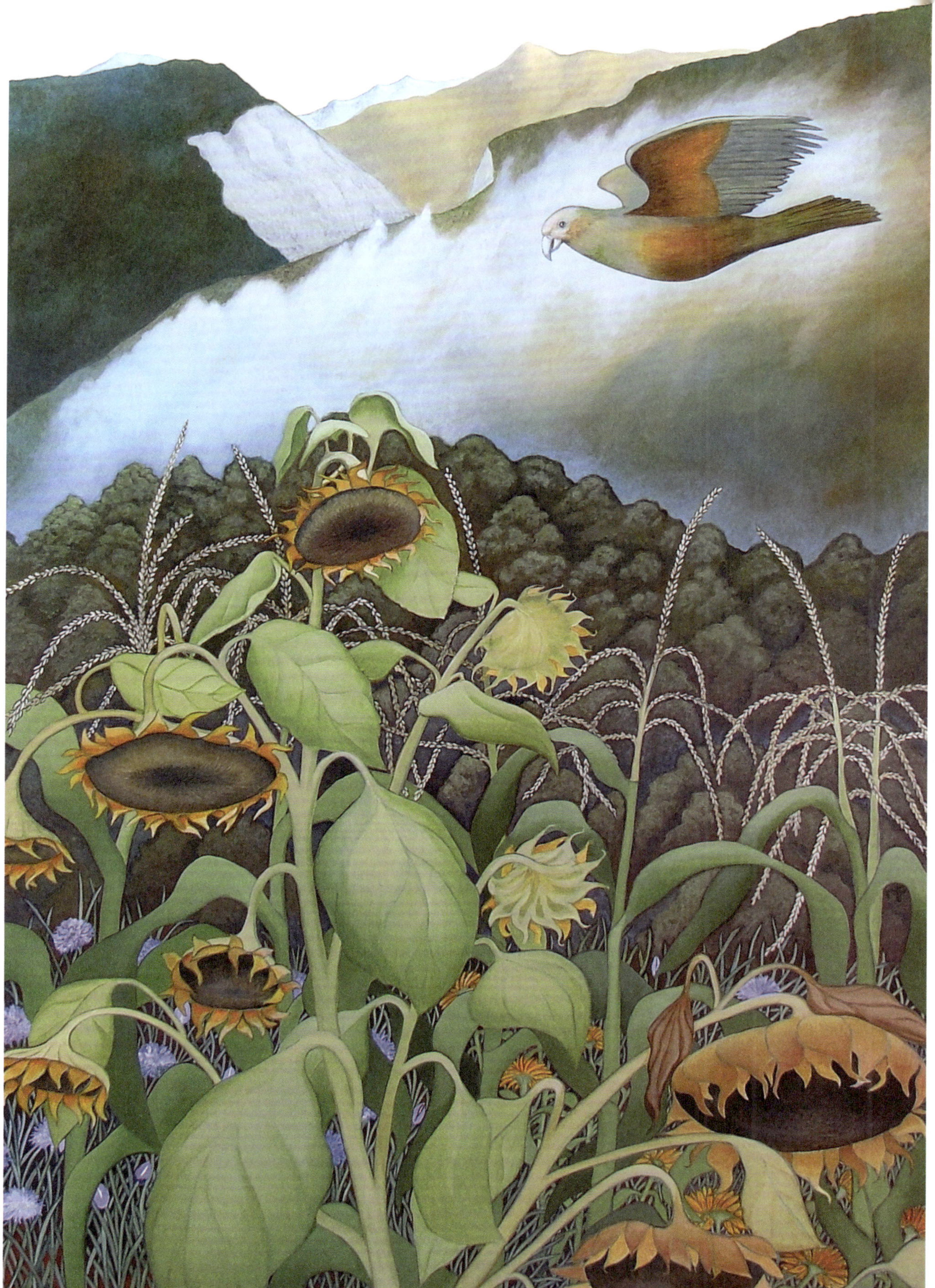

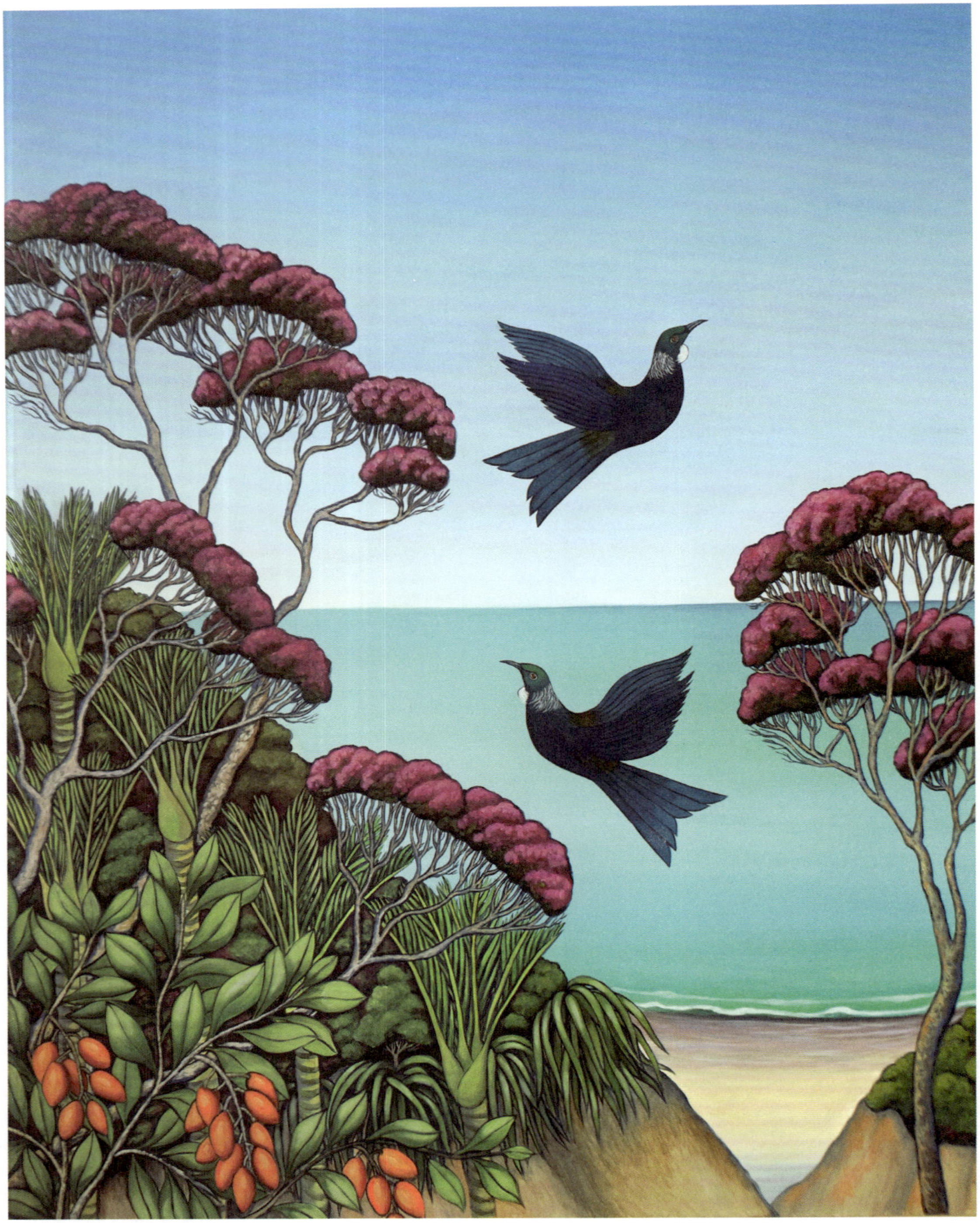

Exuberance 2020
1000 x 800 mm/39¼ x 31½ in

Opposite
At the Pool 2012
800 x 600 mm/31½ x 23½ in

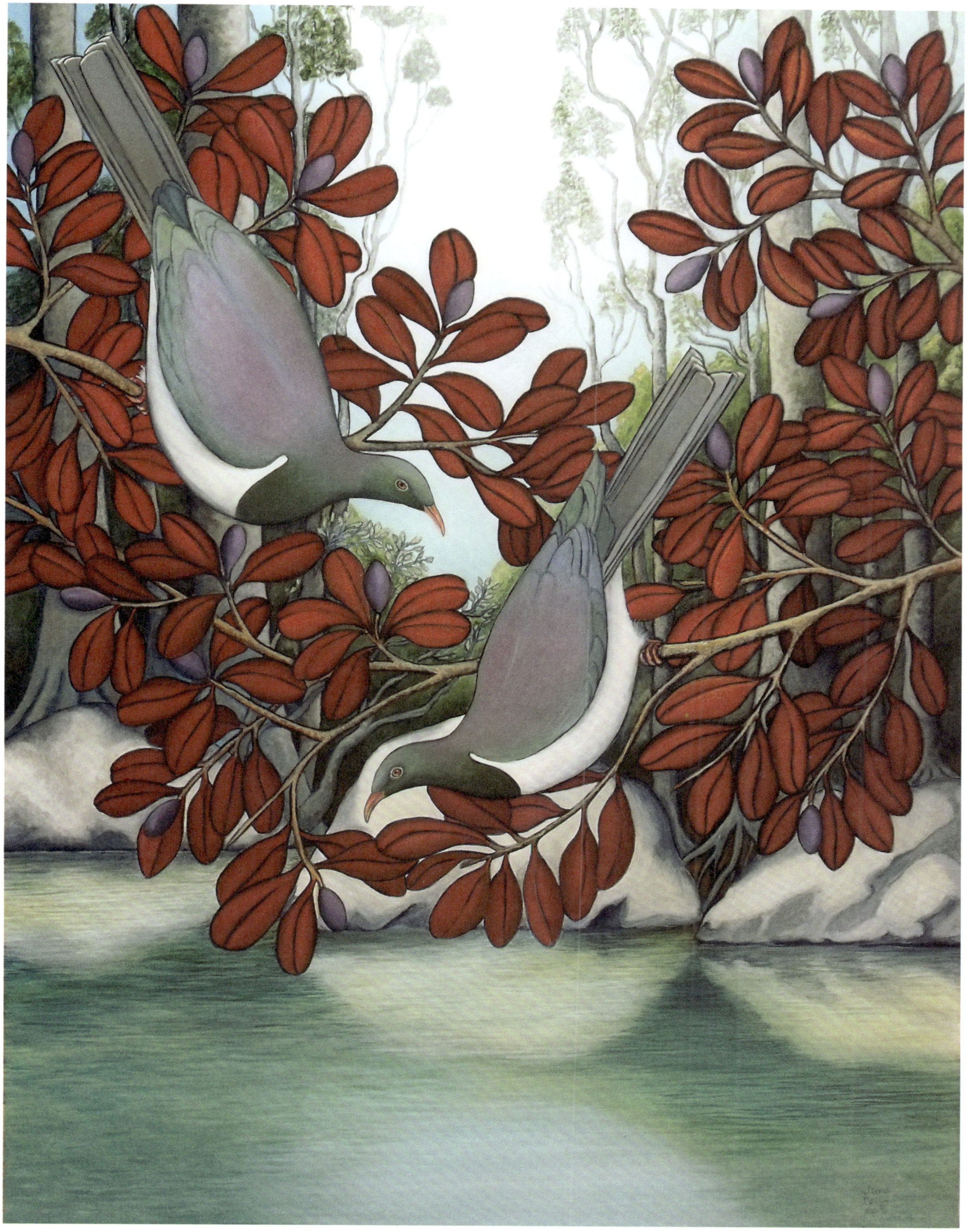

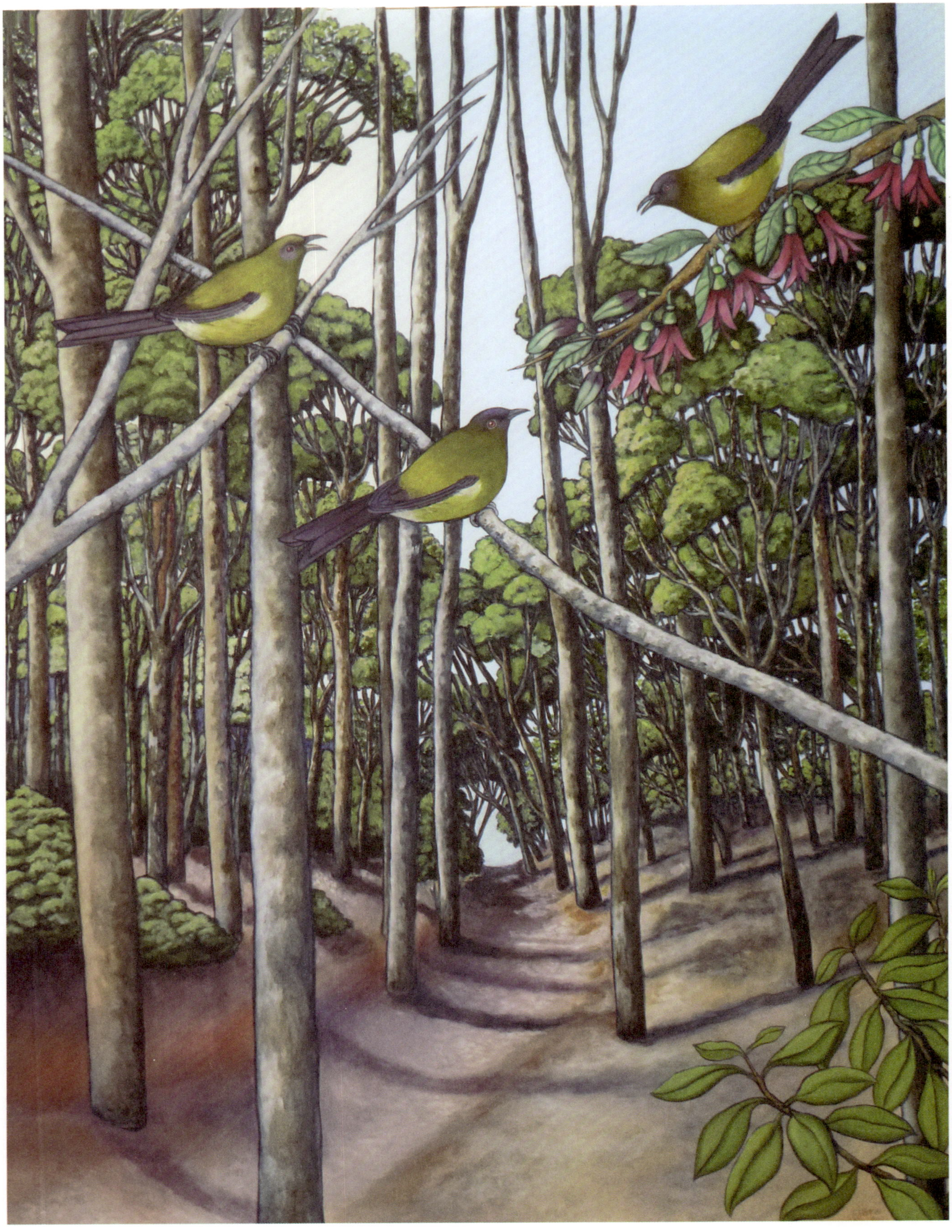

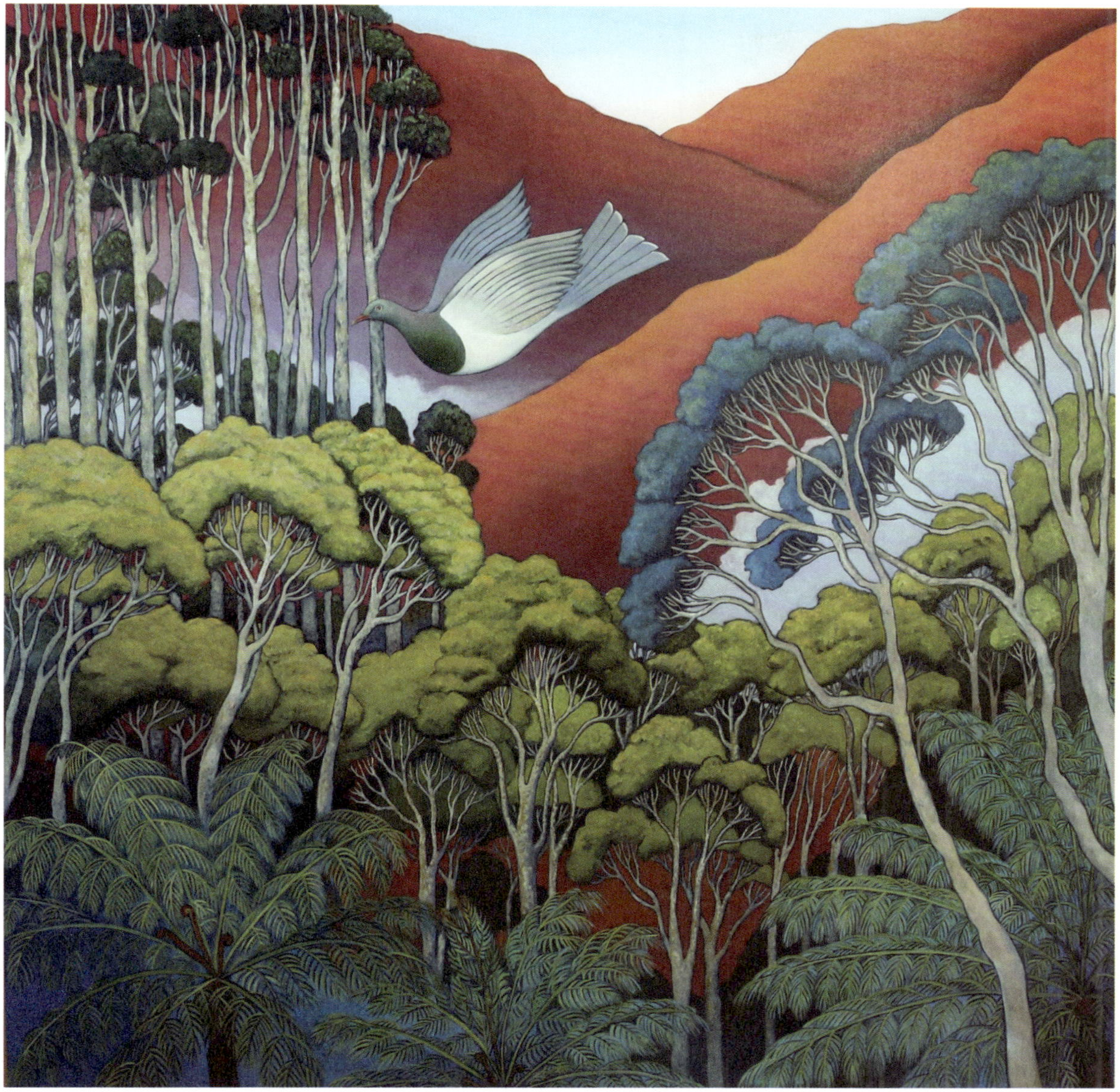

When the Forest Sings 2013
1000 x 1000 mm/39¼ x 39¼ in

Opposite
Singing Of Treasures 2015
800 x 600 mm/31½ x 23½ in

Toutouwai

The South Island robin has a call
that is strong and distinctive
A surprise from such a small bird
He has been calling from my hedgerow
Pecking the ground at my feet.

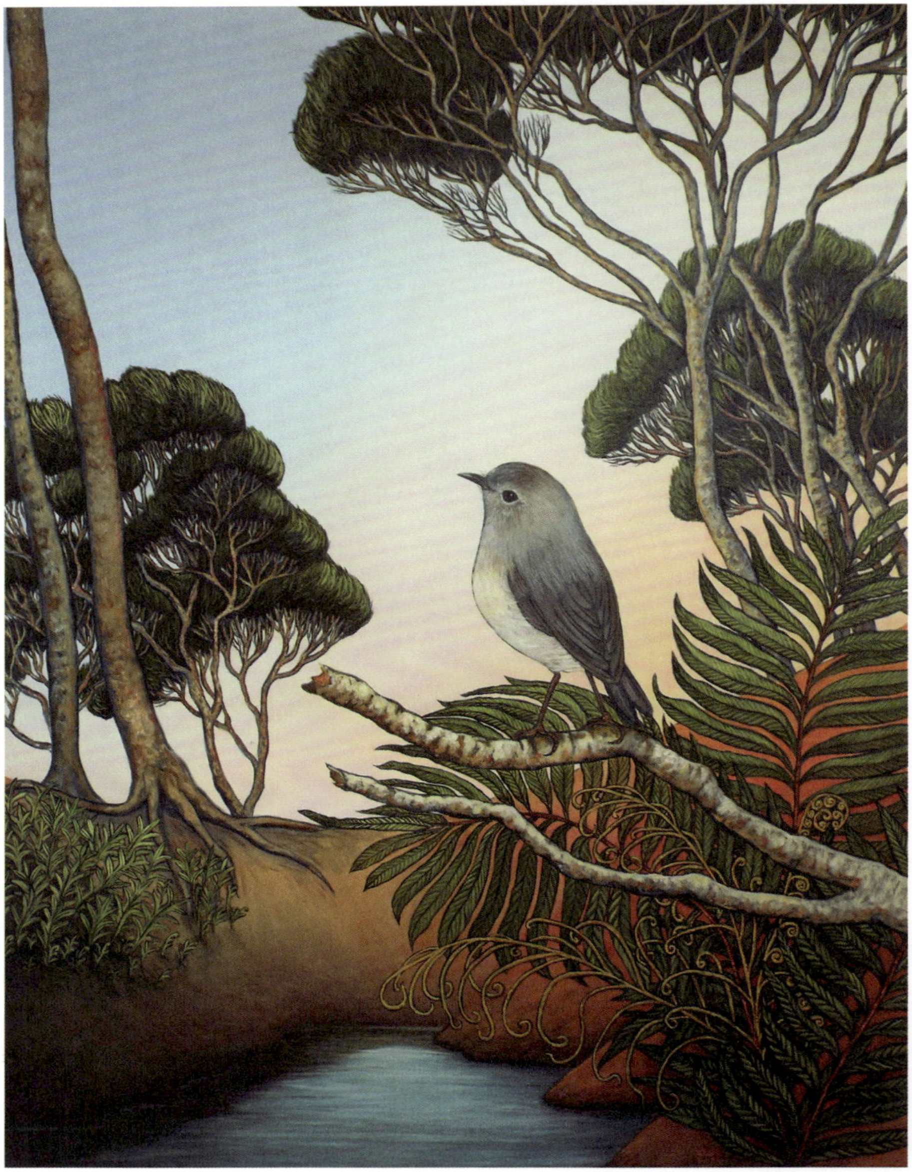

Toutouwai, South Island Robin 2018
800 x 600 mm/31½ x 23½ in

Opposite
Dart River Falcon 2009
1000 x 800 mm/39¼ x 31½ in

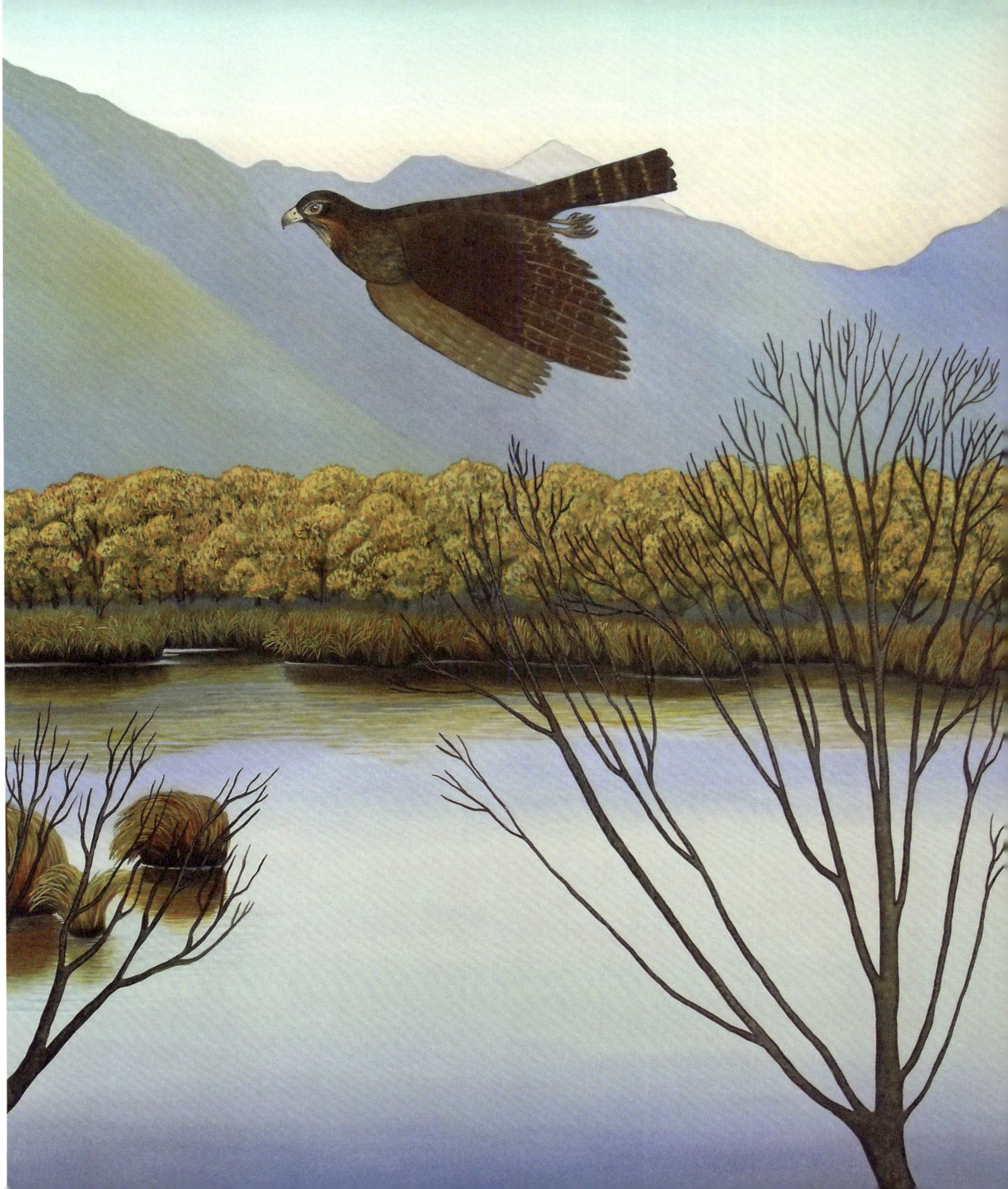

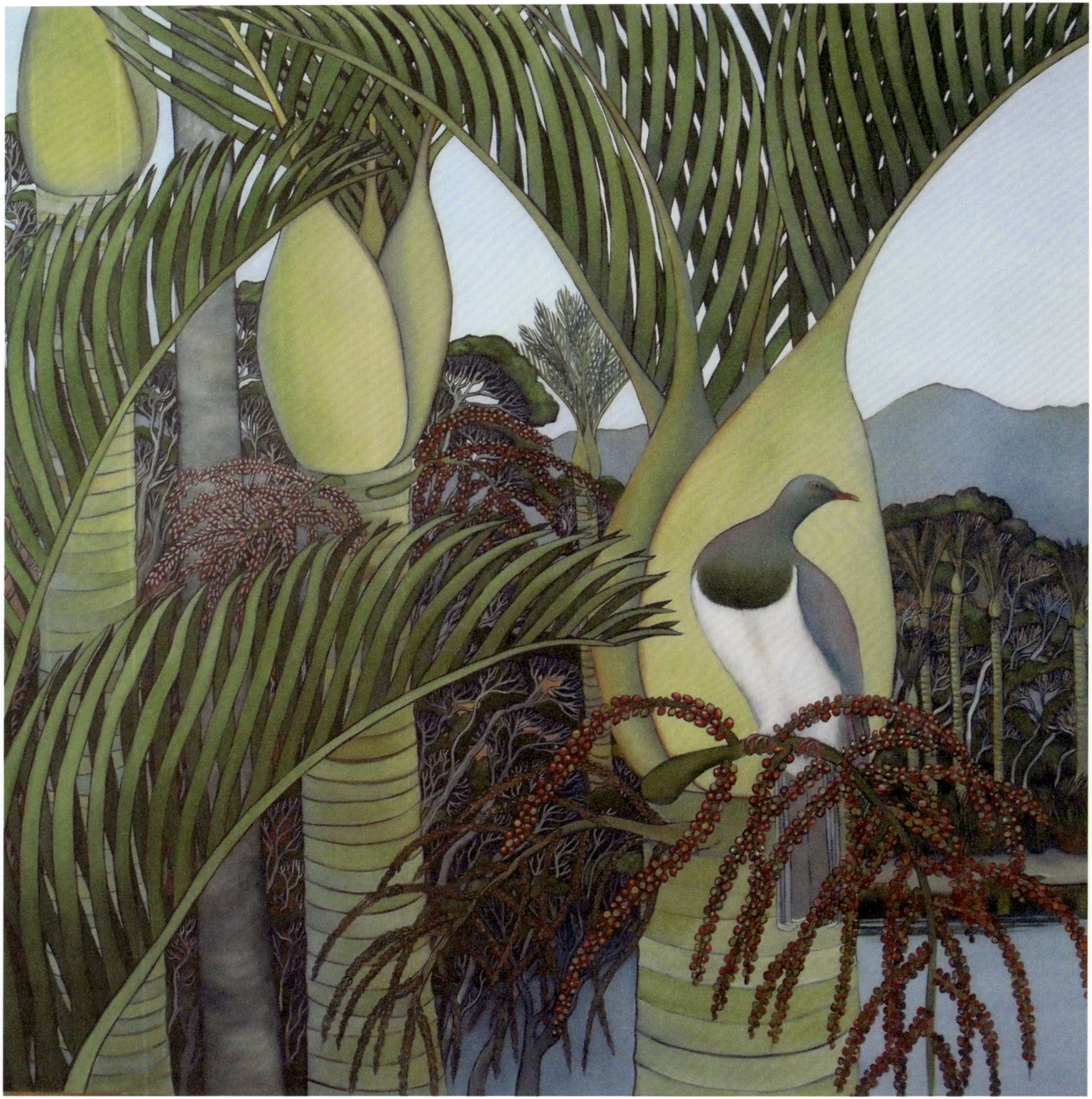

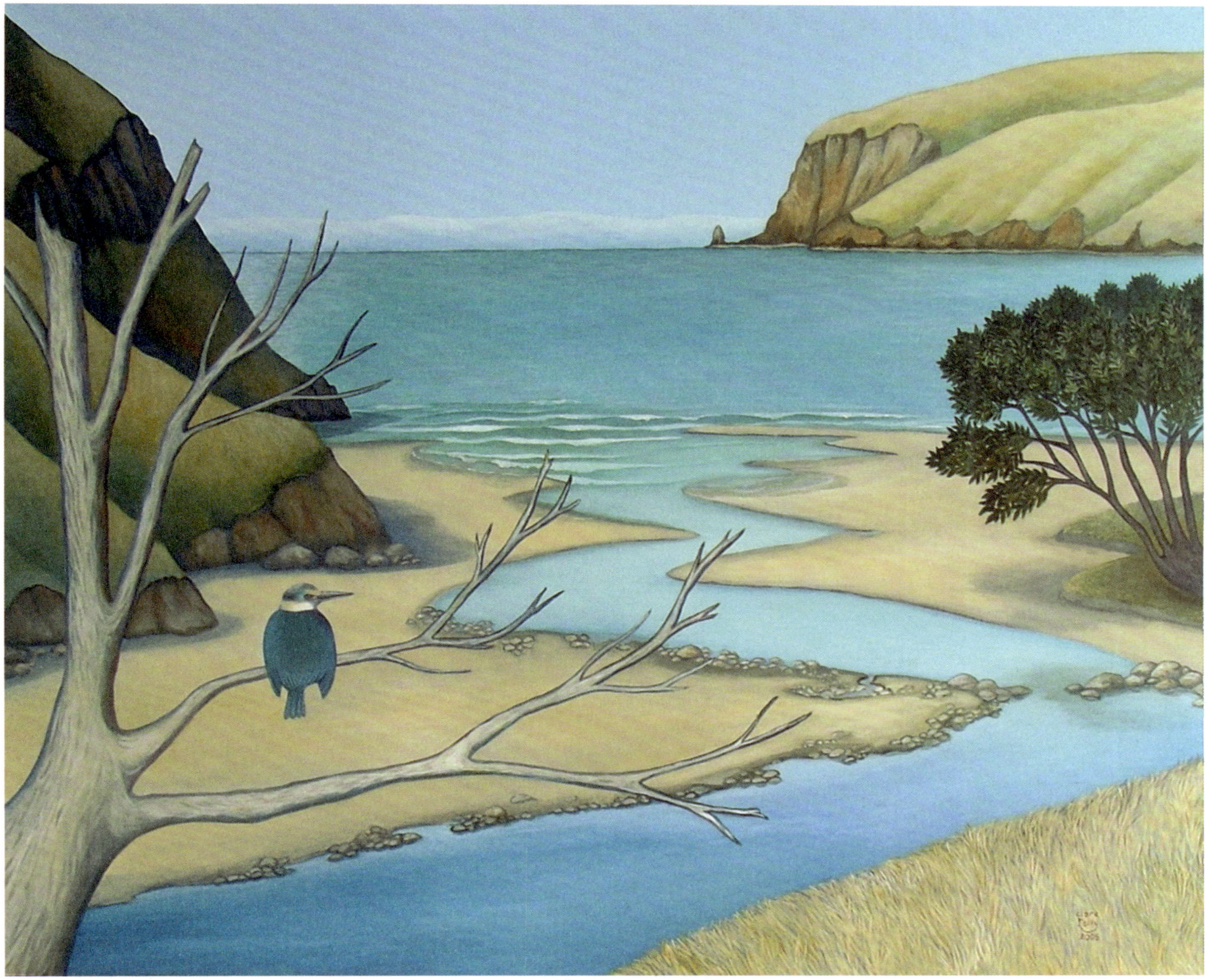

Kingfisher's Bay 2005
840 x 1000 mm/33 x 39¼ in

Opposite
Deep in the Nikau Forest 2013
1000 x 1000 mm/39¼ x 39¼ in

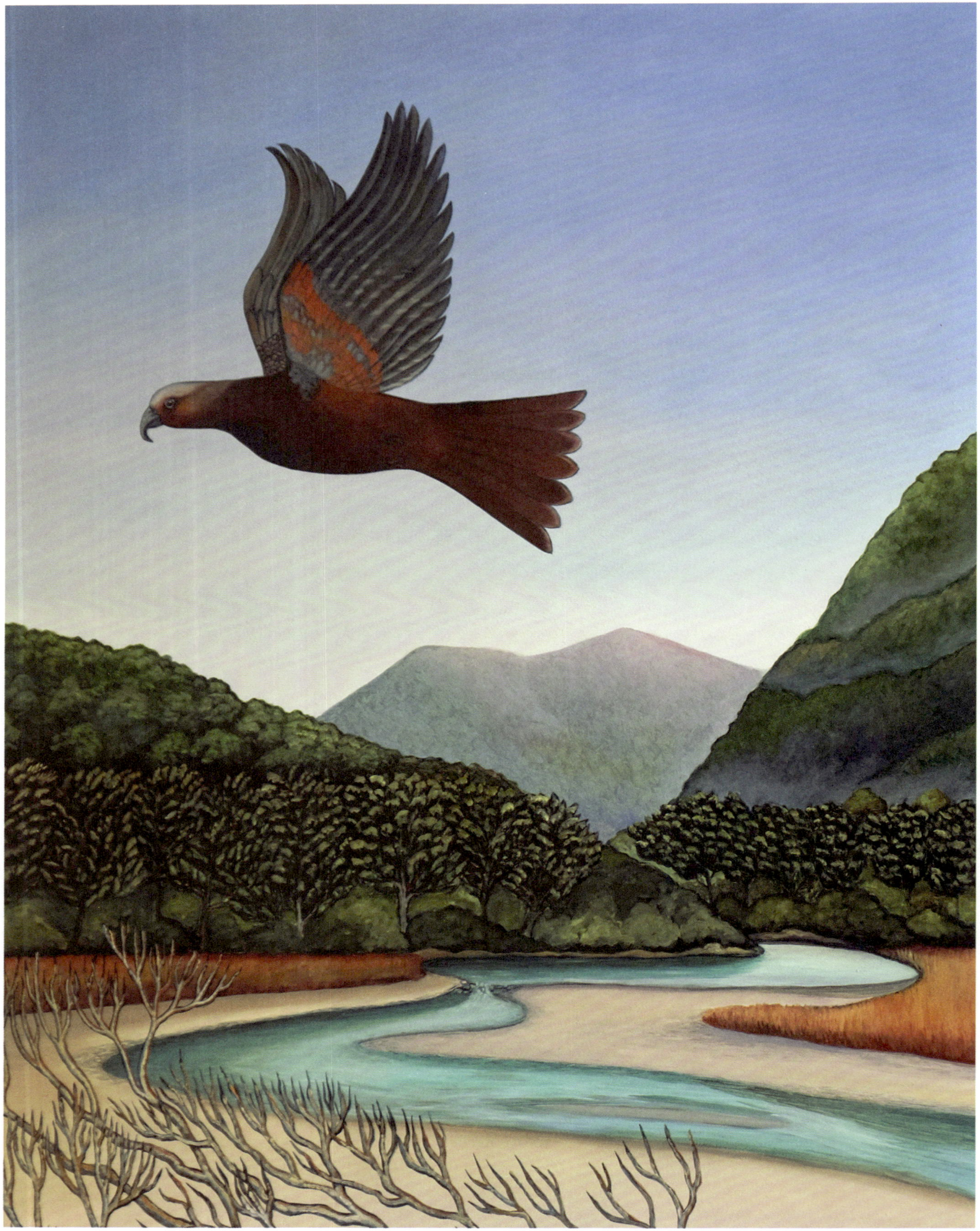

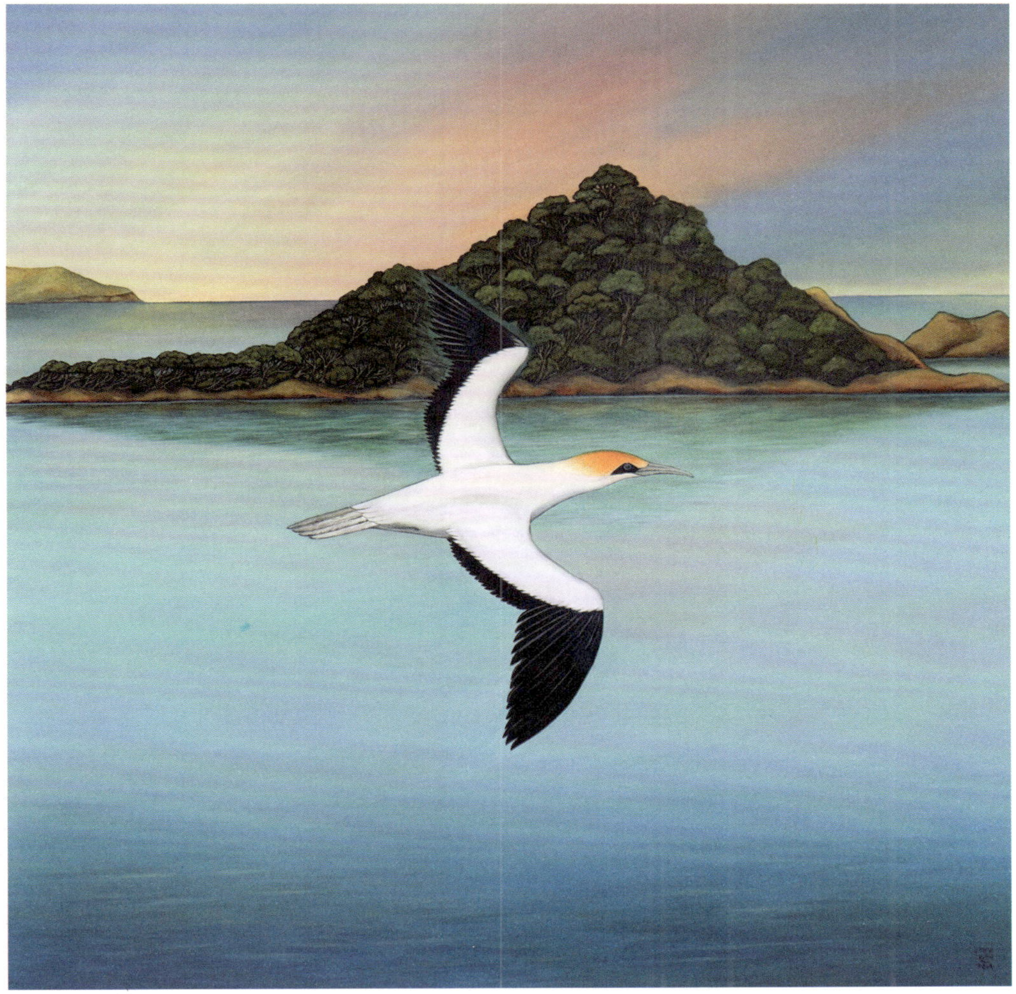

The Quiet Storm of Solitude 2019
1000 x 1000 mm/39¼ x 39¼ in

The Quiet Storm of Solitude

On the horizon a silent storm is brewing
Only noticeable in the unusual colours of sky
The gannet sweeps past in solitude
Not lonely but alone, an observer within
A quiet storm of emotions.

Opposite
Riversong Kākā 2020
1000 x 800 mm/39¼ x 31½ in

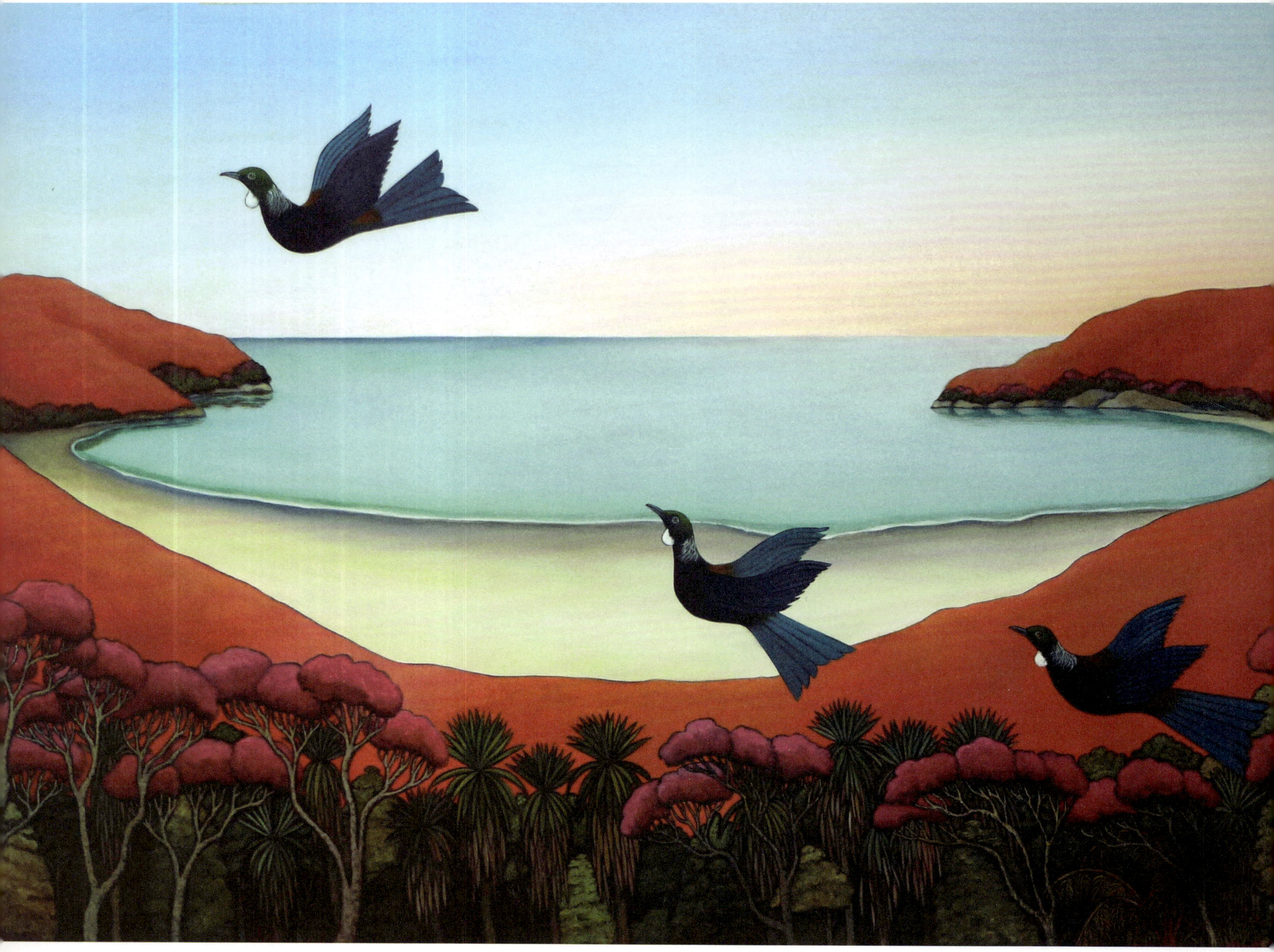

Earthsong 2015
1220 x 800 mm/48 x 31½ in

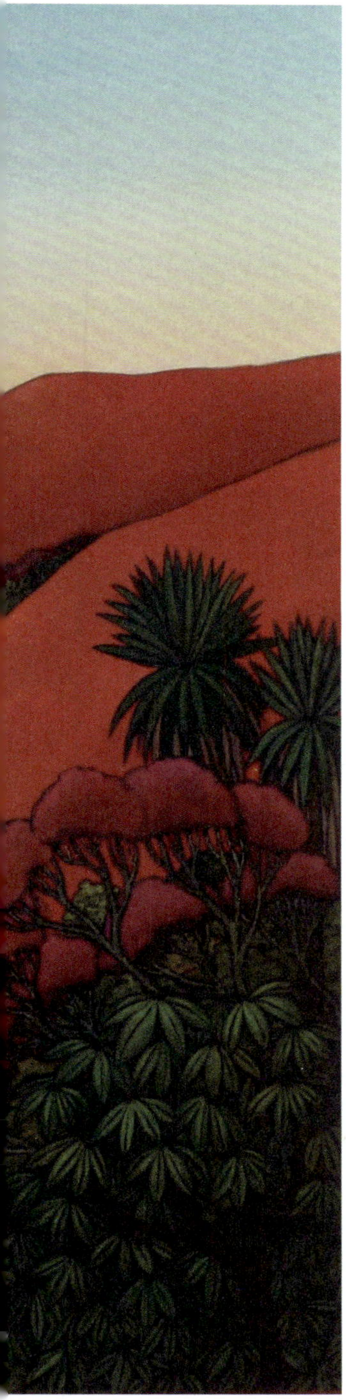

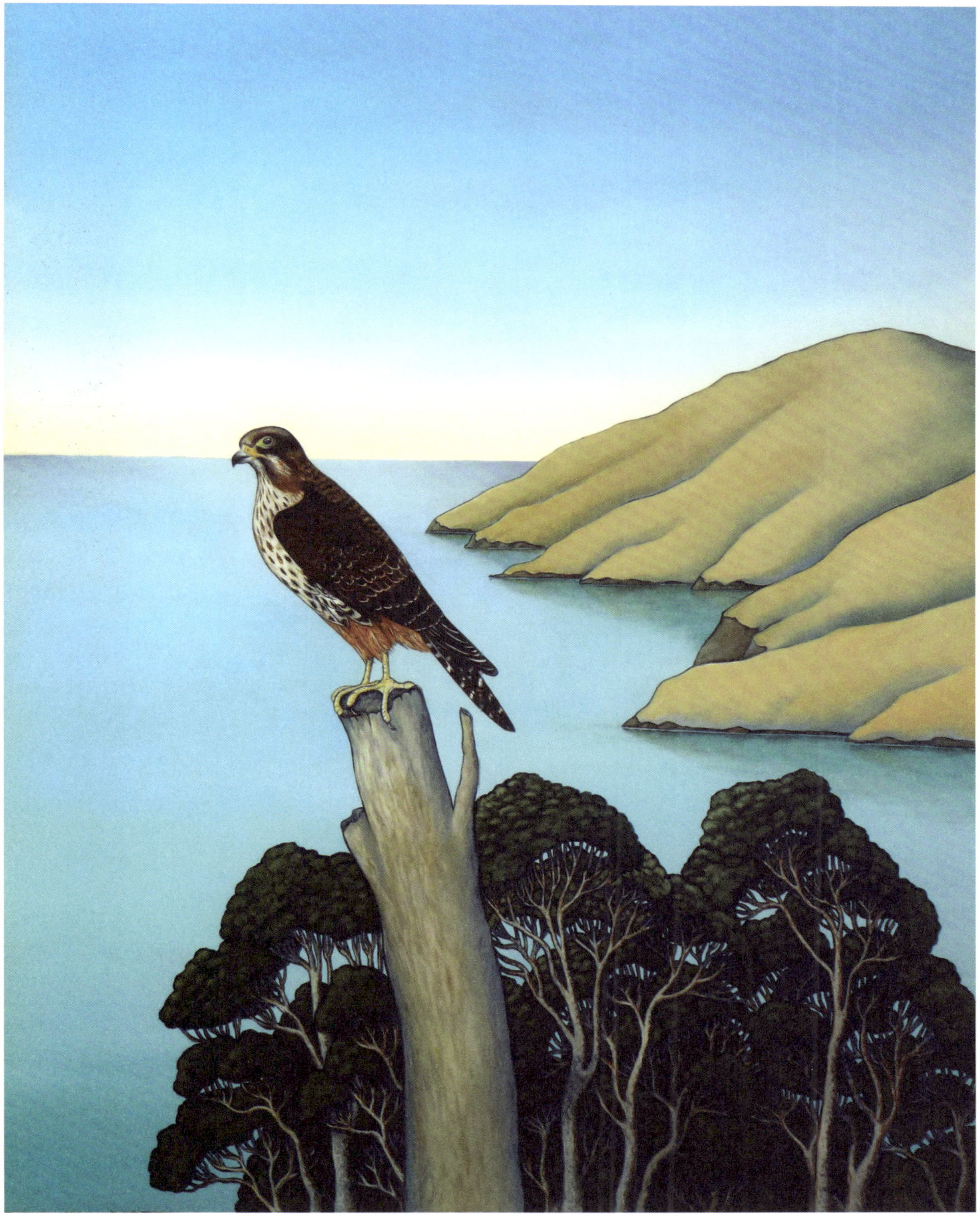

Falcon's Pinnacle 2014
1000 x 800 mm/39¼ x 31½ in

‘Reilly talks of the dreamlike state that she often finds herself in when she is inspired by a particular physical environment, and it is her experience of this that she seeks to communicate in what she refers to as the “naive, childlike, magical qualities” of her paintings.’

— **Zoe Reeves, *West to East*, paintings by Clare Reilly 2003**

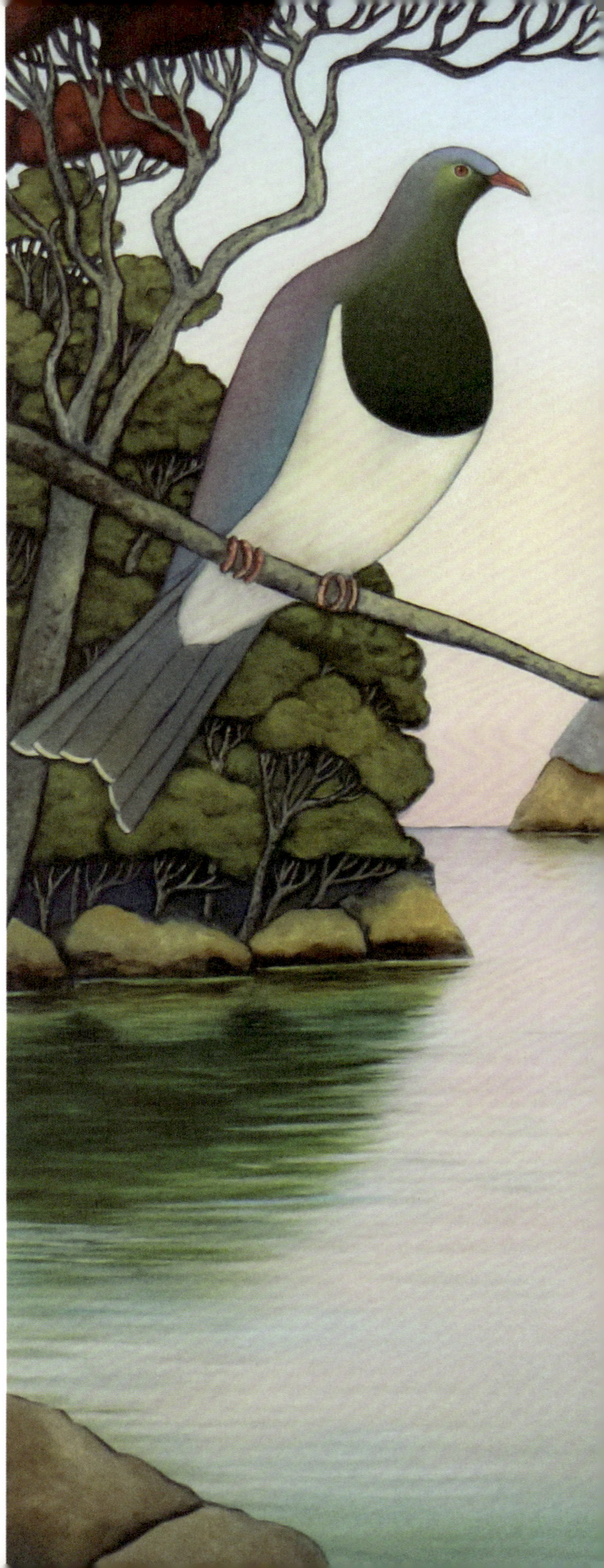

The Hidden Gifts of Life 2016
800 x 1000 mm/31½ x 39¼ in

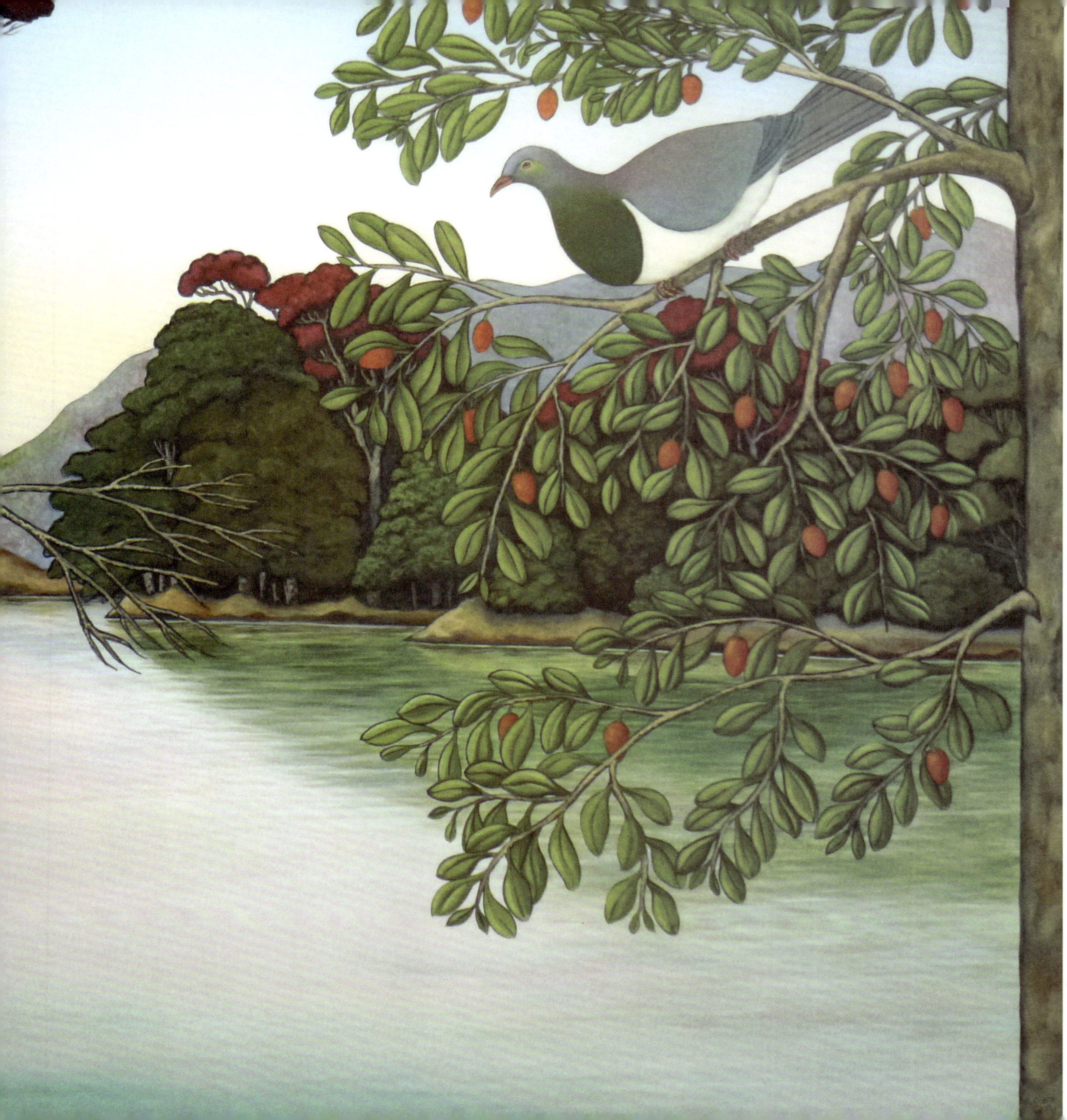

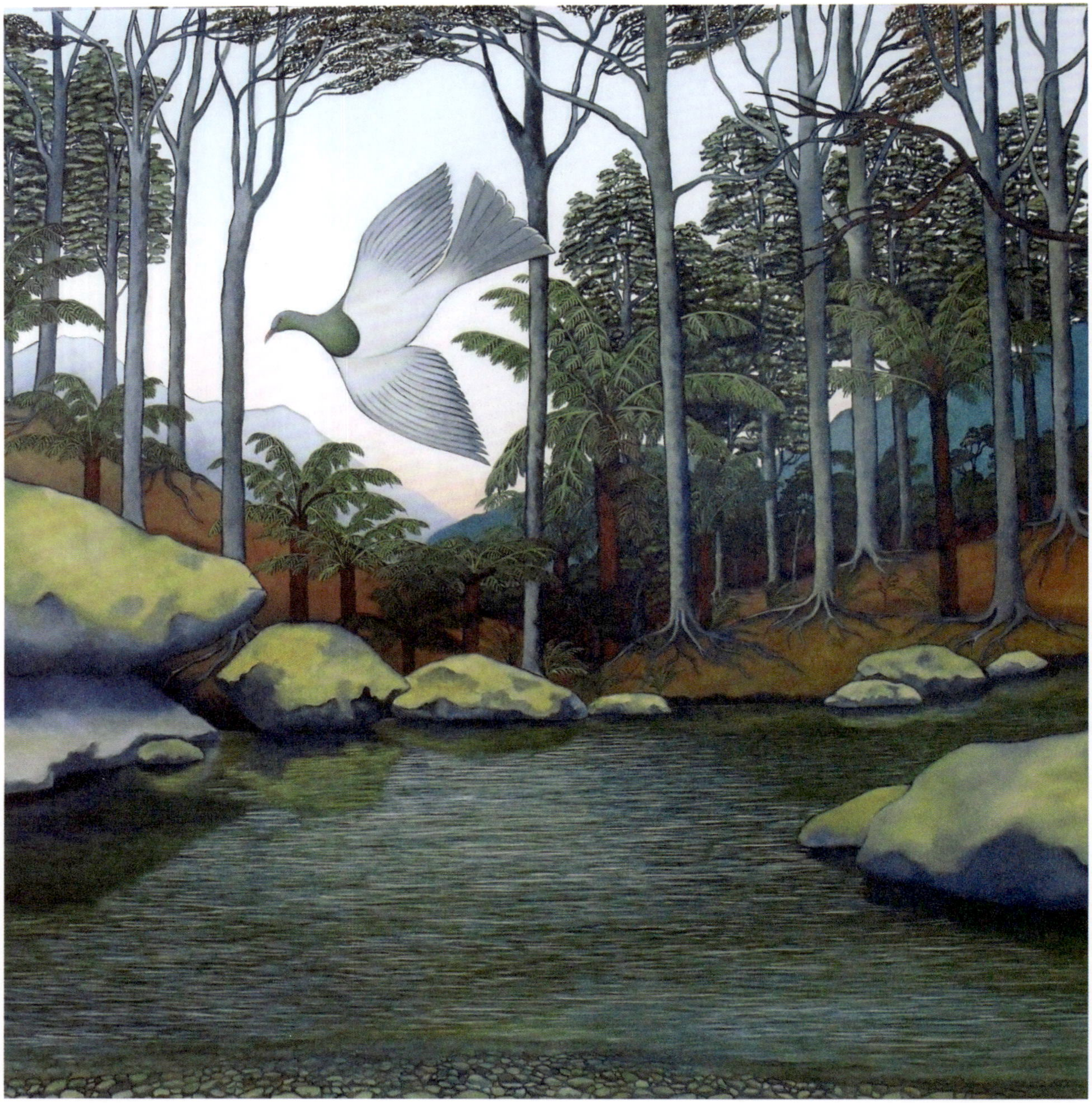

Primavera 2013
1000 x 1000 mm/39¼ x 39¼ in

Opposite
Optimism For A New Day 2020
1000 x 1000 mm/39¼ x 39¼ in

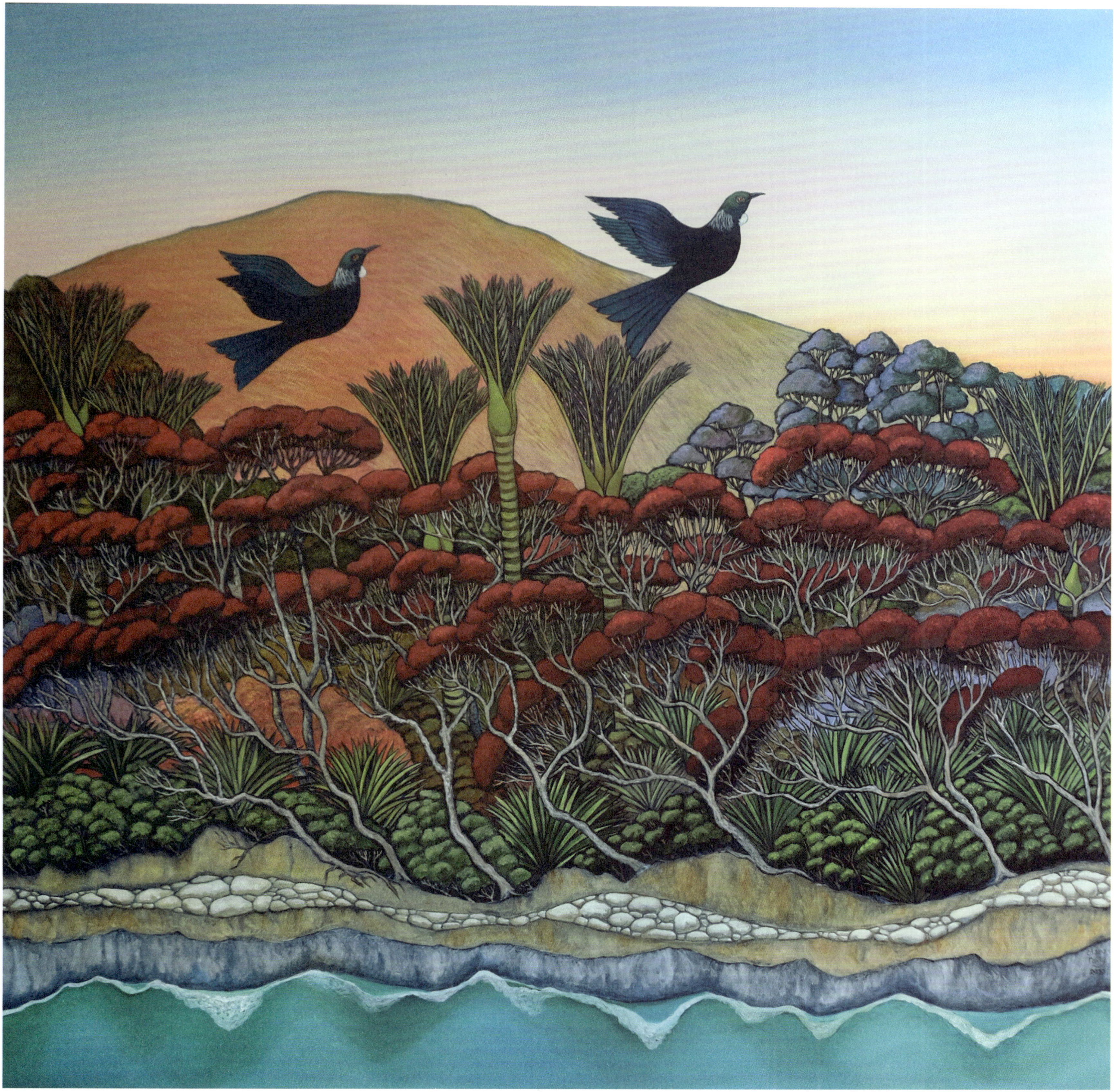

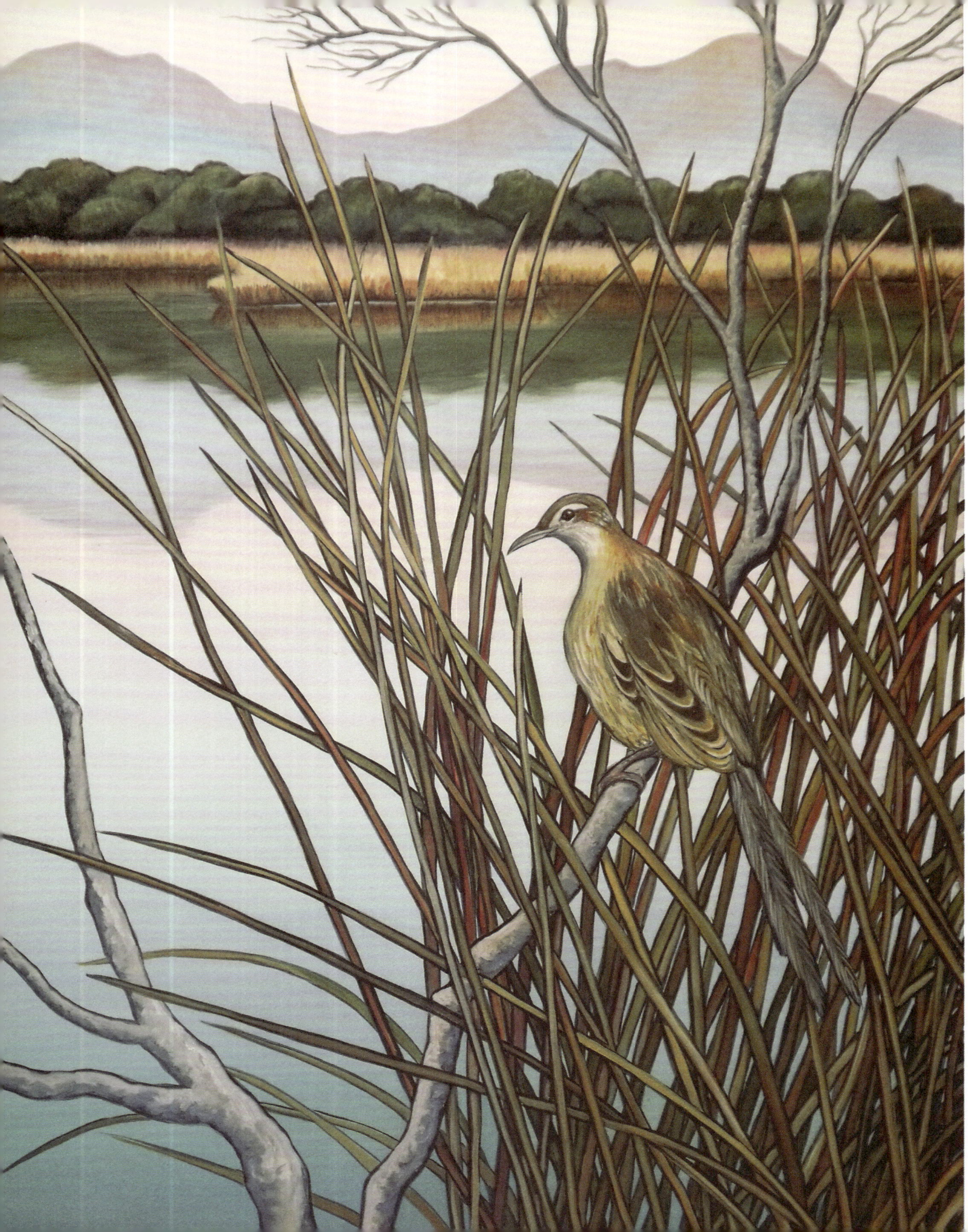

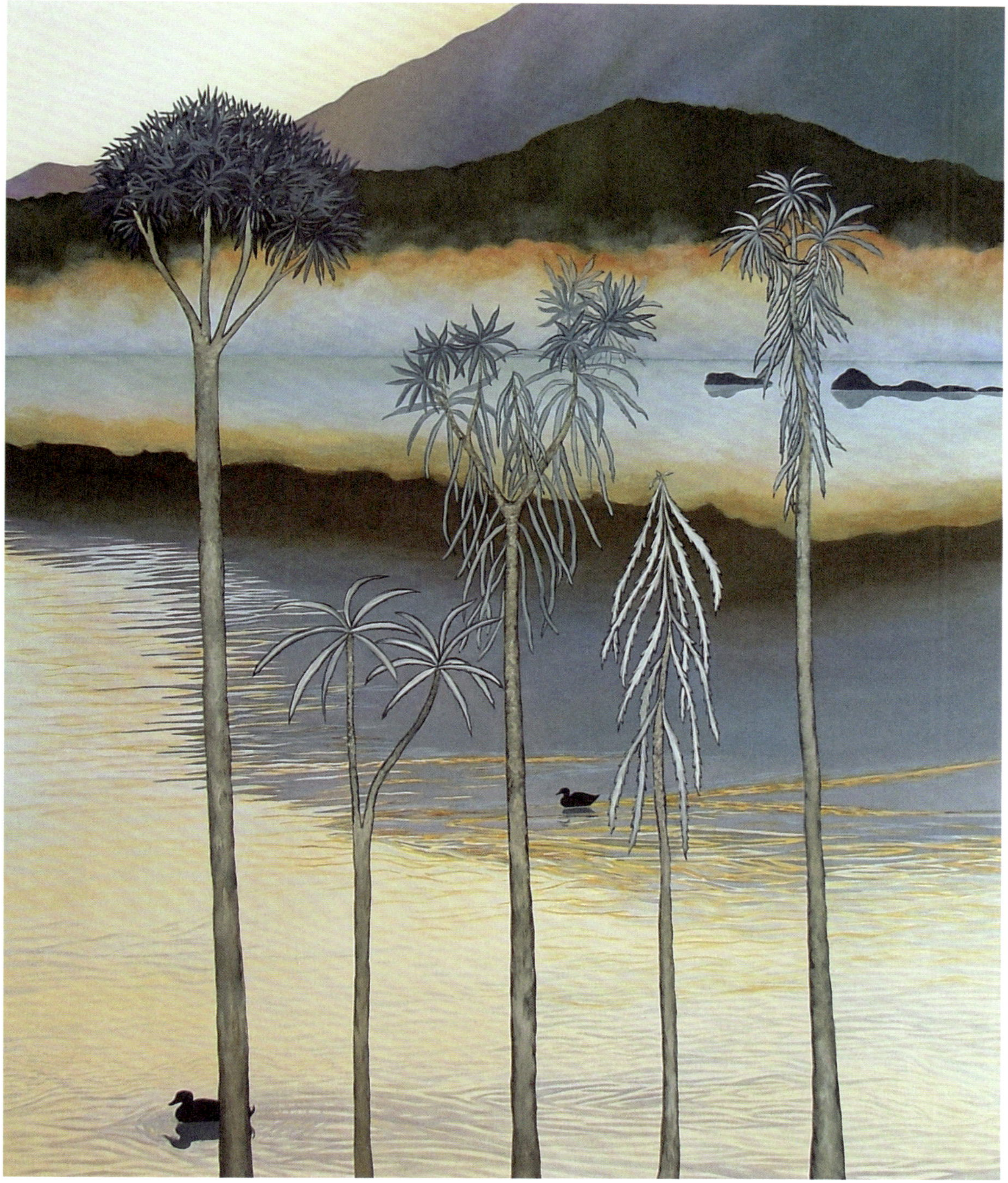

Five Stages of Wisdom 2008
1000 x 800 mm/39¼ x 31½ in

Opposite
Fernbird 2015
650 x 450 mm/25½ x 17¾ in

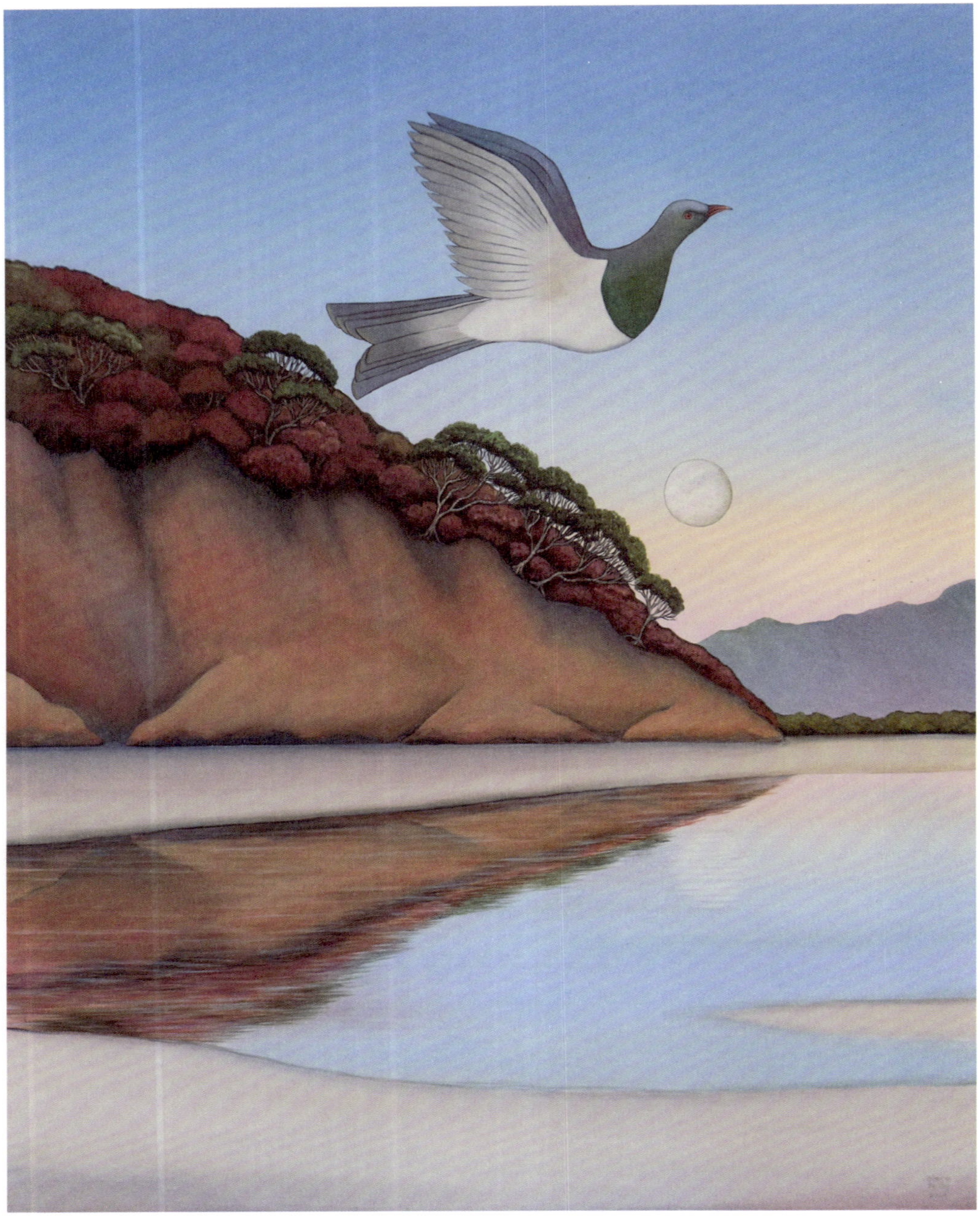

Over the Moon

Crisp winter dawn
Rich colour on the horizon
Ice crystals encrust the sand
A creamy full moon sinks towards
The mountains
Jubilant flight as the kererū
Momentarily suspends mid-air
Over the moon
Joyous rush of energy
To be alive in this moment.

Over the Moon 2019
1000 x 800 mm/39¼ x 31½ in

Opposite
Leaving the Pleasure Garden 2019
1000 x 1000 mm/39¼ x 39¼ in

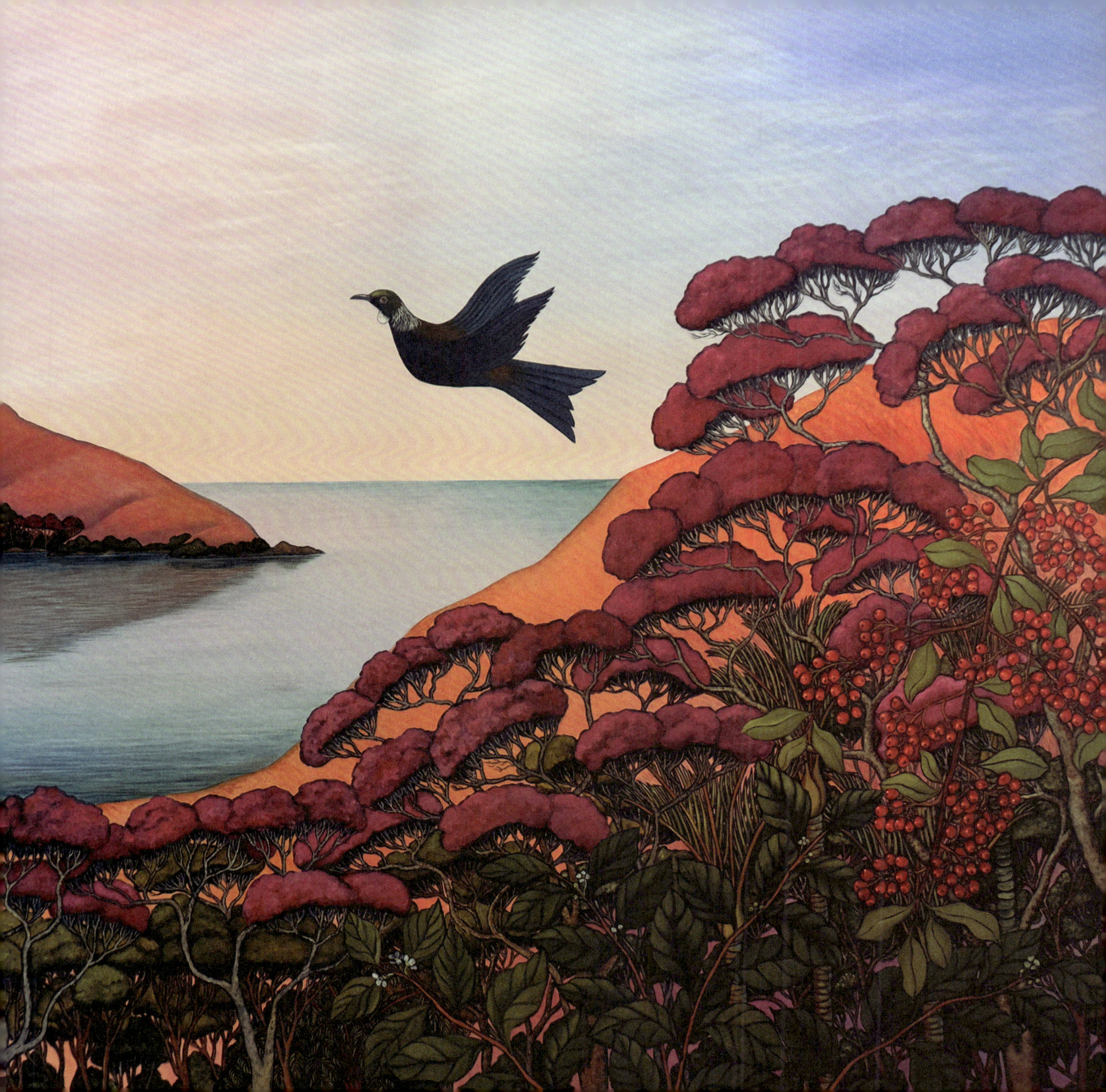

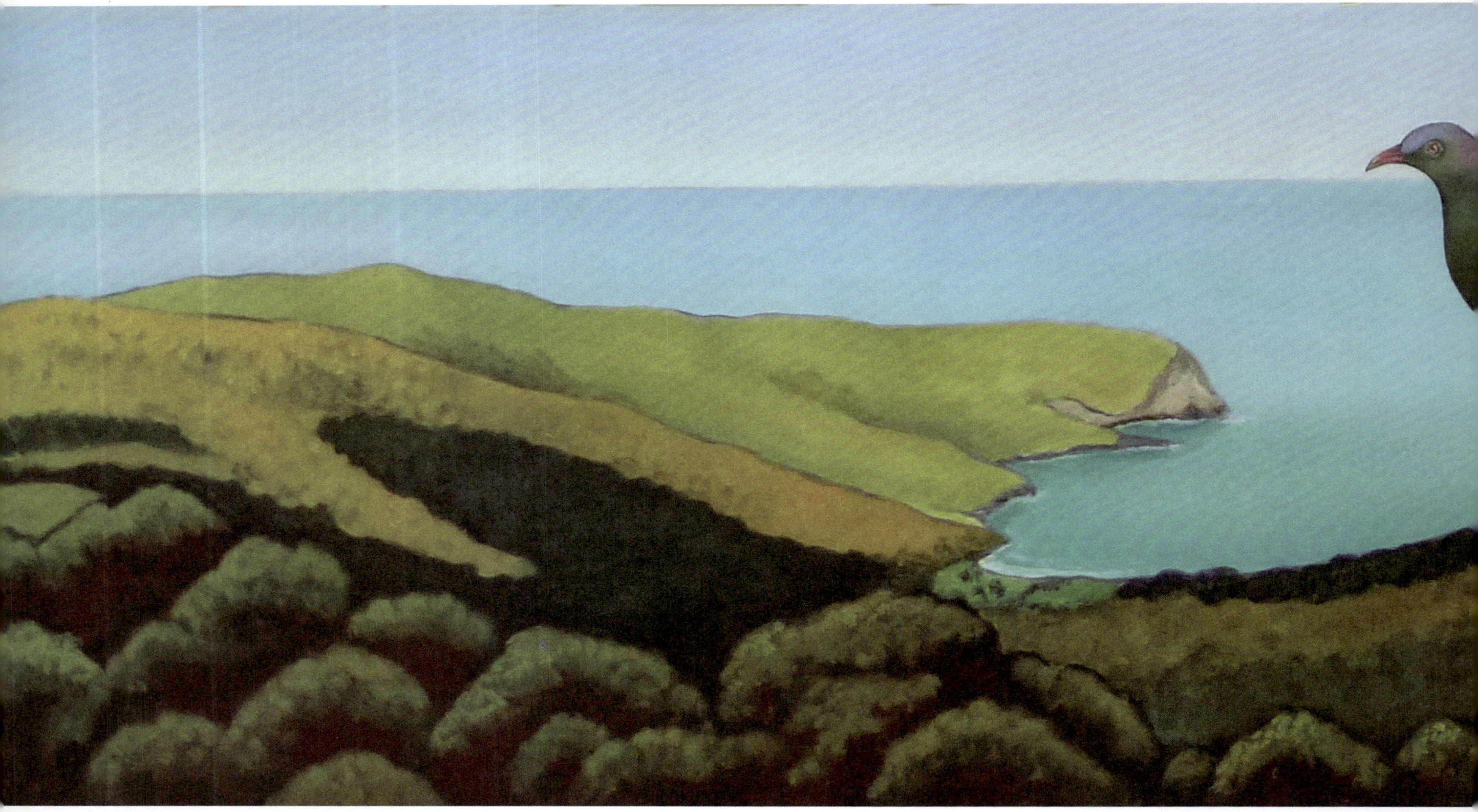

We Will Re-cloak the Land

We Will Re-cloak the Land 2011
500 x 800 mm/19½ x 31½ in

The environmental impact of the recent arrival of humans to the pristine land of New Zealand, particularly in the last one hundred and fifty years, caused devastation to the native flora and fauna.

Forests were felled leaving huge scars on the land. While timber was needed for the construction of new towns and cities, very little thought was given to the resulting environmental impact. Fortunately, the kererū, our native wood pigeon, survived and plays a vital role in seed dispersal. These birds feed on many larger seeds and fruits of our native trees and are able to ingest and expel the seeds in a way that is beneficial to the viability of plant germination.

The kererū is a key player in assisting new forests to once again re-cloak the land.

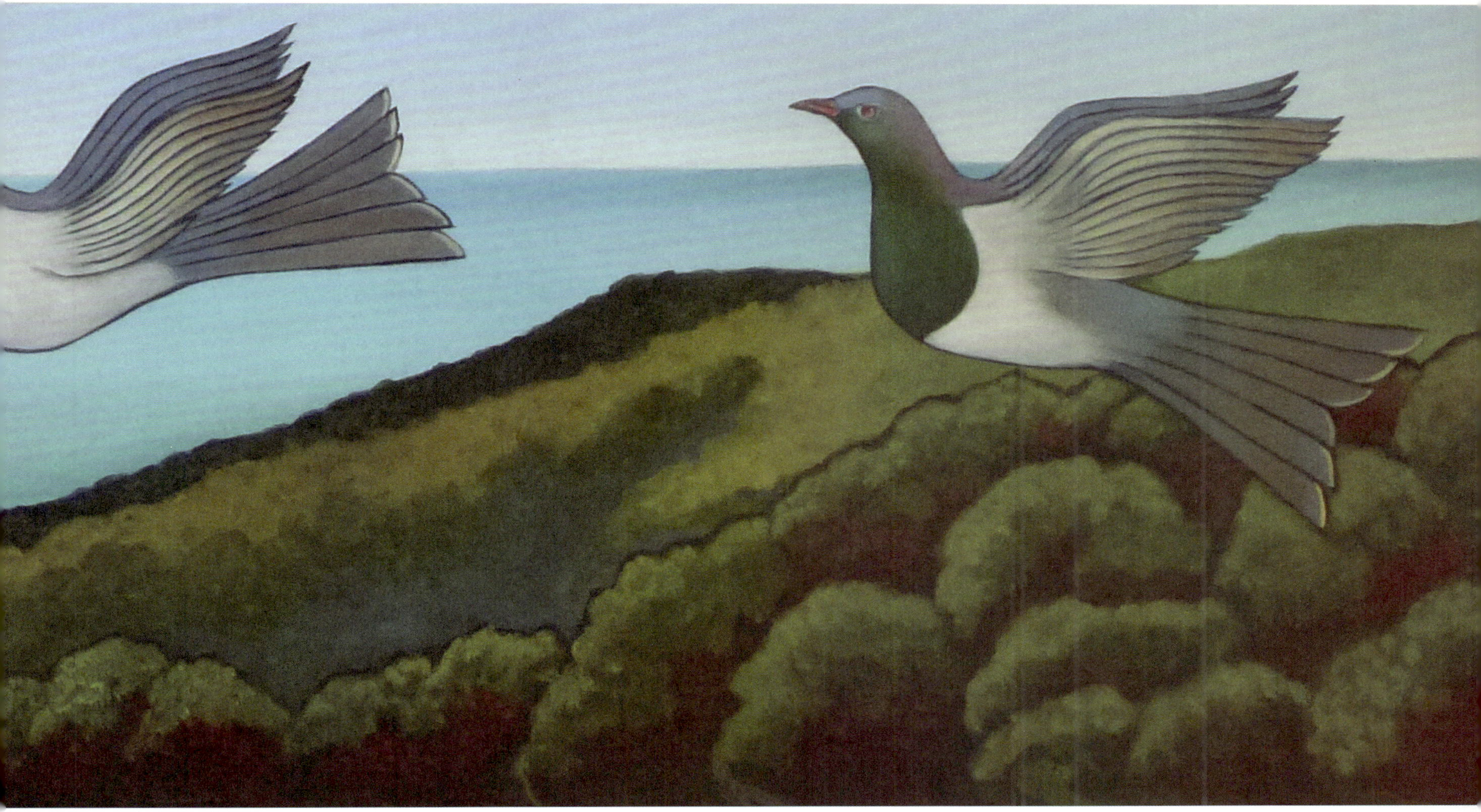

'Suffusing her paintings with light to evoke a spiritually-charged luminosity is a recurrent feature of Reilly's art.'

— **Gail Ross, *Eye of the Calm* catalogue, published 2009 by Primitive Bird Group**

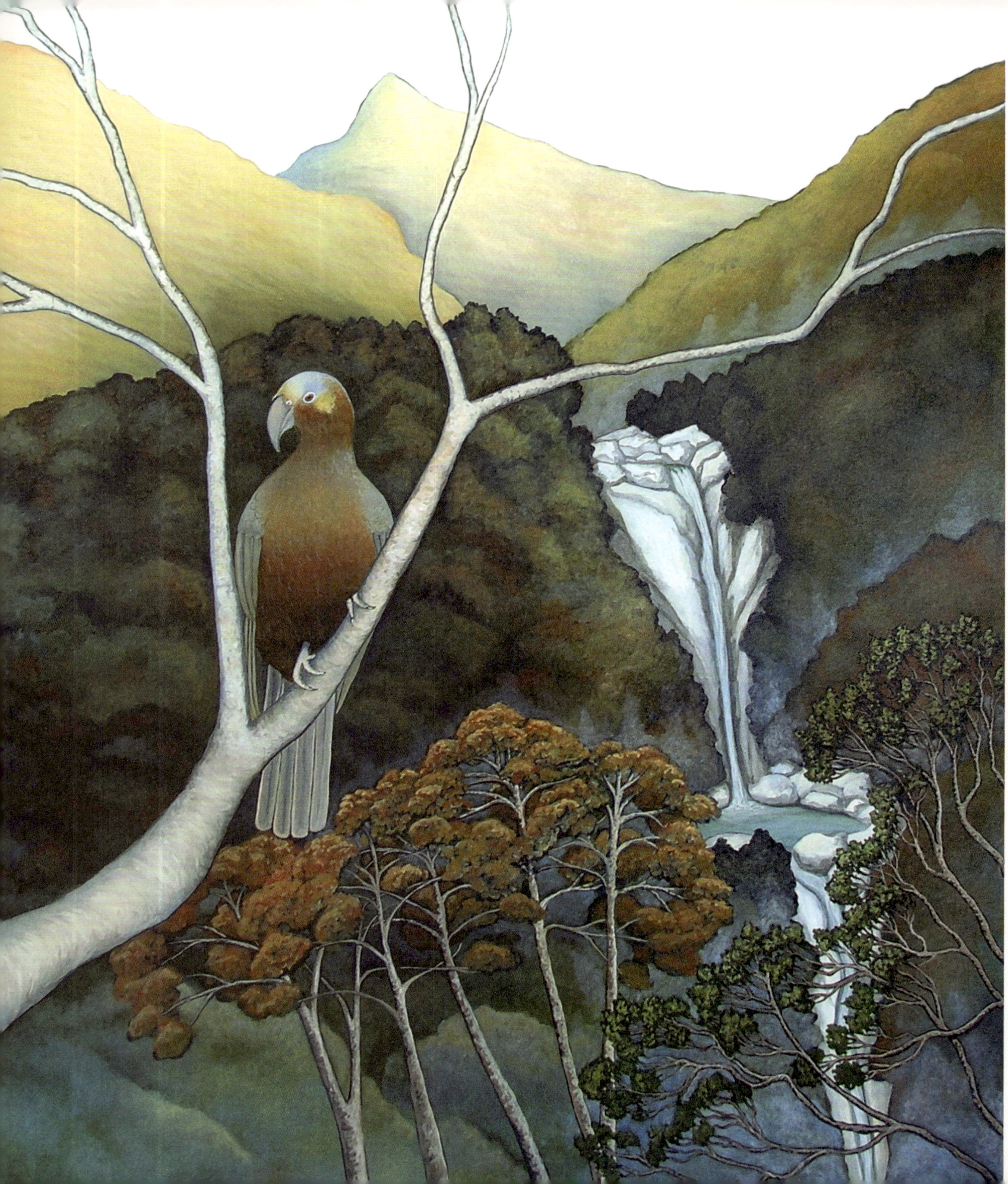

Dance of Grace

Tūī flight is bold, definite and powerful
When coupling is in the air
It becomes a pure dance of grace.

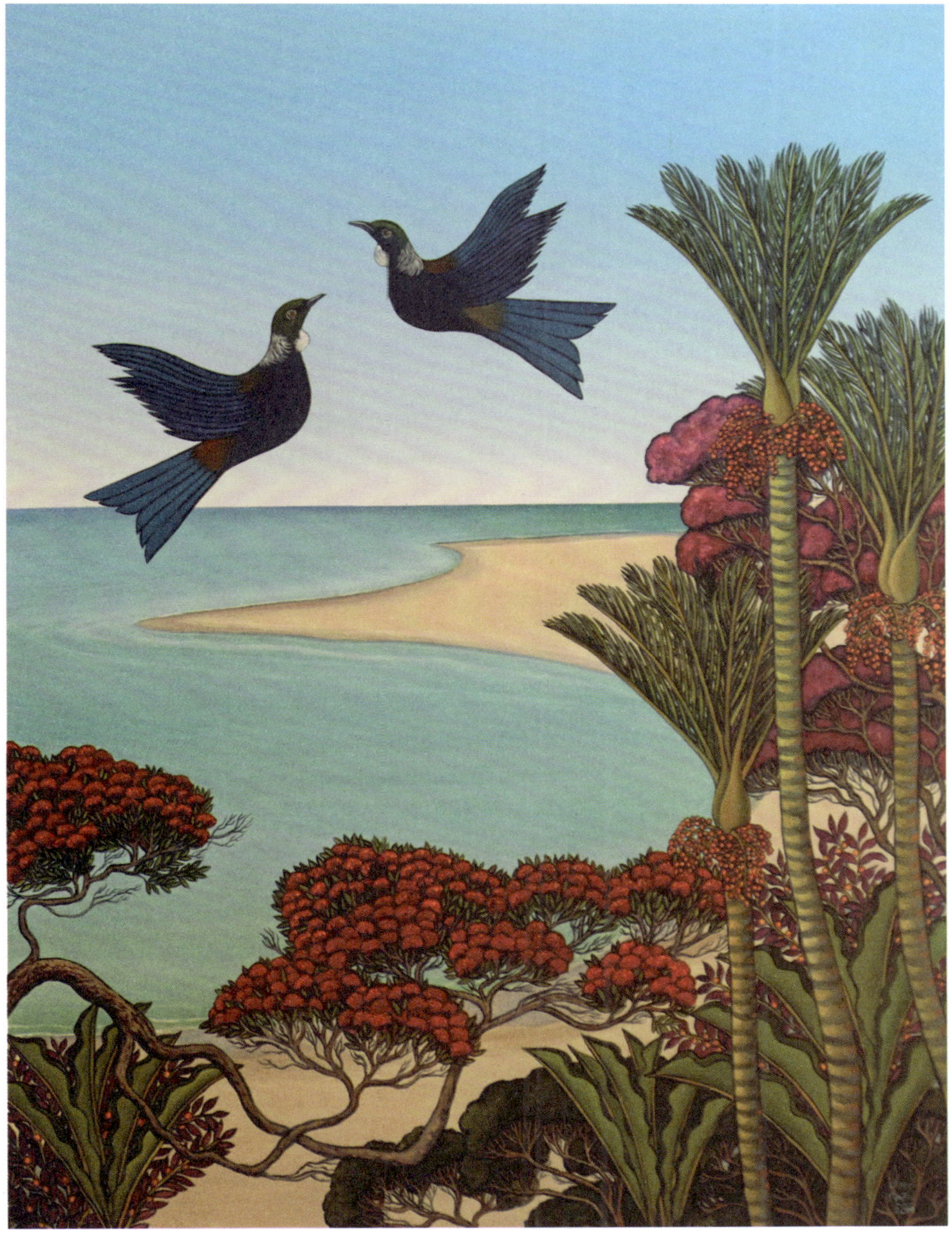

Dance of Grace 2019
800 x 600 mm/31½ x 23½ in

Opposite
Bushline Kākā 2008
1000 x 800 mm/39¼ x 31½ in

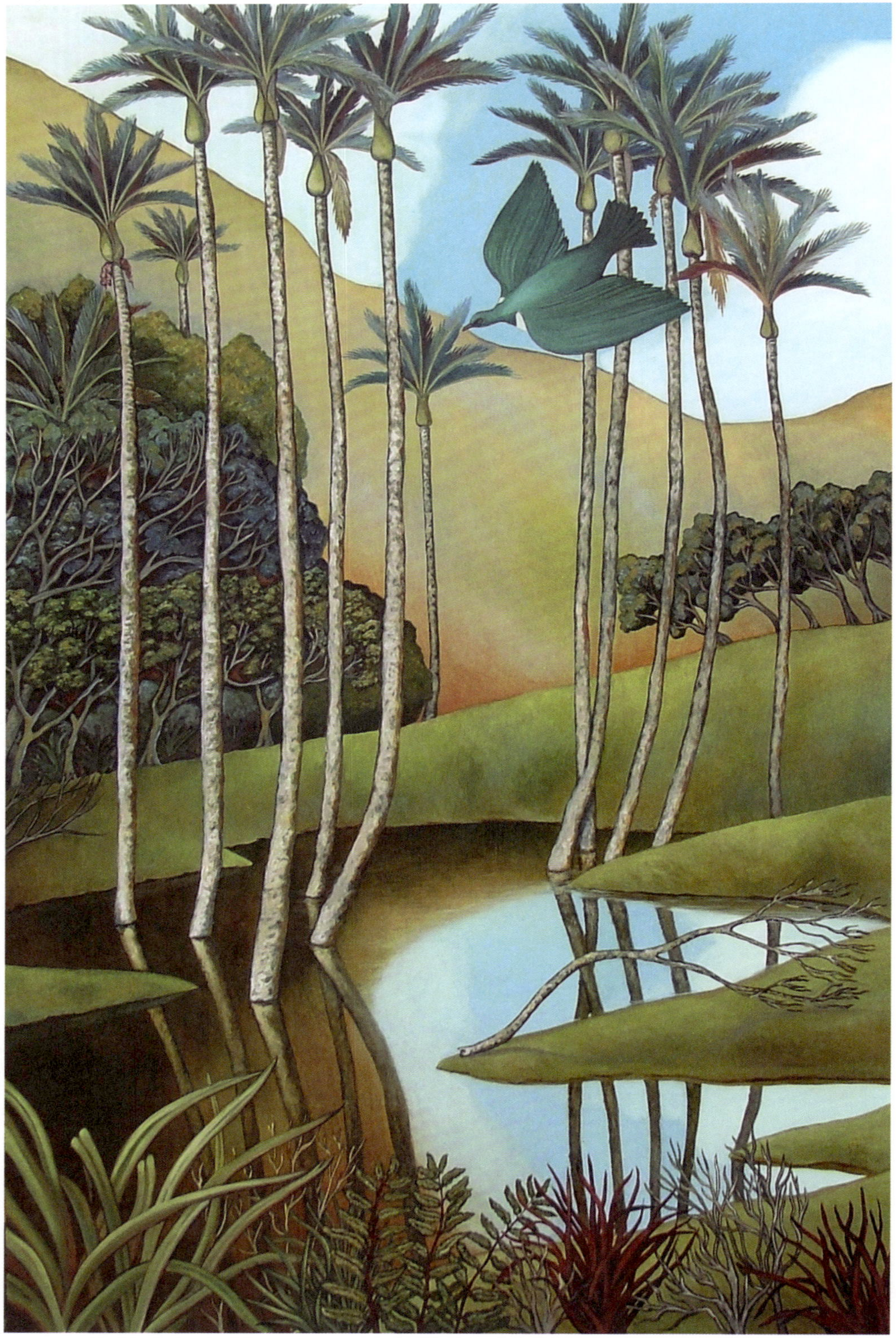

Still Water Pond 2003
1220 x 800 mm/48 x 31½ in

Opposite
Crested Grebes 2008
1000 x 800 mm/39¼ x 31½ in

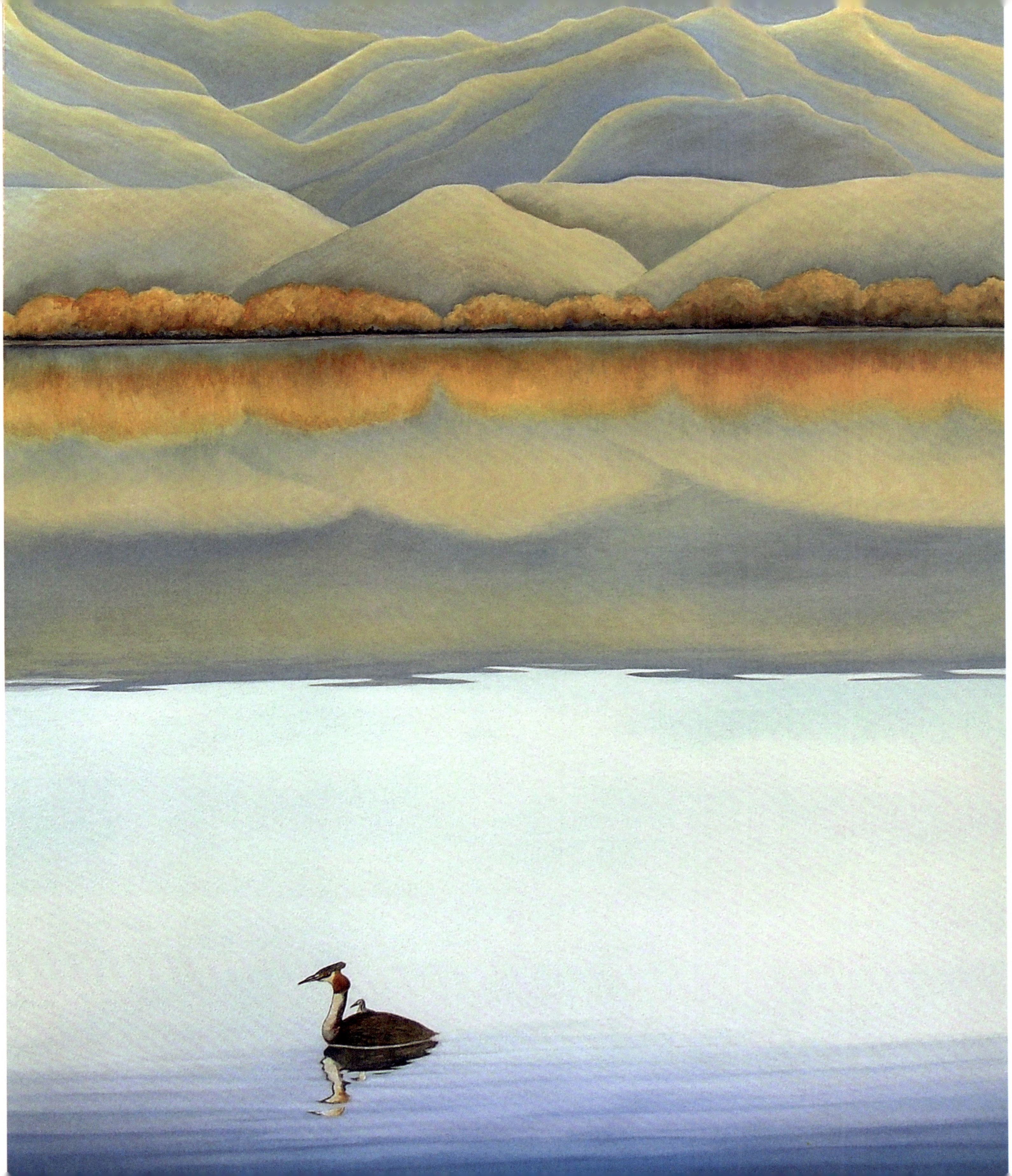

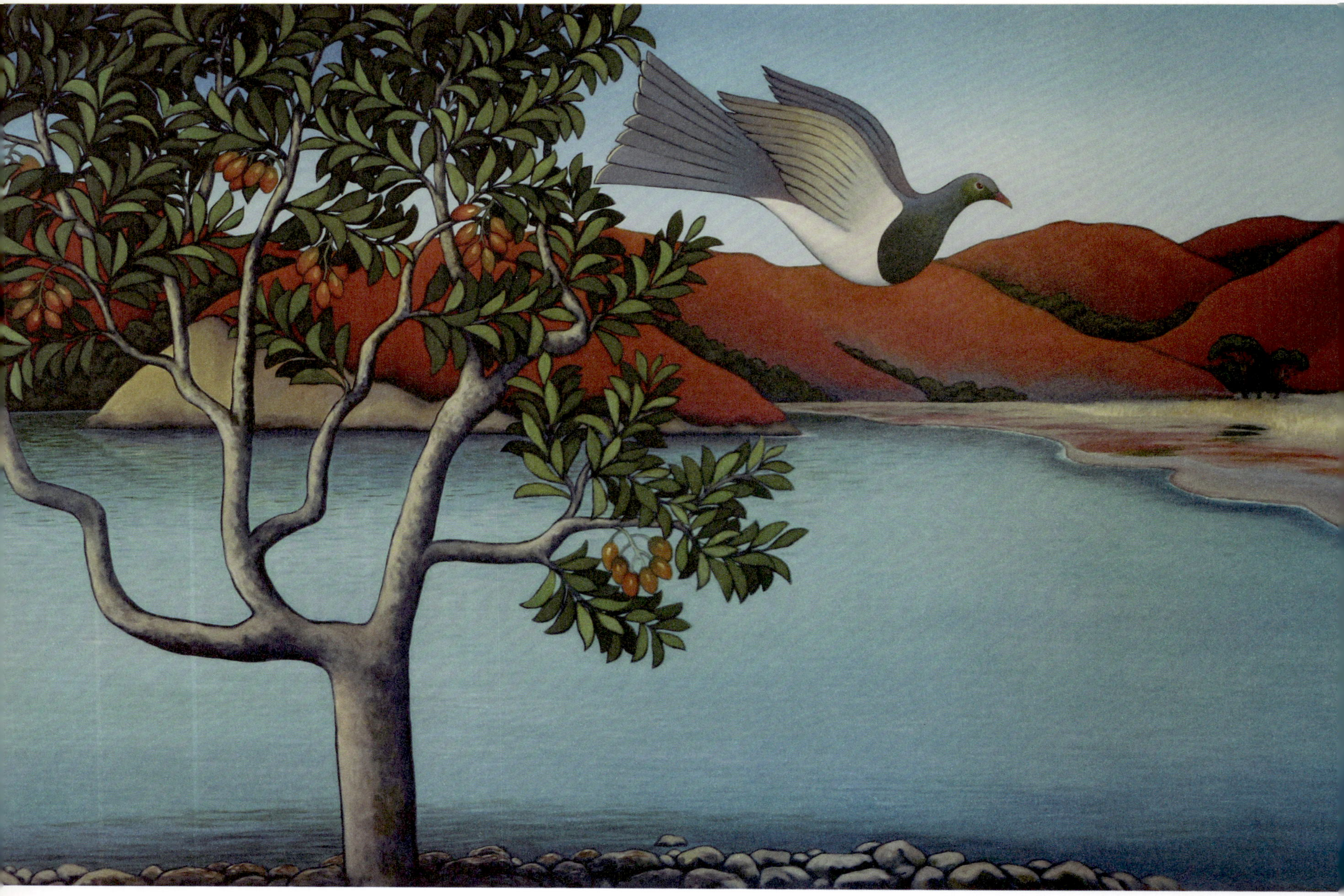

Karaka Summer 2014
800 x 1220 mm/31½ x 48 in

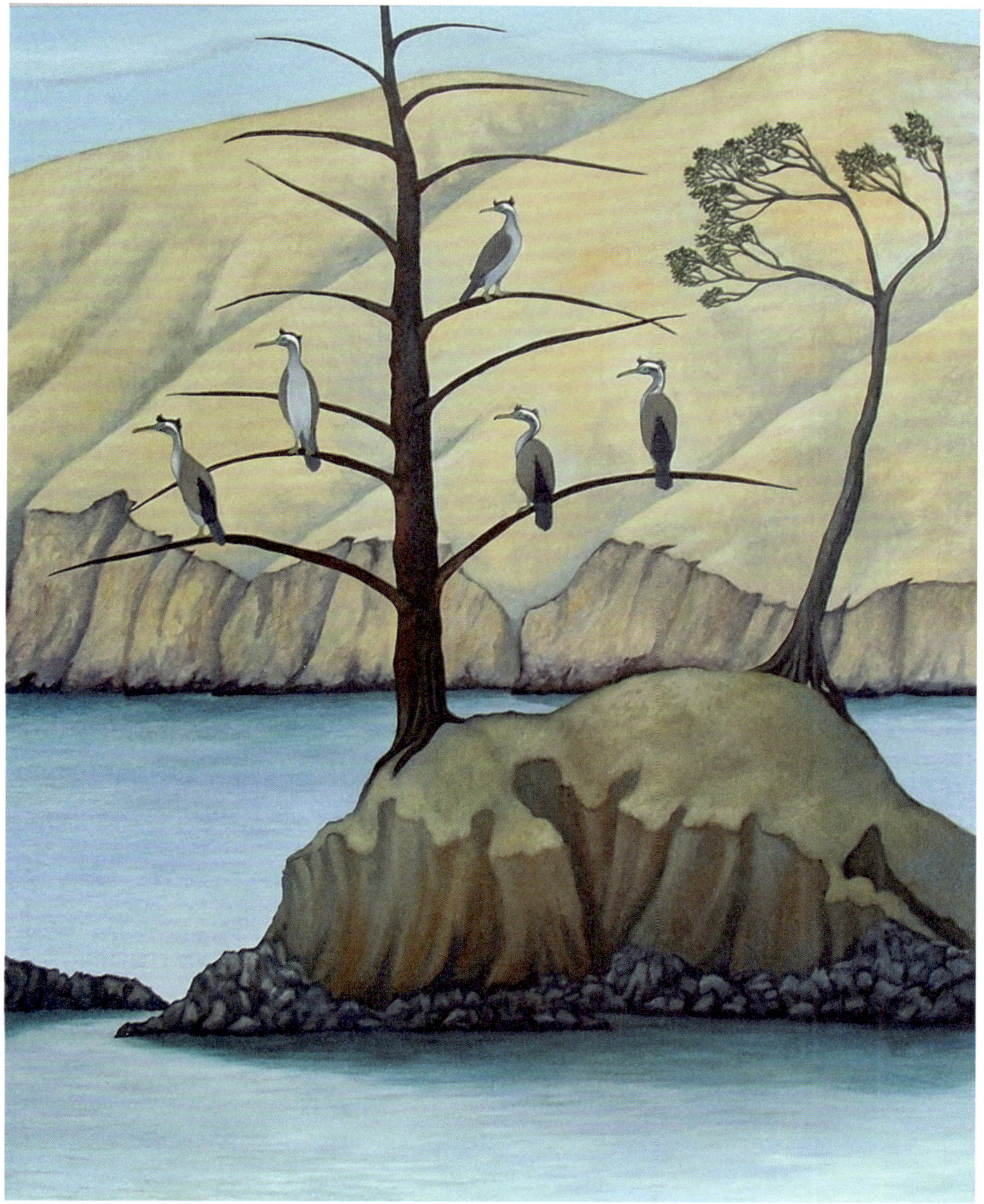

Island 2004
1000 x 840 mm/39¼ x 33 in

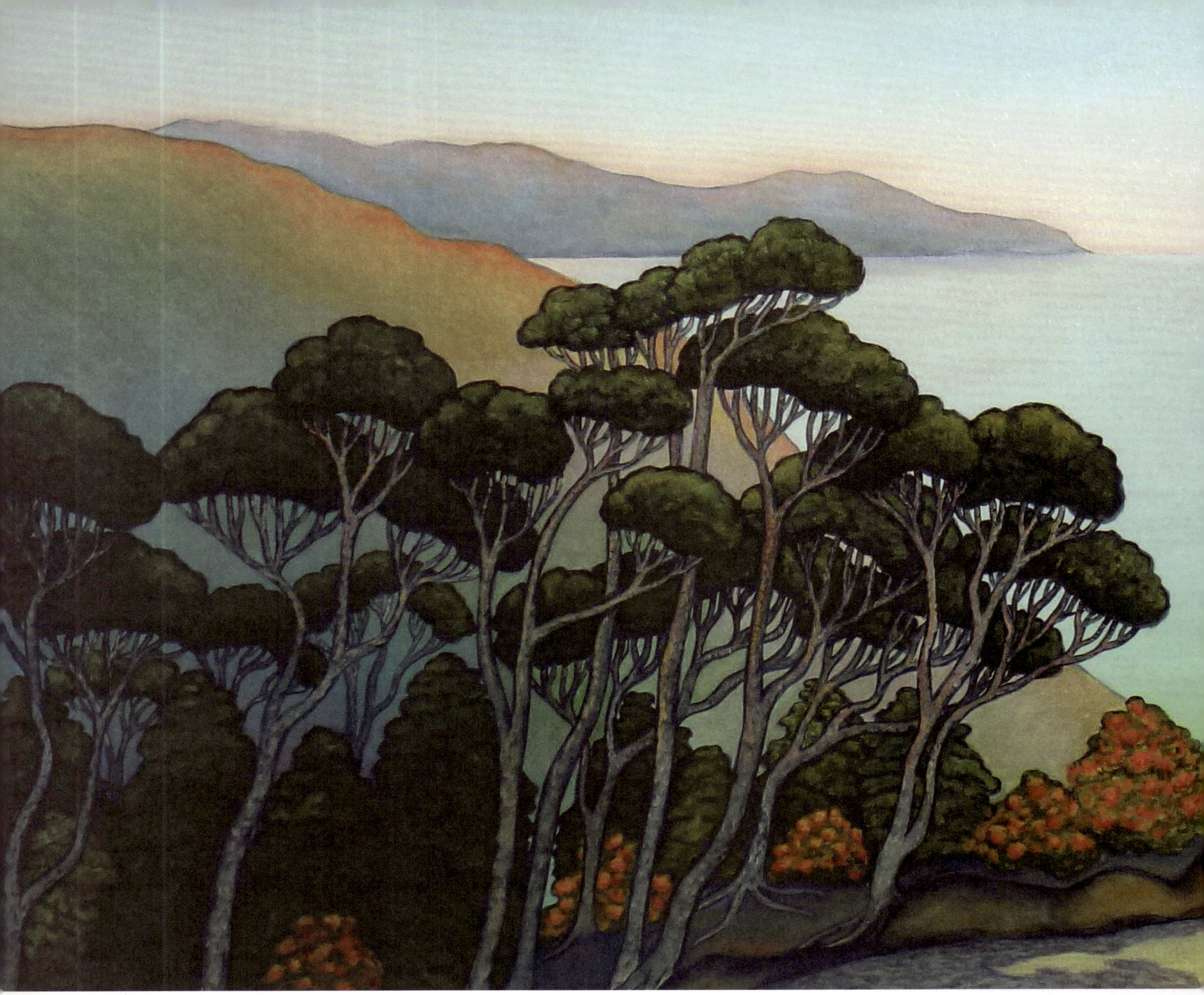

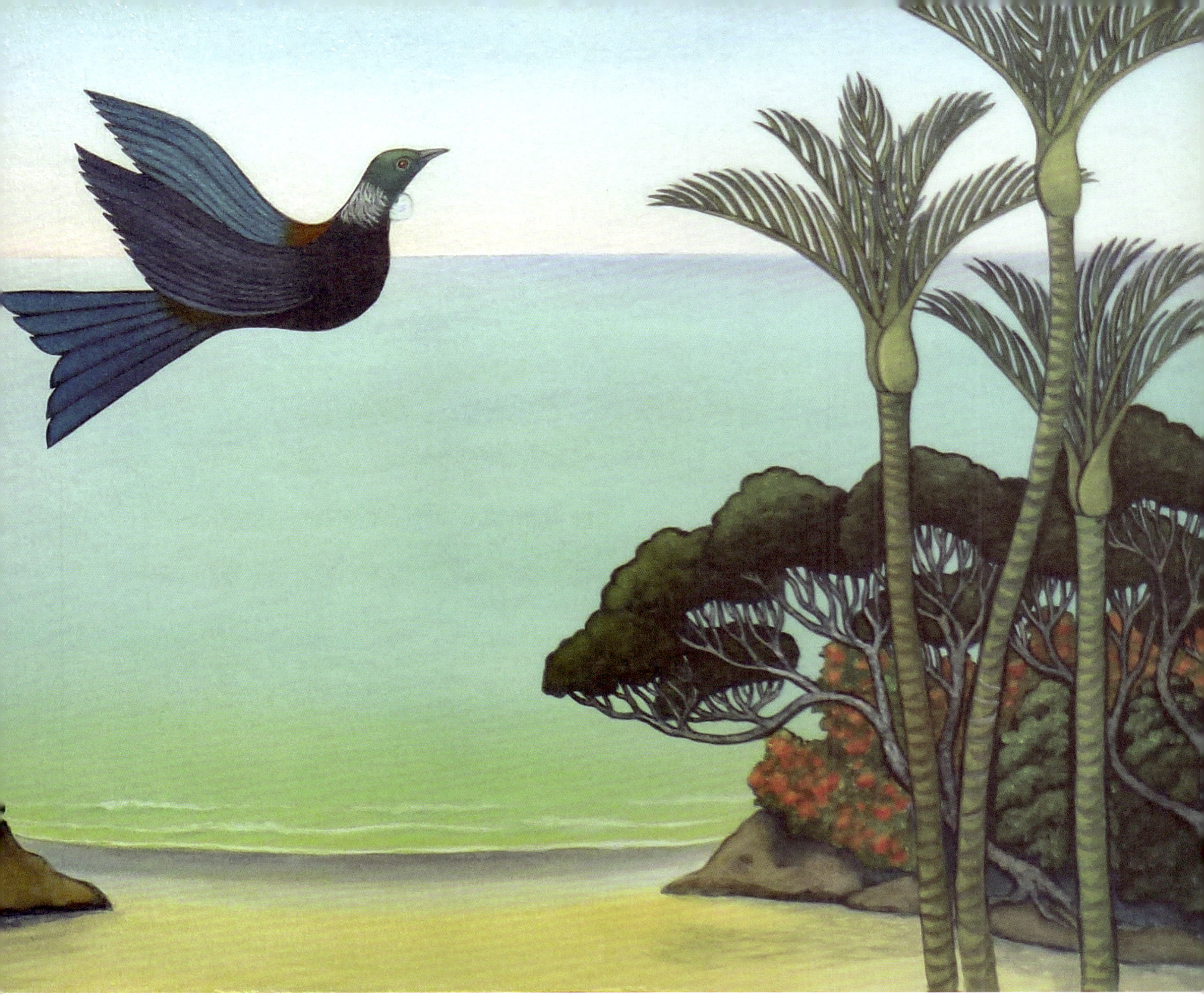

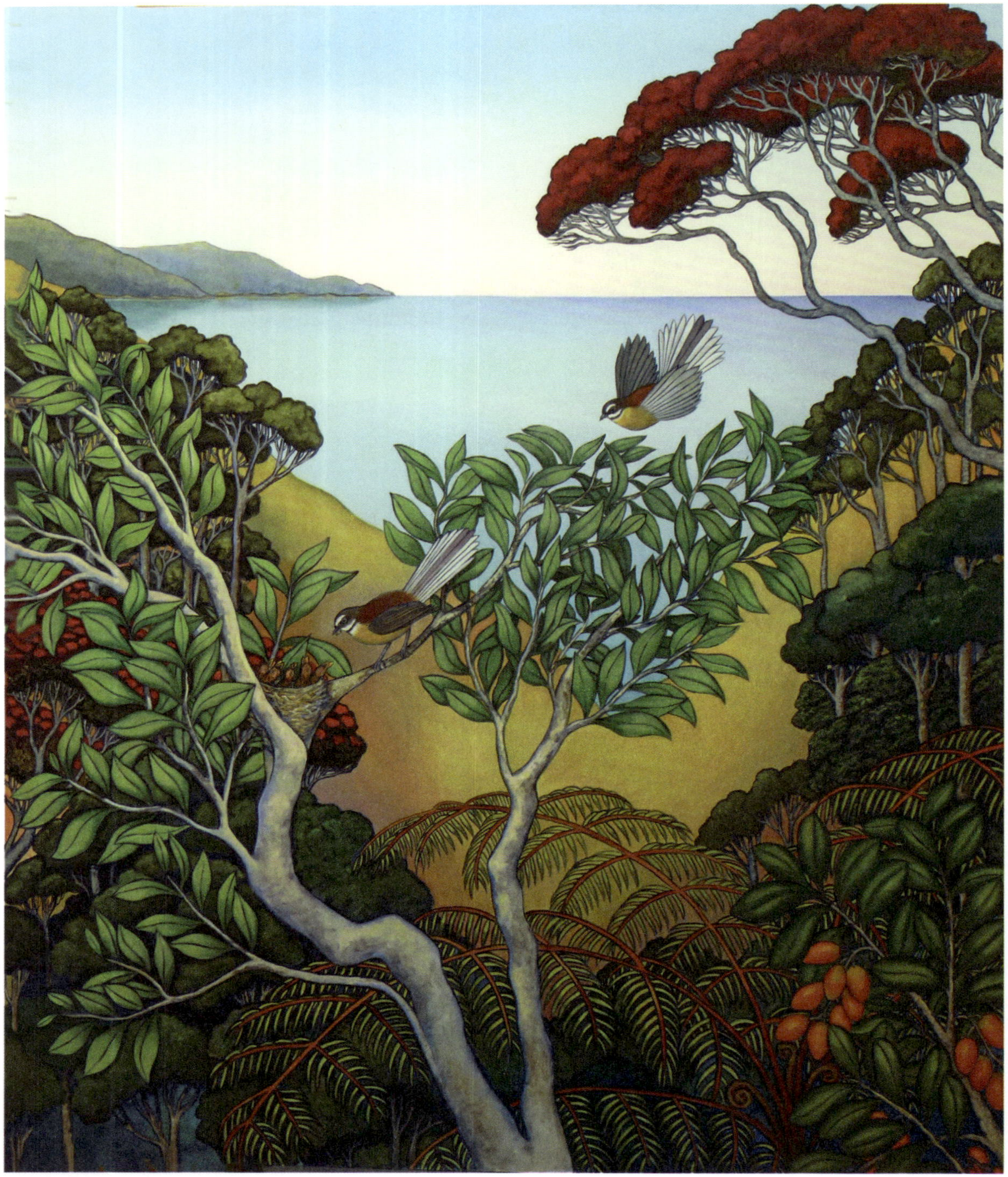

Renewal 2015
1000 x 840 mm/39¼ x 33 in

Opposite

Last Evening Flight 2009
1000 x 800 mm/39¼ x 31½ in

Previous page

A Vigorous Flight 2015
500 x 800 mm/19½ x 31½ in

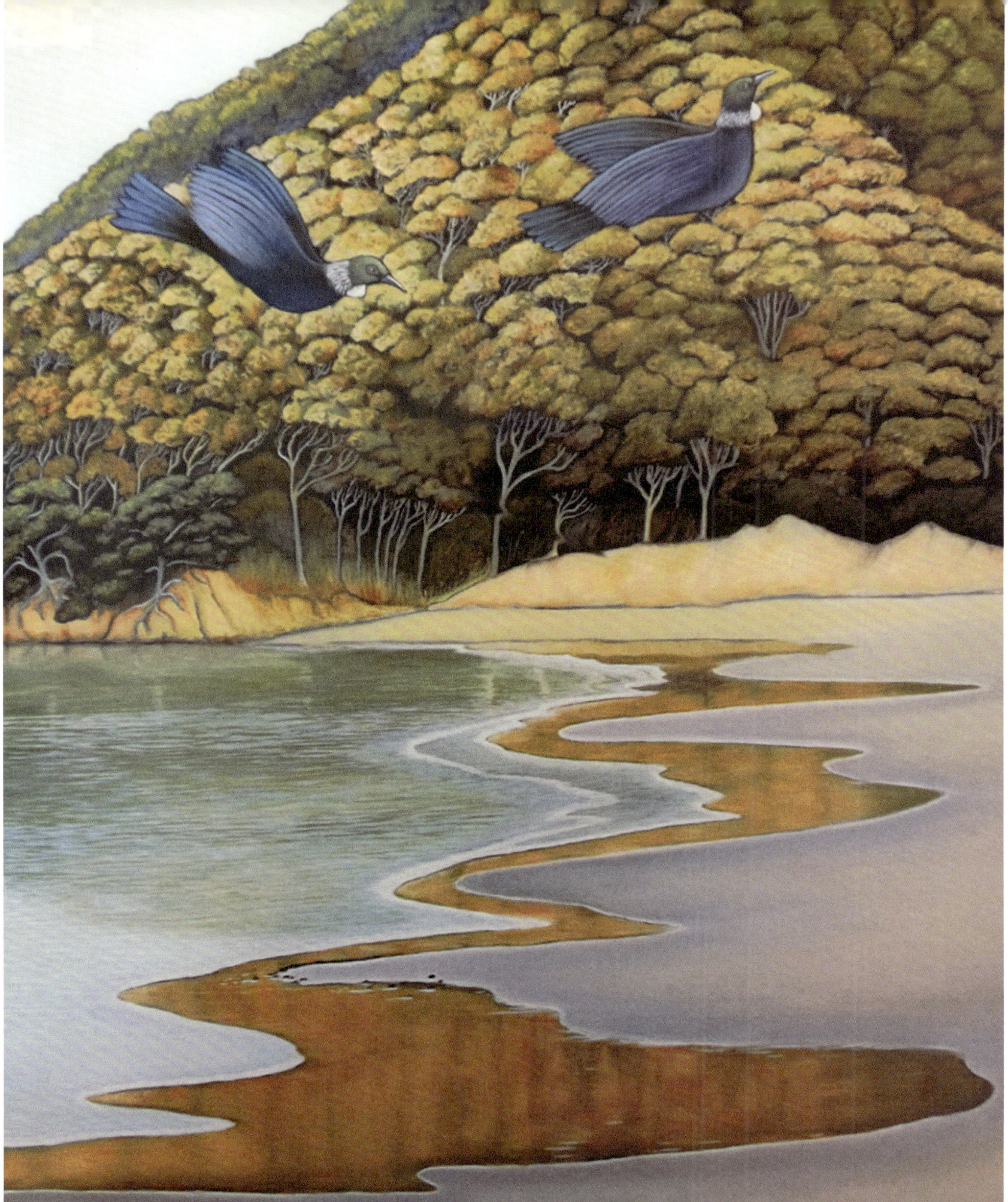

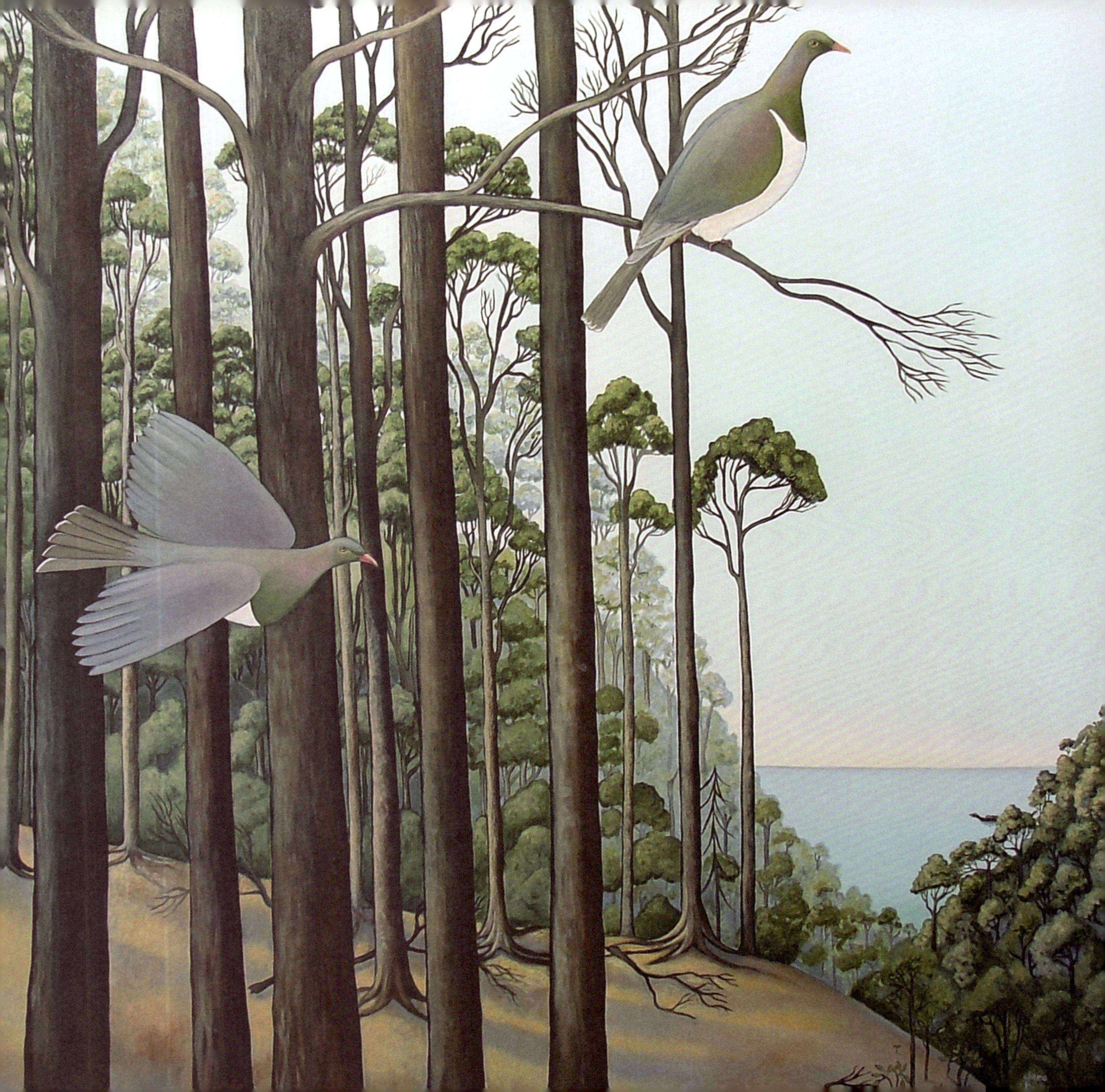

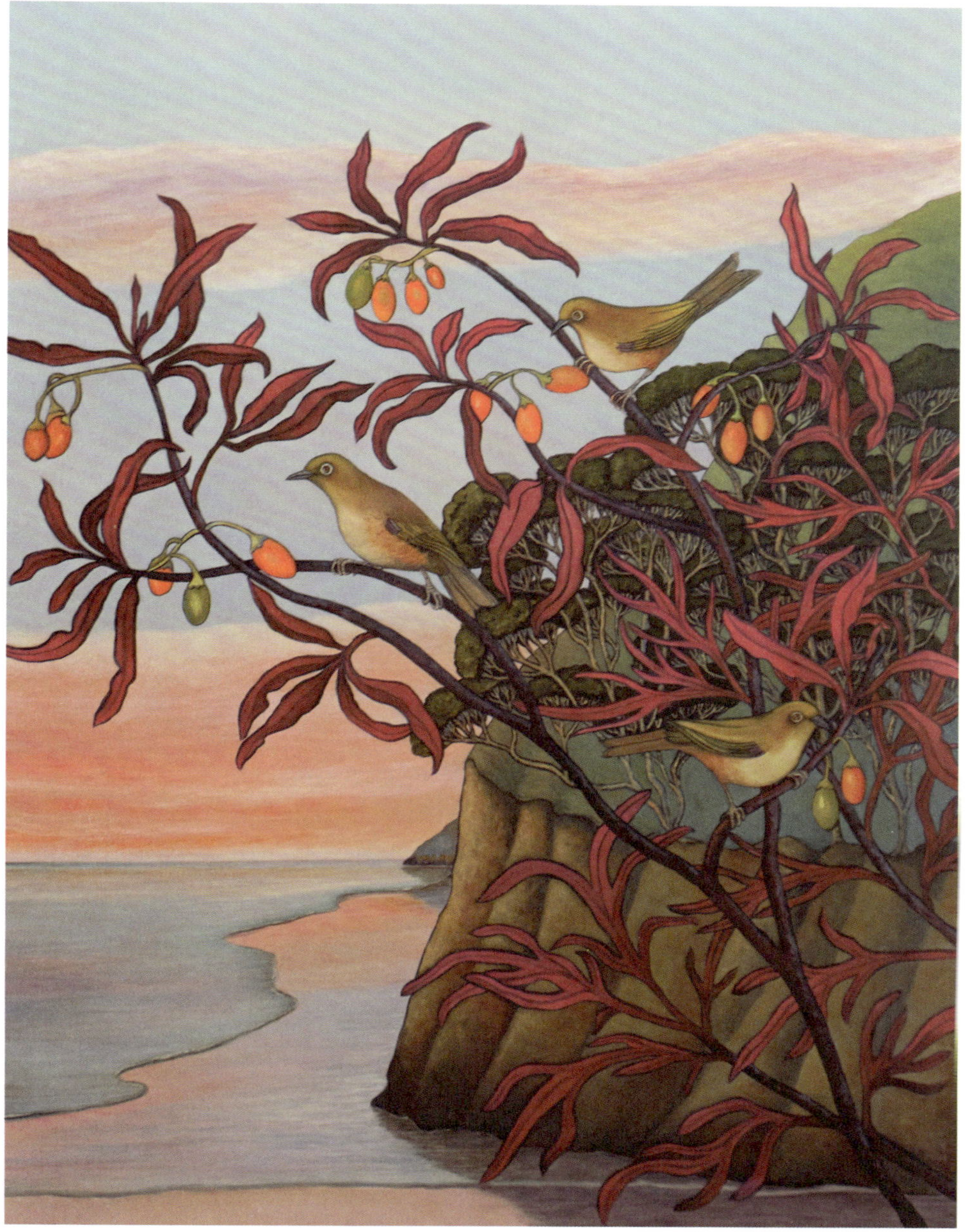

Waxeyes in the Poroporo

Winter dawn when the colours intensify
Food is scarce but the poroporo tree is alive
with activity as waxeyes eagerly feast
on poroporo fruit
A winter gift of abundance.

Waxeyes in the Poroporo 2019
800 x 600 mm/31½ x 23½ in

Opposite
Once, Our Land 2009
1000 x 1000 mm/39¼ x 39¼ in

Paradise Dreams

The derelict house sat abandoned on a lush, grassy hillside overlooking Hoopers Inlet on the Otago Peninsula. As with many country dwellings, this small, unassuming house had ceased to hold any economic value and was gradually decaying into the landscape, each year slowly disintegrating in all weathers.

What struck me about this particular house was how barren the dwelling was in its surroundings. There was no sign of a garden or trees to soften its walls. Possibly the sheep that grazed the hillside had nibbled away at any remnants of vegetation, but it didn't look like any had been there.

What had been the hopes and dreams of the people who had built this house and lived here, in what is a magnificent setting? Where had their lives taken them and how had the decline happened? Had families lived here or was it a sole farm worker's cottage? I imagined the house provided the most basic of shelter and probably very little comfort, a place to fall exhaustedly into bed after a long day's work and early morning starts, with only dreams of a better time and place to look forward to.

Paradise ducks now strutted in the foreground, down below the house, their chests thrust forward as they called hauntingly across the bay. They enjoyed the charms of the location, overlooking the water, raising their yearly flock of young.

Most of us seem to have 'Paradise Dreams': that desire to find a place in the country, a view of water, and away from the bustle and stresses of city life. A place where the landscape stretches out, and where the isolation is welcomed by the meditative mind.

We had that dream of a place in the country when in 1976 we struck out for the South Island, young, vigorous and naive, all our worldly possessions in the packs on our backs. Oh, we could do that … find a little run-down cottage on a piece of land and live a simple life and paint our paradise dreams!

Opposite
Paradise Dreams 2004
1220 x 800 mm/48 x 31½ in

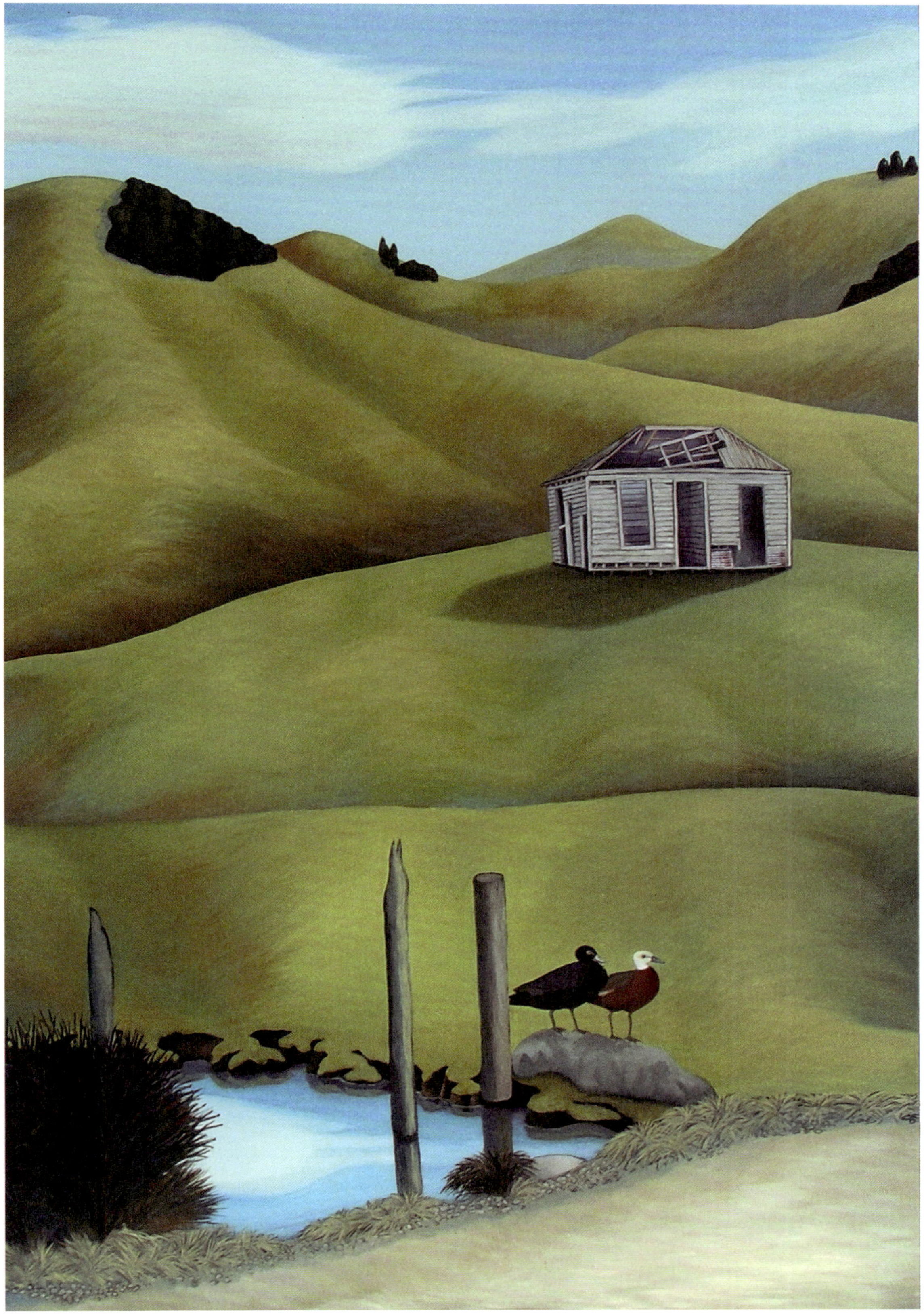

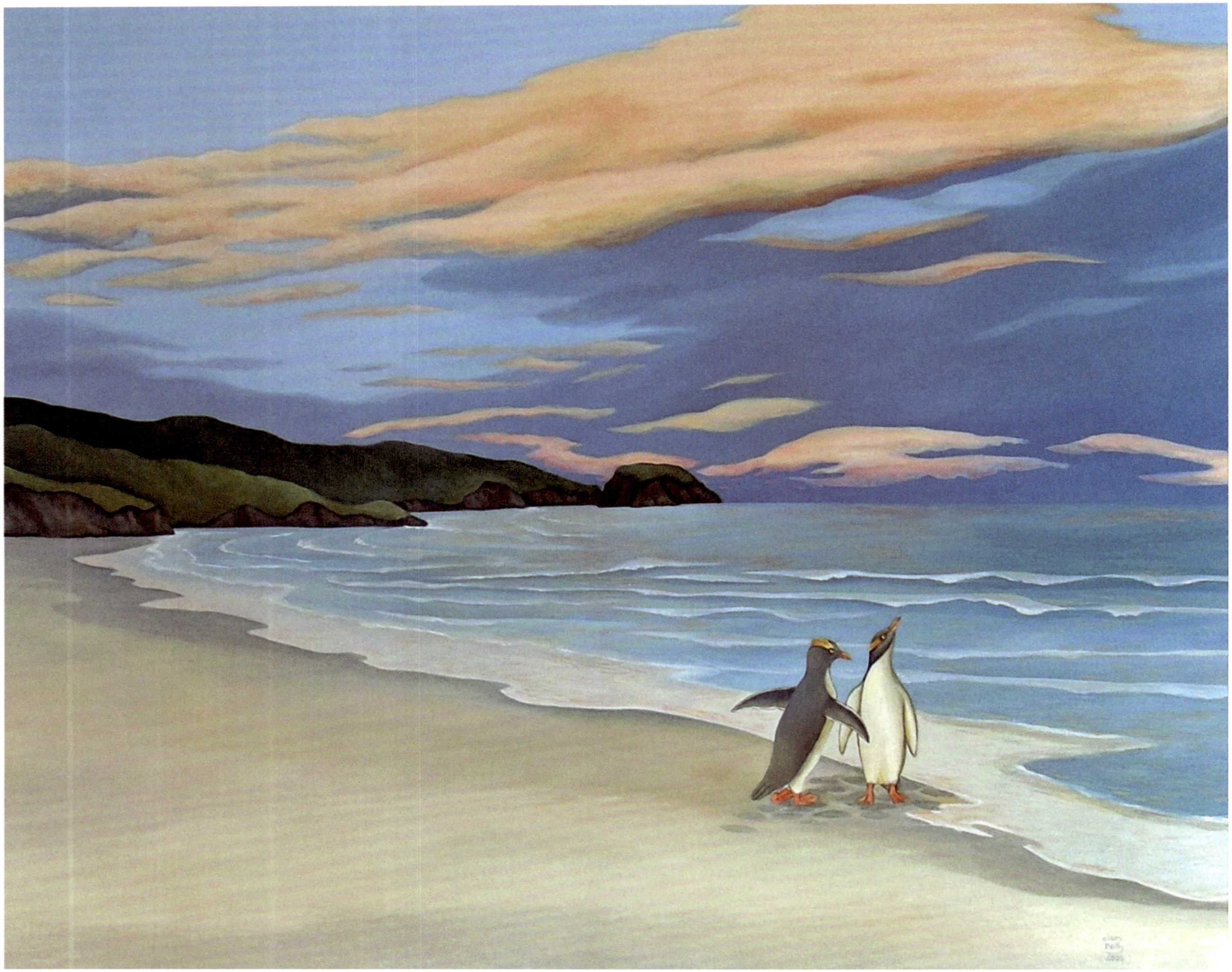

Hoiho's Return 2005
800 x 1000 mm/31½ x 39¼ in

Opposite
Fernbirds. Are You Listening? 2017
1000 x 840 mm/39¼ x 33 in

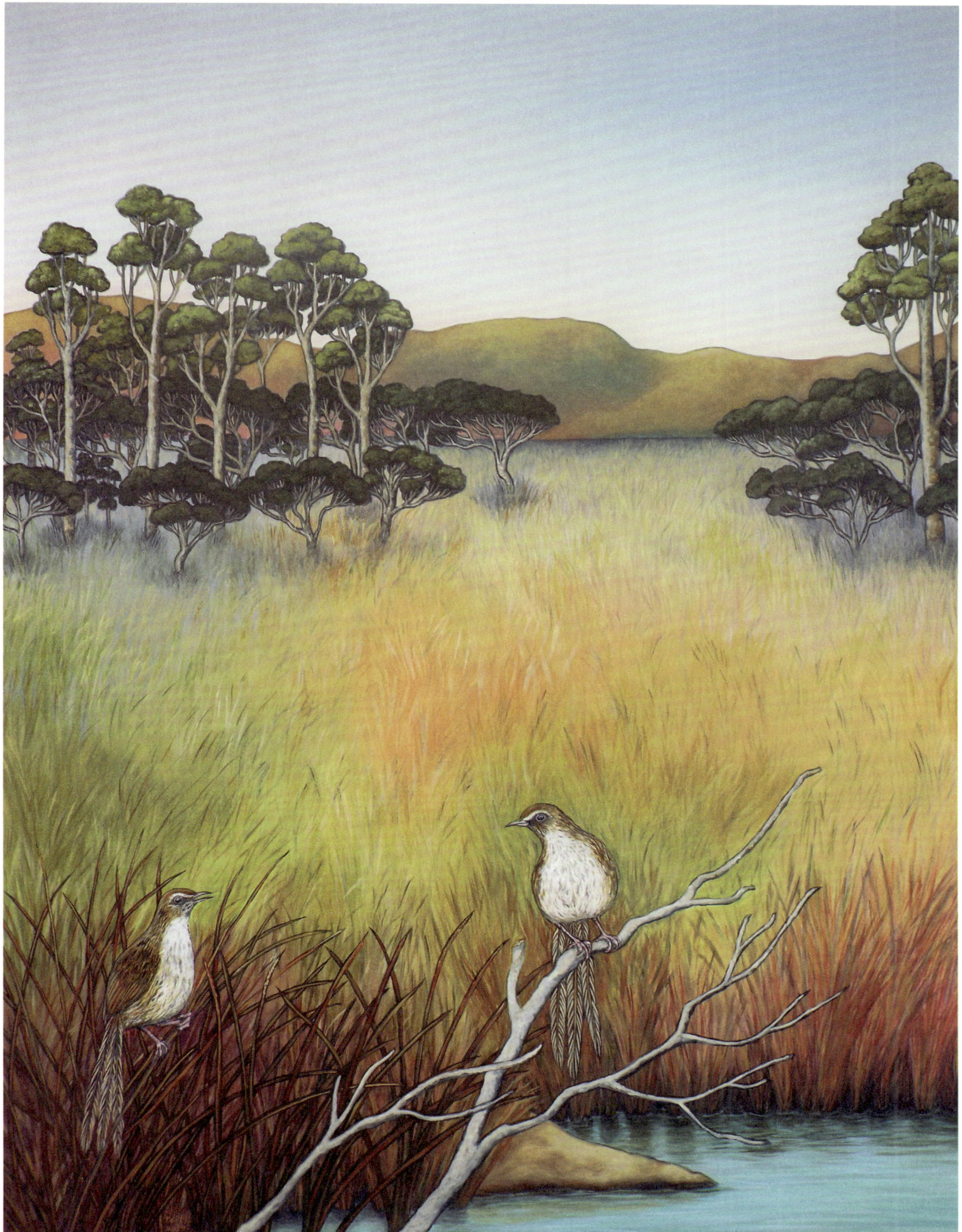

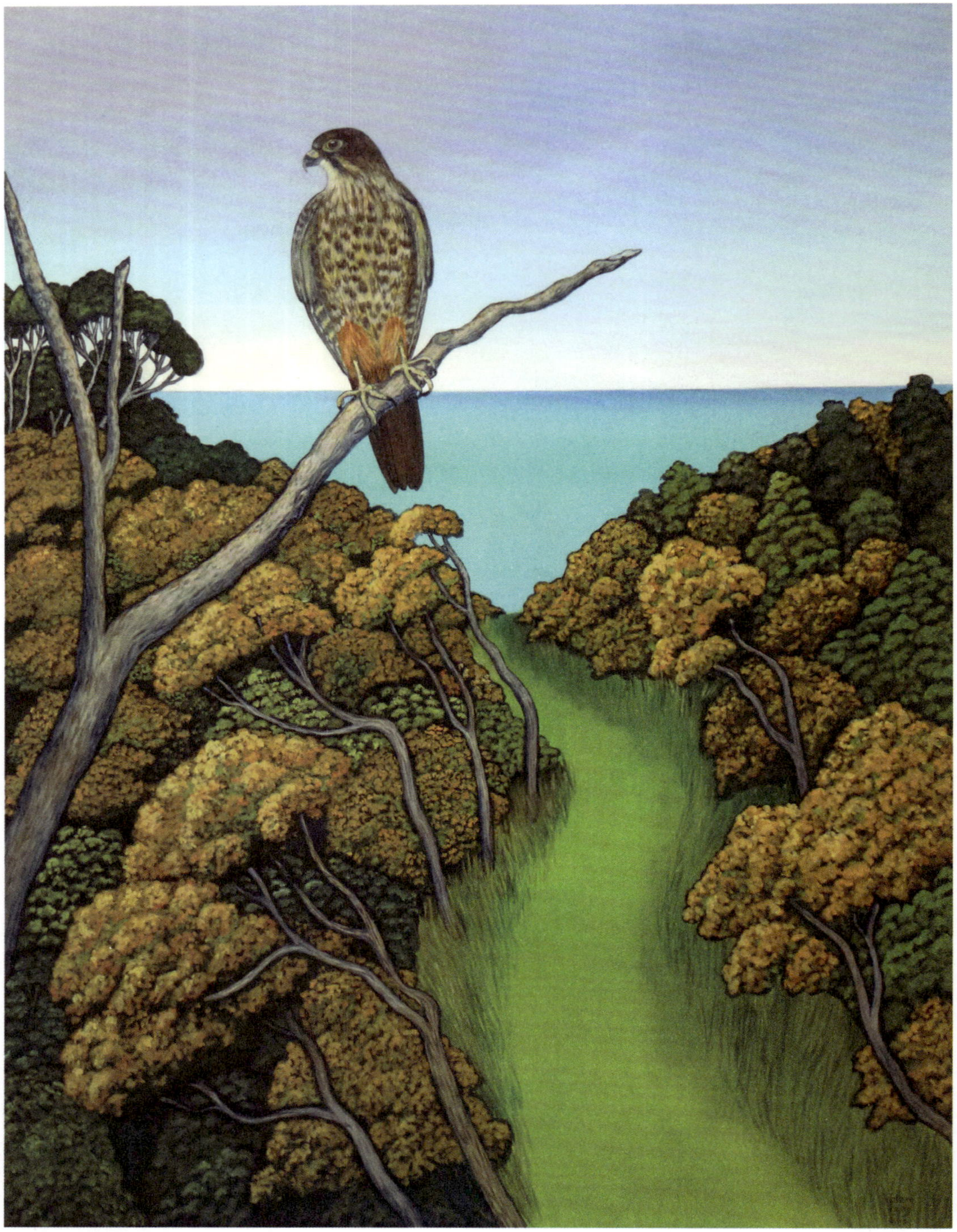

Young Kārearea and the Golden Gorse 2015
1000 x 800 mm/39¼ x 31½ in

Opposite

The River Widens Here 2015
600 x 800 mm/23½ x 31½ in

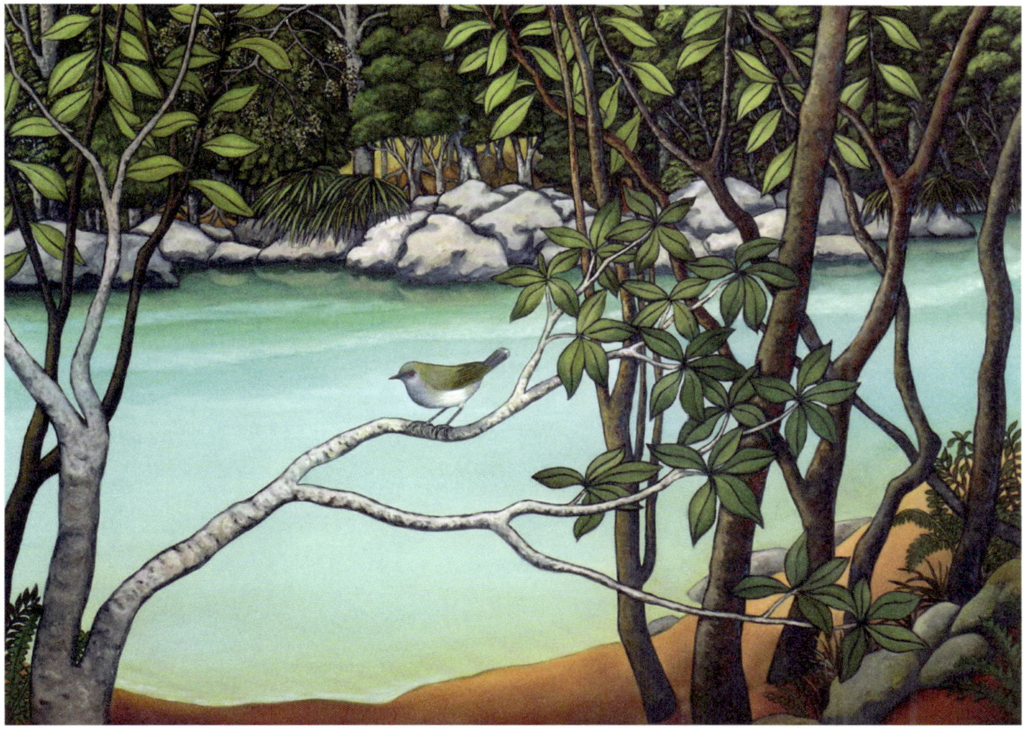

The River Widens Here

The river widens here
released from the tight
chasm of the roaring gorge.

The water, a milky aquamarine,
carries a slick of white foam,
bubbling lazily on the surface,
while the deep undercurrent
races seaward.

The sky is a heavy, steely grey,
a patter of rain drips off
the towering rock faces causing
tiny cascades to splash into the
mosses and lichens that
cover every surface.

Where the path falls away
into the river below, the beech trees
cling onto the vertical bank.
Their leaves shiver slightly in the updraft,
releasing droplets that soak
into the spongy ground.

From an overhanging branch,
Riroriro sings a sweet song that
rises above the tumult of the river,
his refrain is absorbed into the rich green
denseness of this West Coast rainforest.

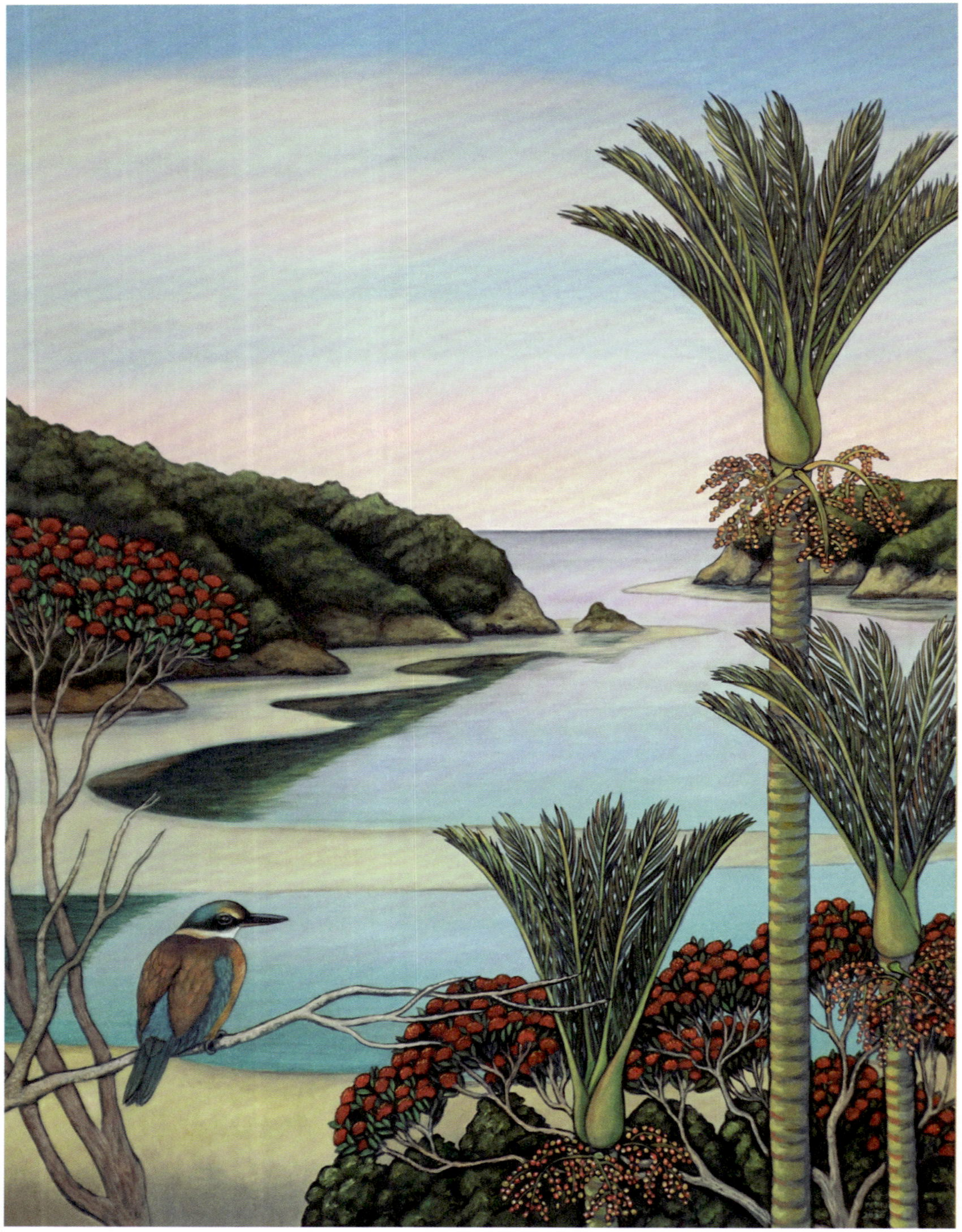

Kōtare's Perch 2020
800 x 600 mm/31½ x 23½ in

Opposite
Call of the Light 2019
1000 x 1000 mm/39¼ x 39¼ in

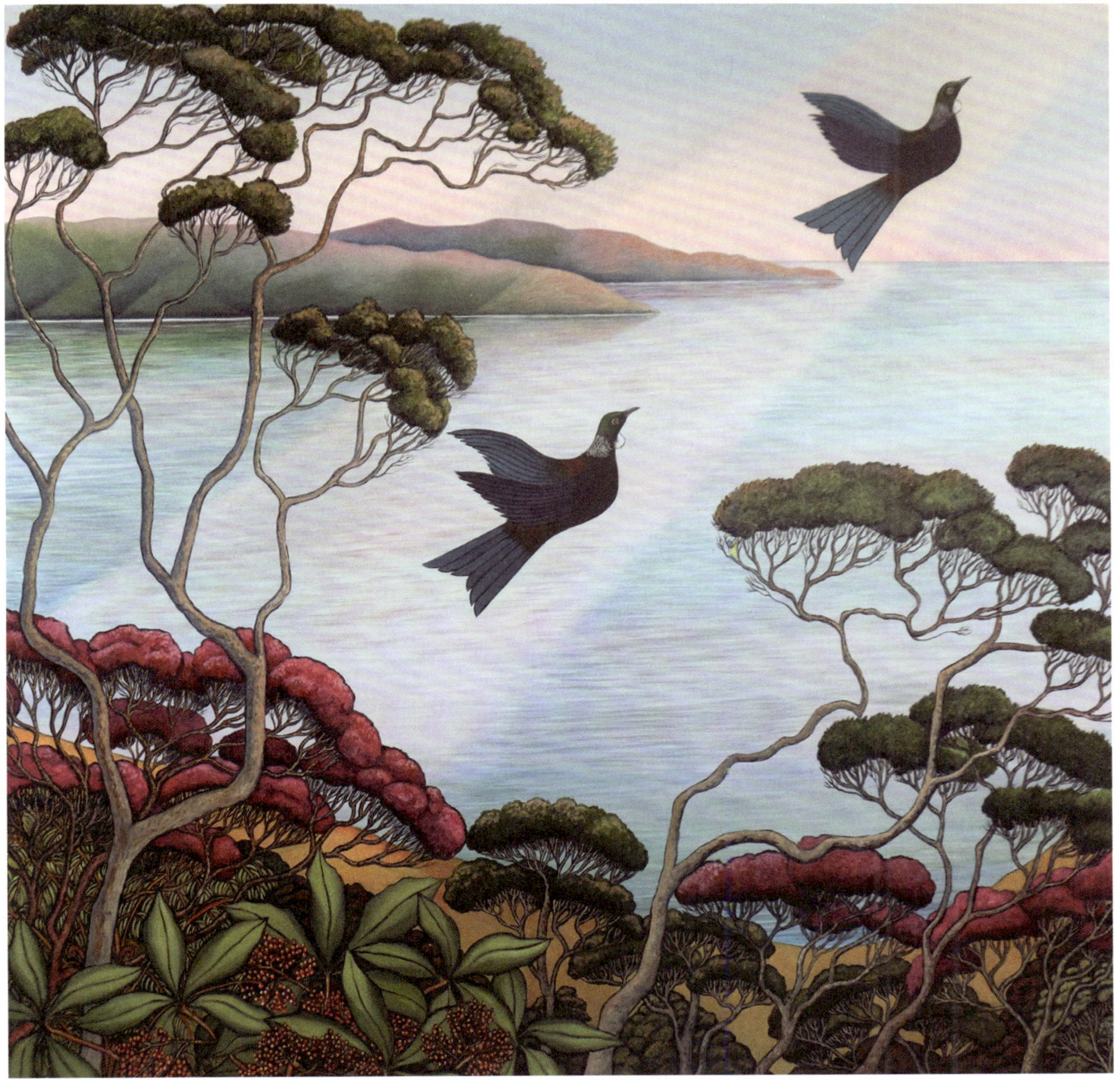

Call of the Light

An illuminating shaft of light
Reveals a path forward
Giving a sense of clarity and purpose
Drawing the present moment
Forward into another world of existence.

‘Approaching the indigenous landscape and its flora and fauna with unusual humility, Clare Reilly creates paintings imbued with a poetic stillness.’

— Gail Ross, *Eye of the Calm* catalogue, published 2009 by Primitive Bird Group

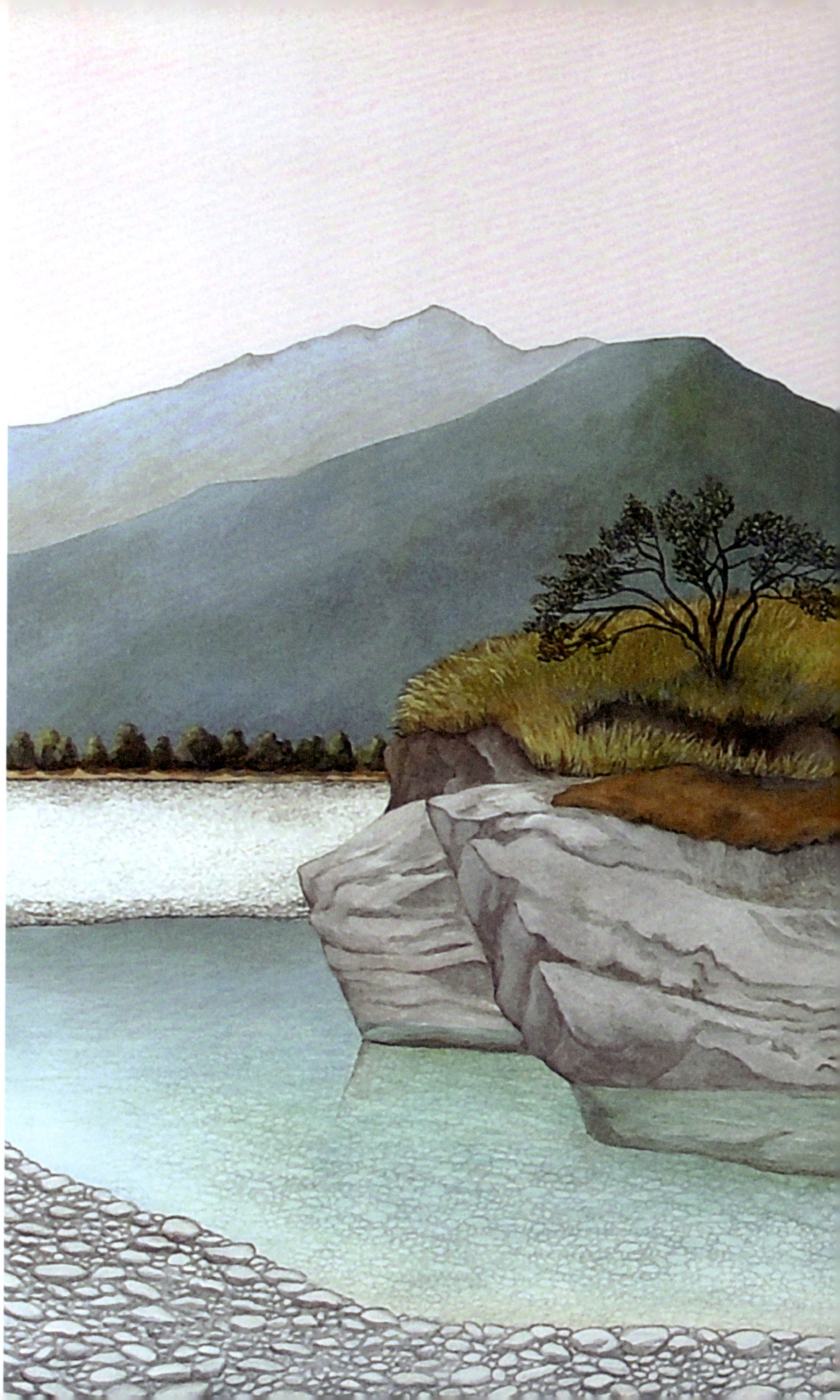

Yellow-crowned Parakeets, Mātukituki 2008
840 x 1000 mm/33 x 39¼ in

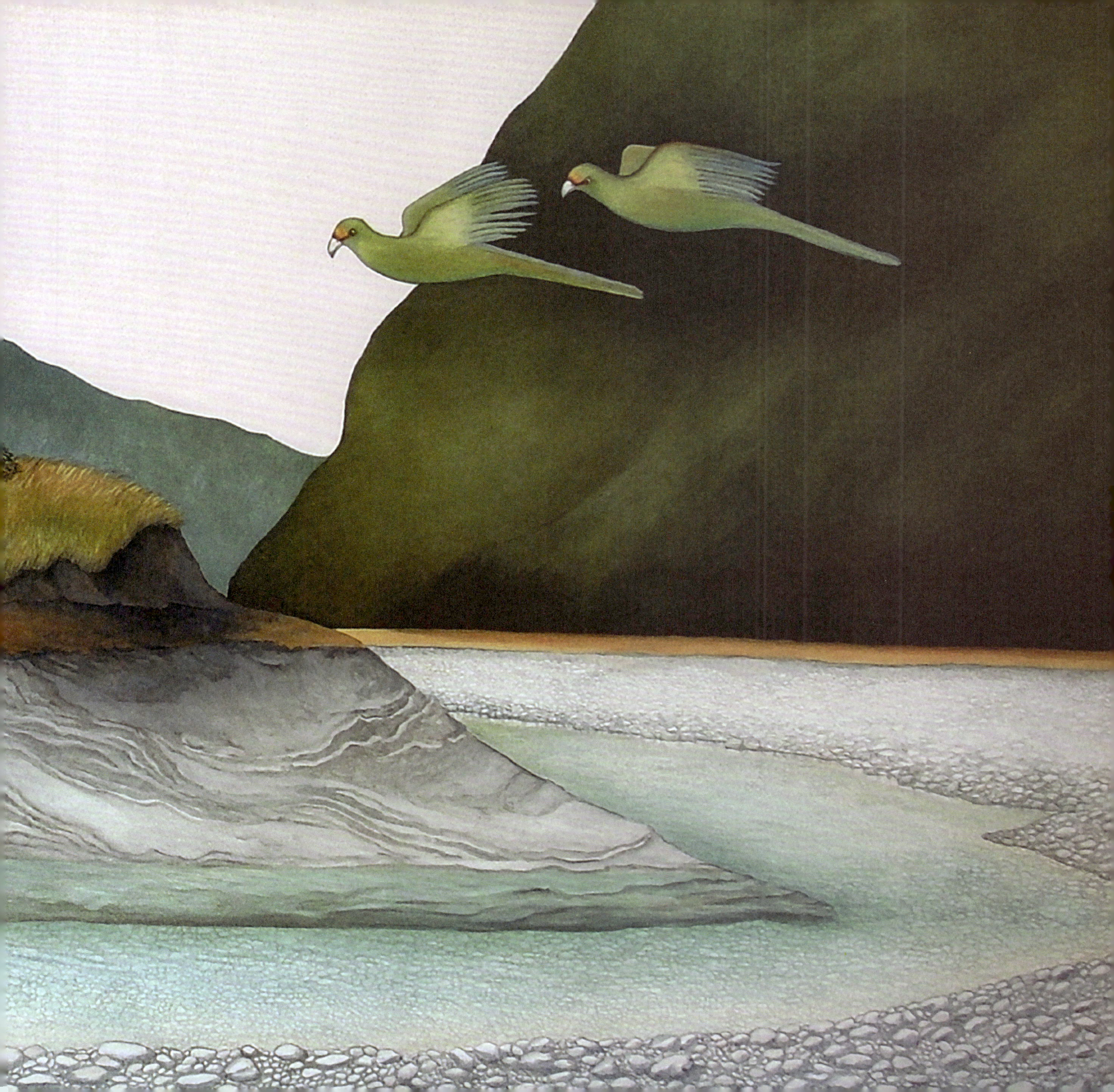

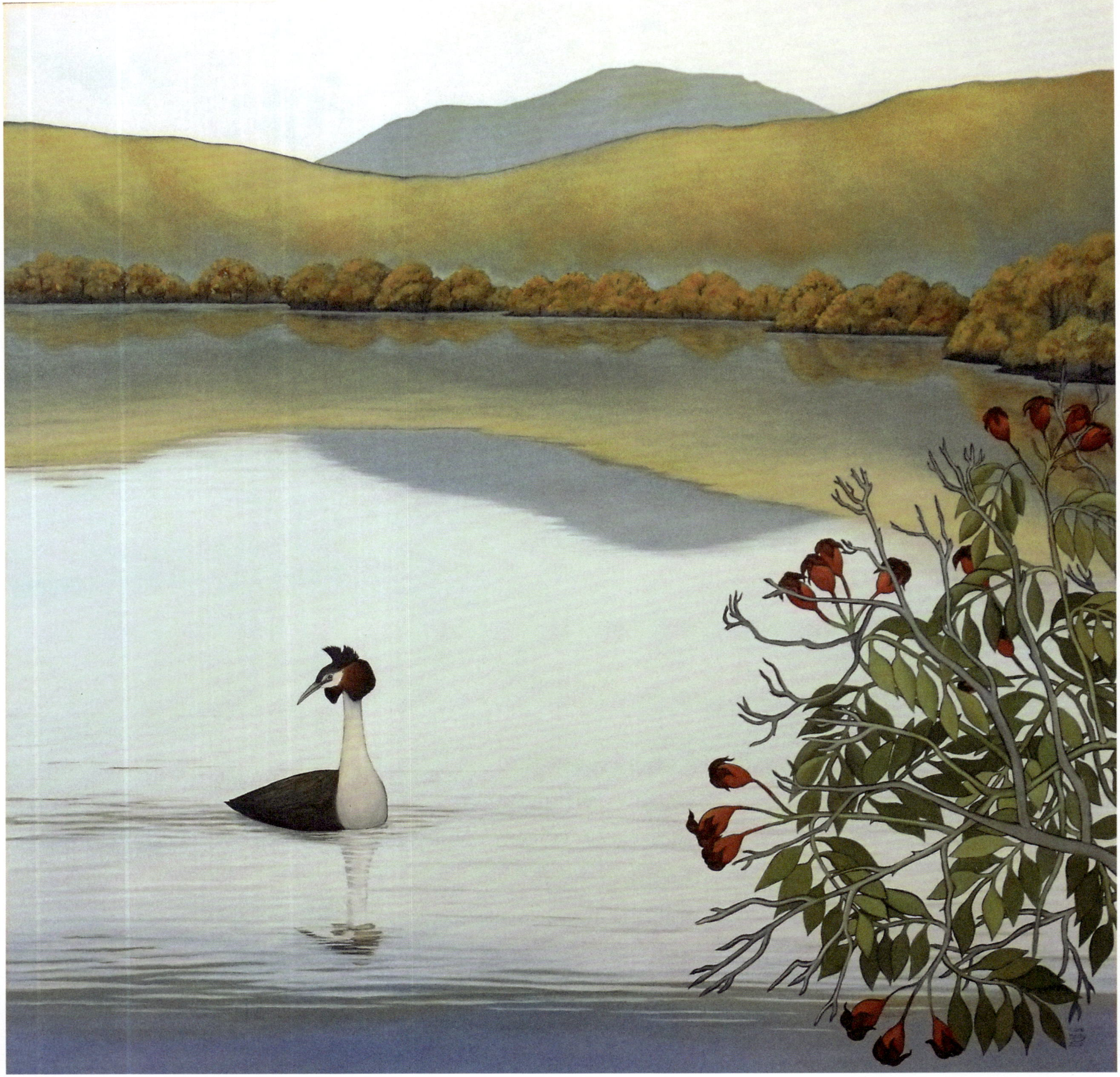

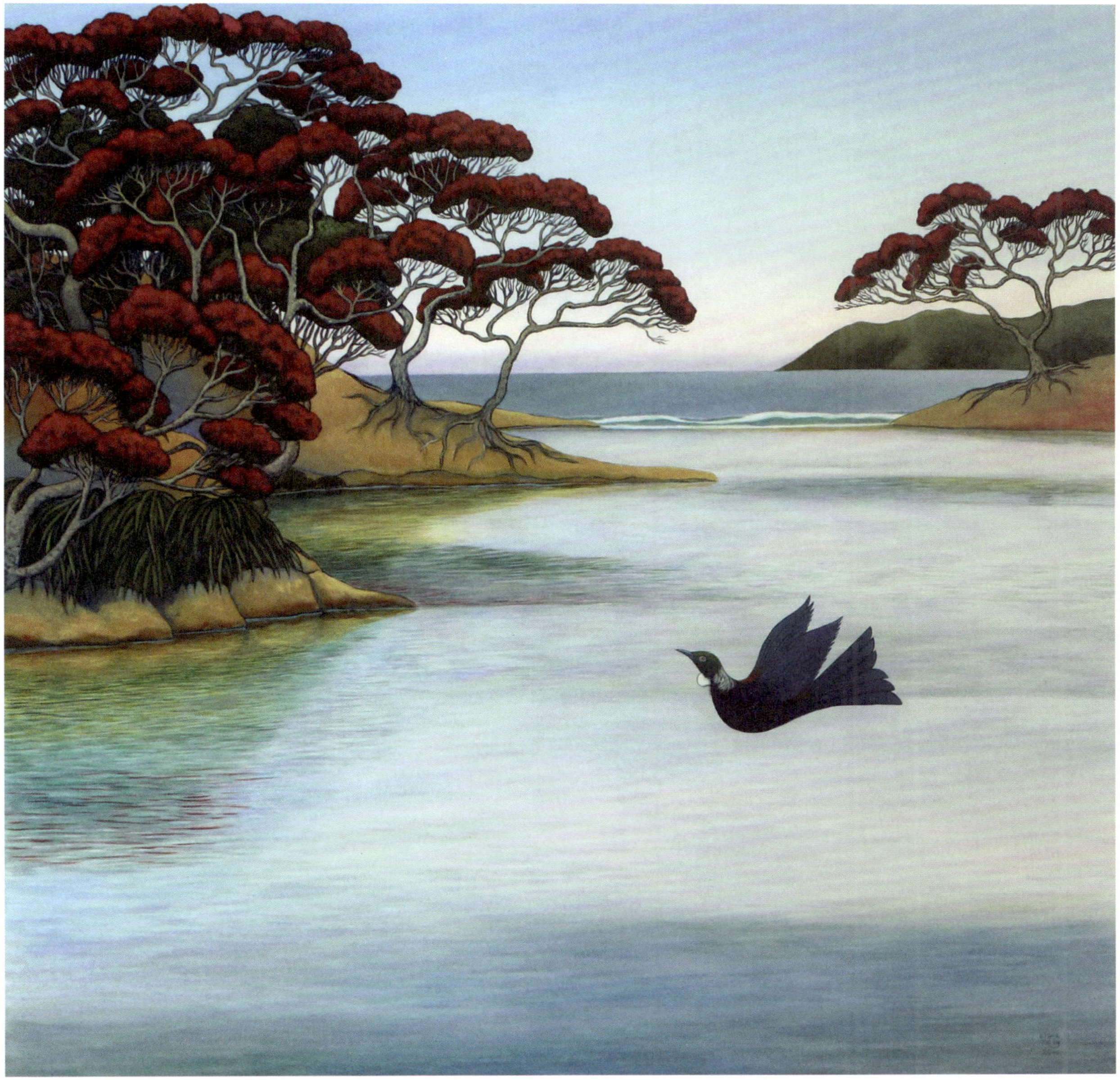

The Blazing Pōhutukawa Bay 2014
1000 x 1000 mm/39¼ x 39¼ in

Opposite
Wild Rosehips 2010
1000 x 1000 mm/39¼ x 39¼ in

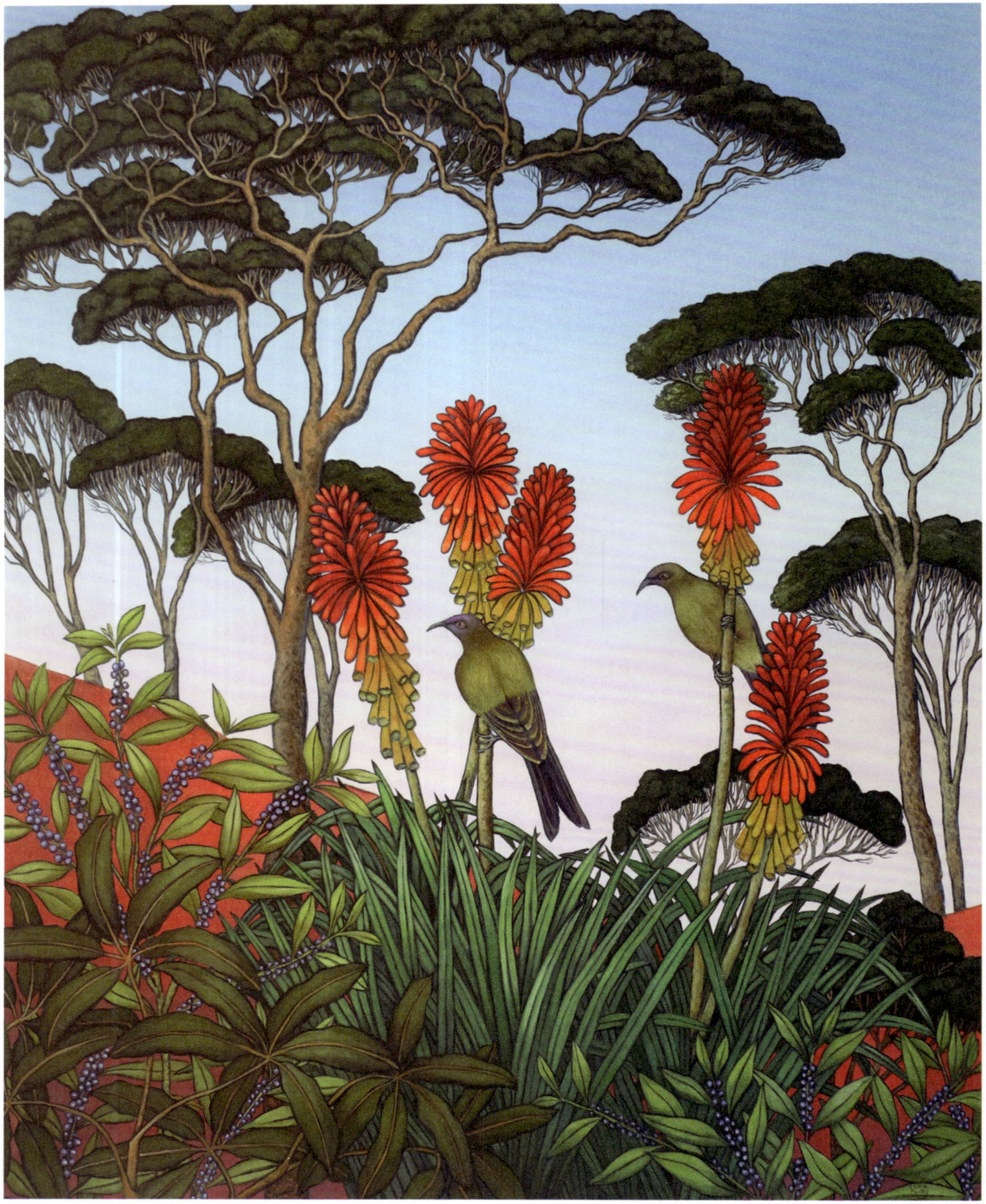

Korimako in the Kniphofia 2021
1000 x 800 mm/39¼ x 31½ in

Opposite

Calling in the Kākā 2020
1000 x 1000 mm/39¼ x 39¼ in

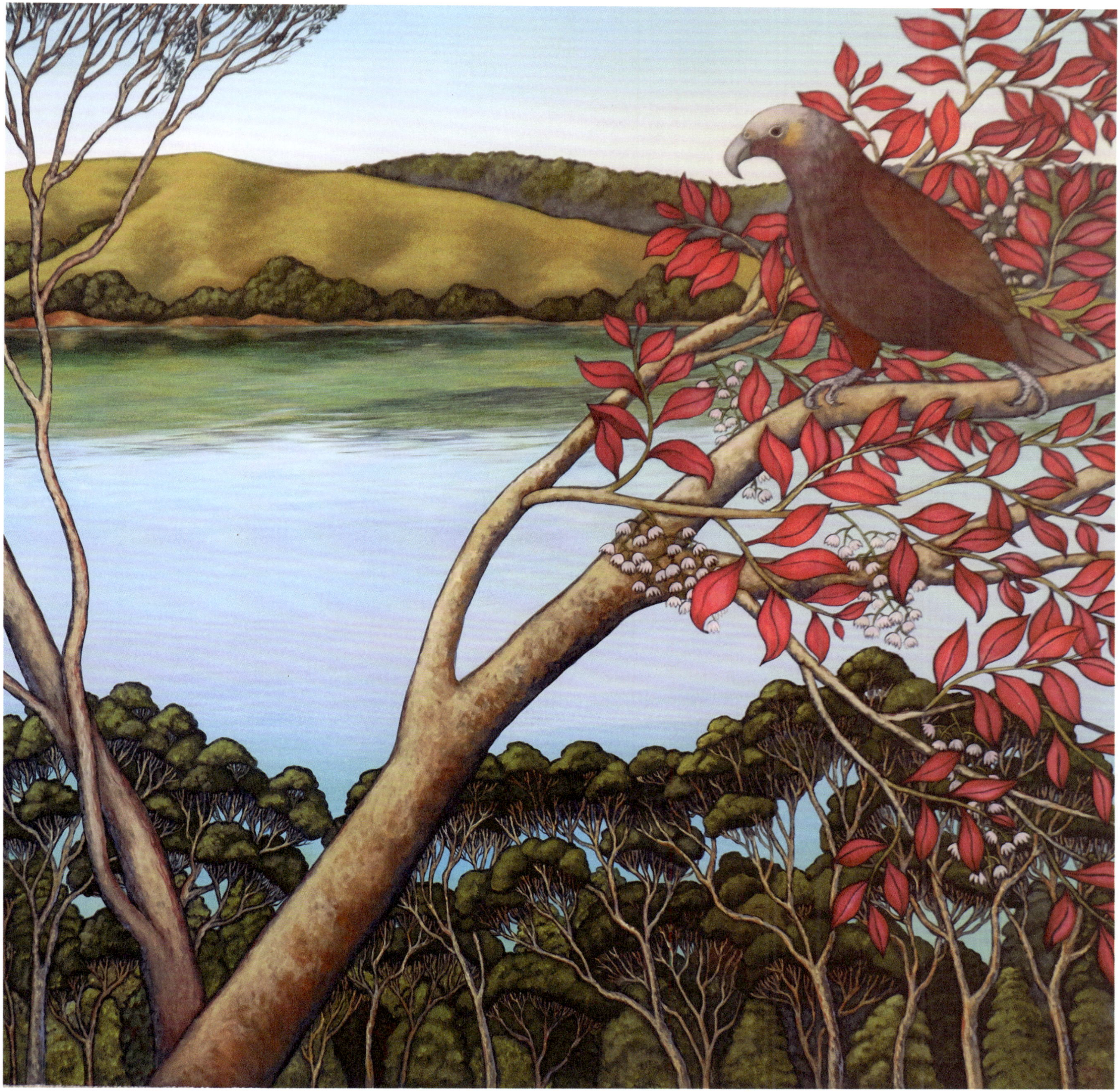

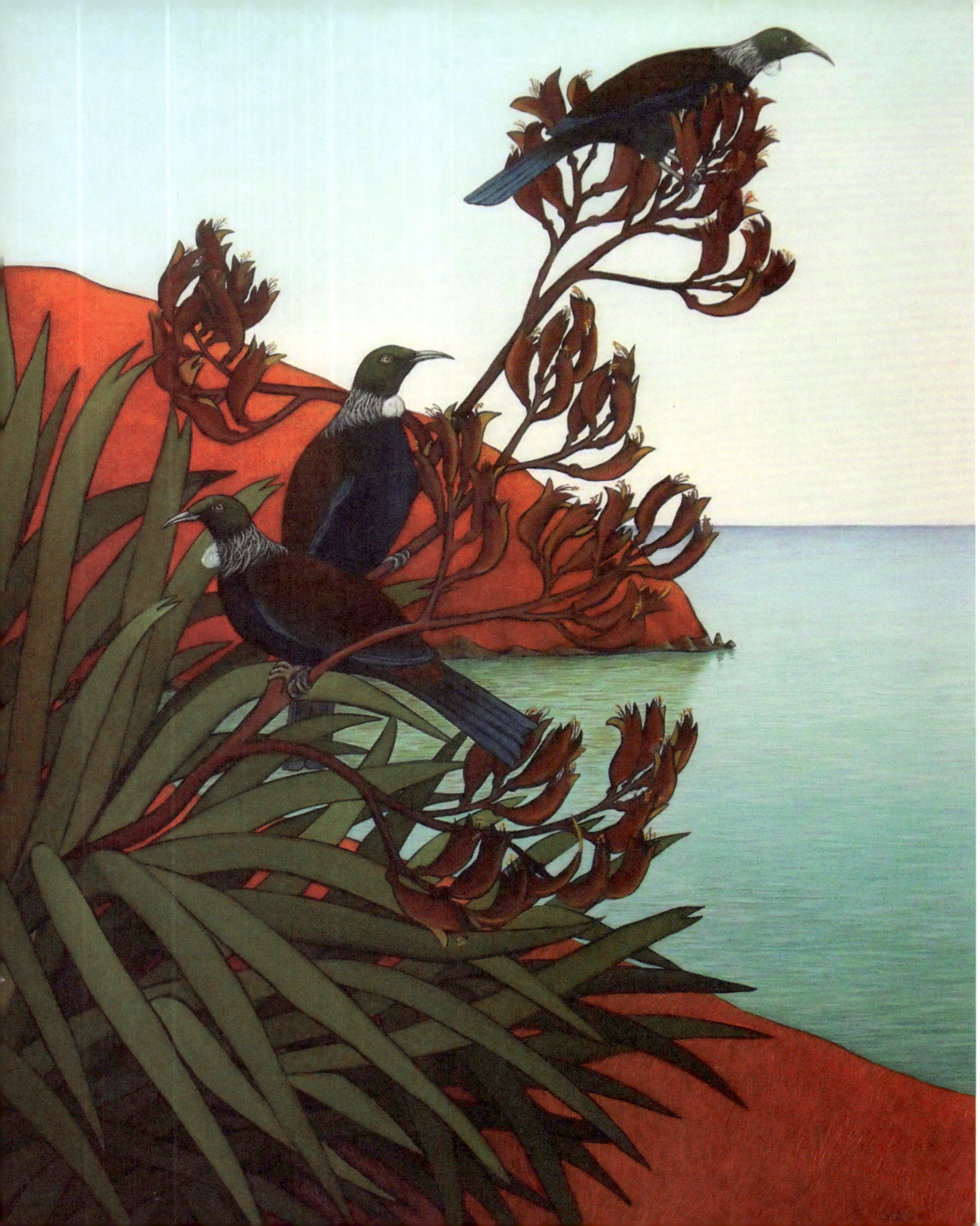

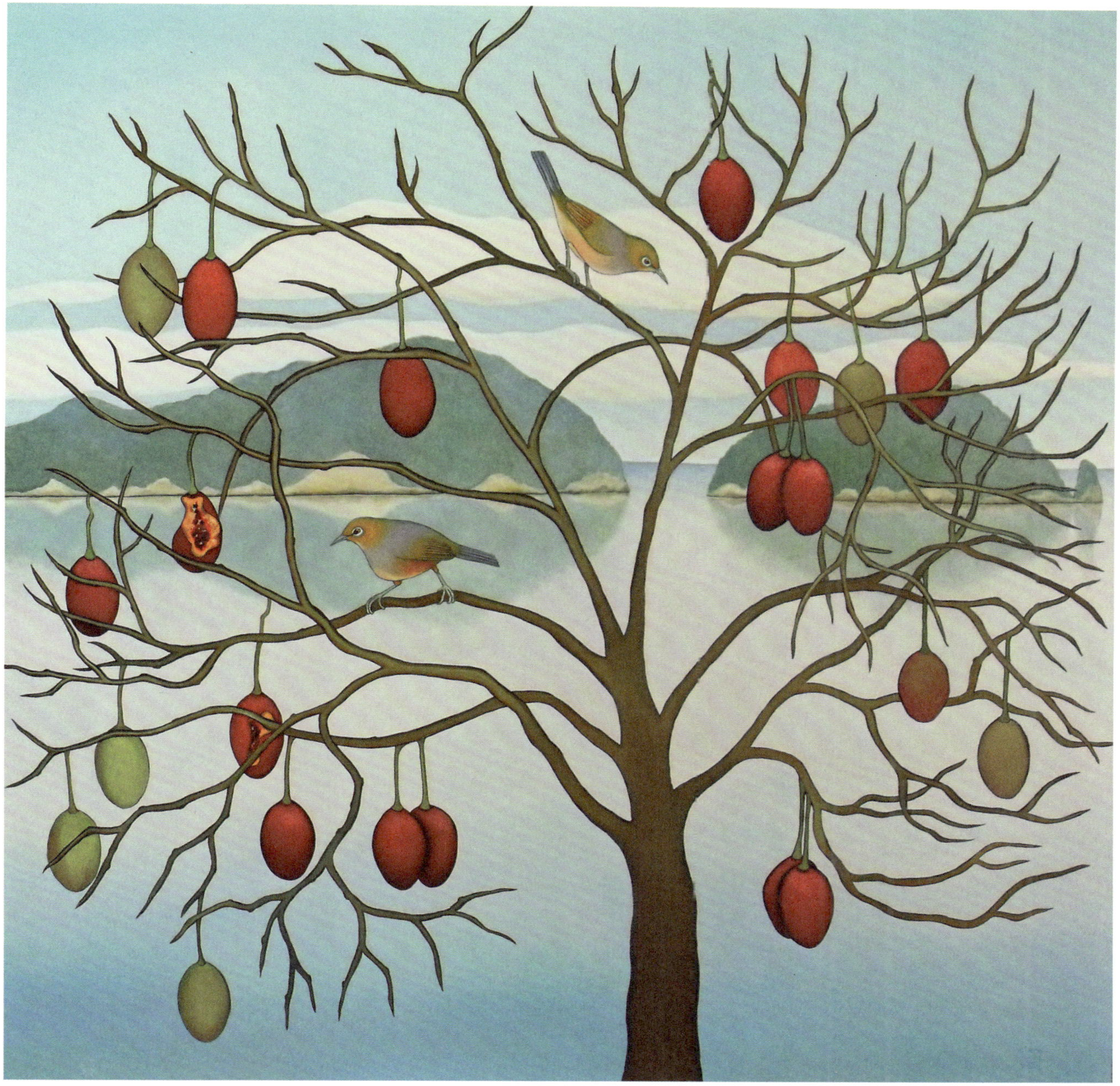

Opposite

This Strange New Land 2009

800 x 600 mm/31½ x 23½ in

The Tamarillo Tree 2009

1000 x 1000 mm/39¼ x 39¼ in

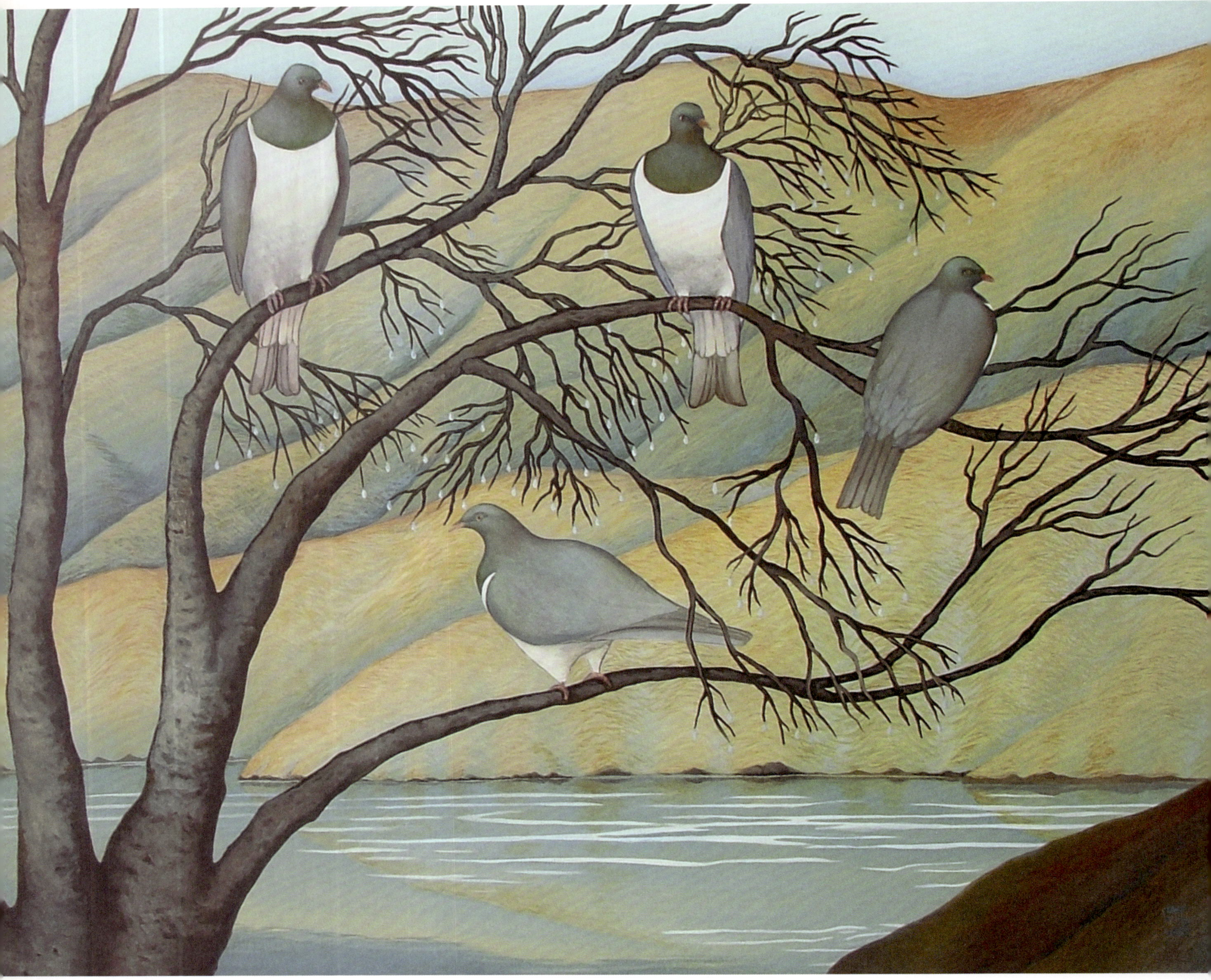

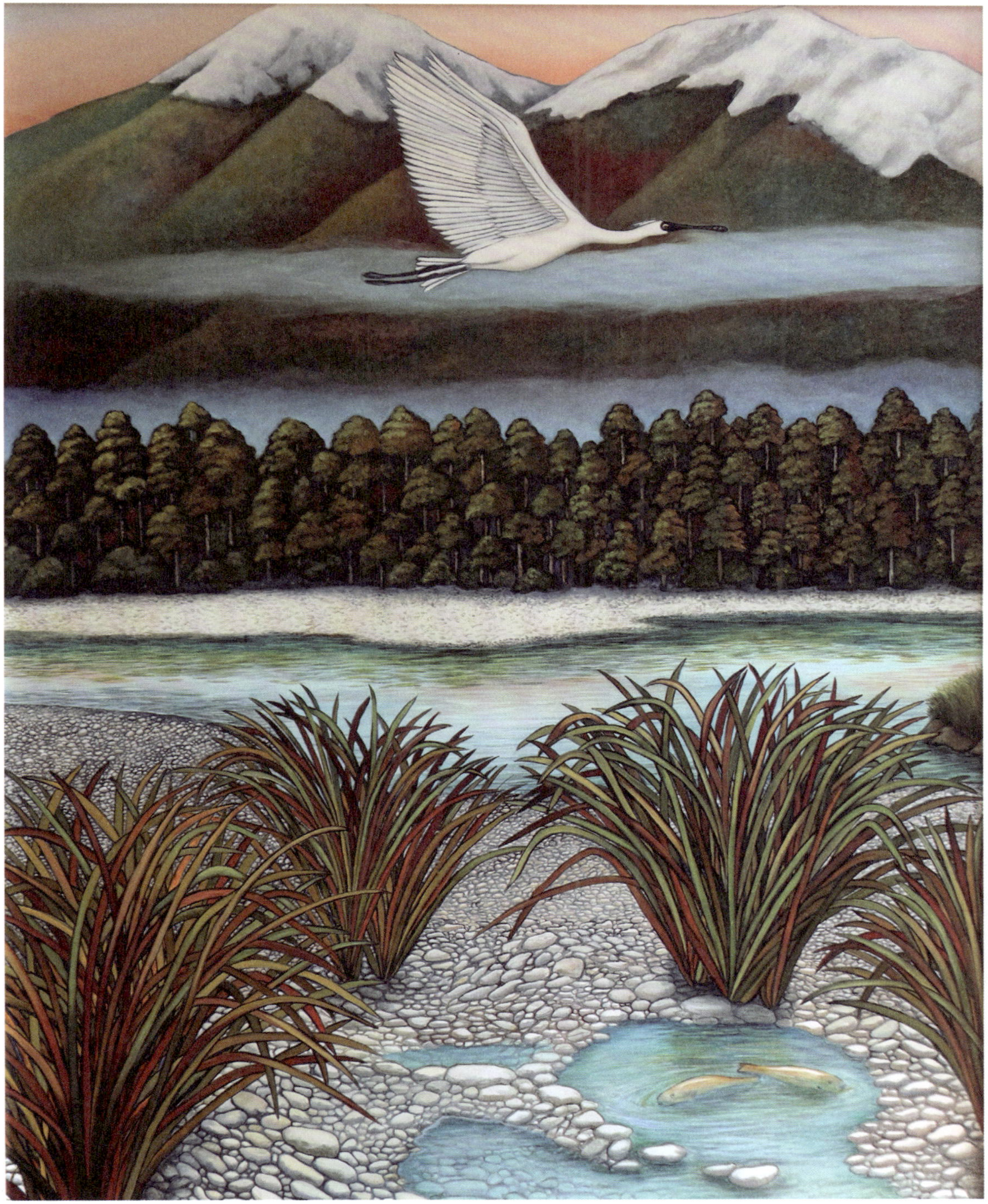

Journeying Inland 2020
1000 x 800 mm/39¼ x 31½ in

Opposite

After the Rain 2005
800 x 1000 mm/31½ x 39¼ in

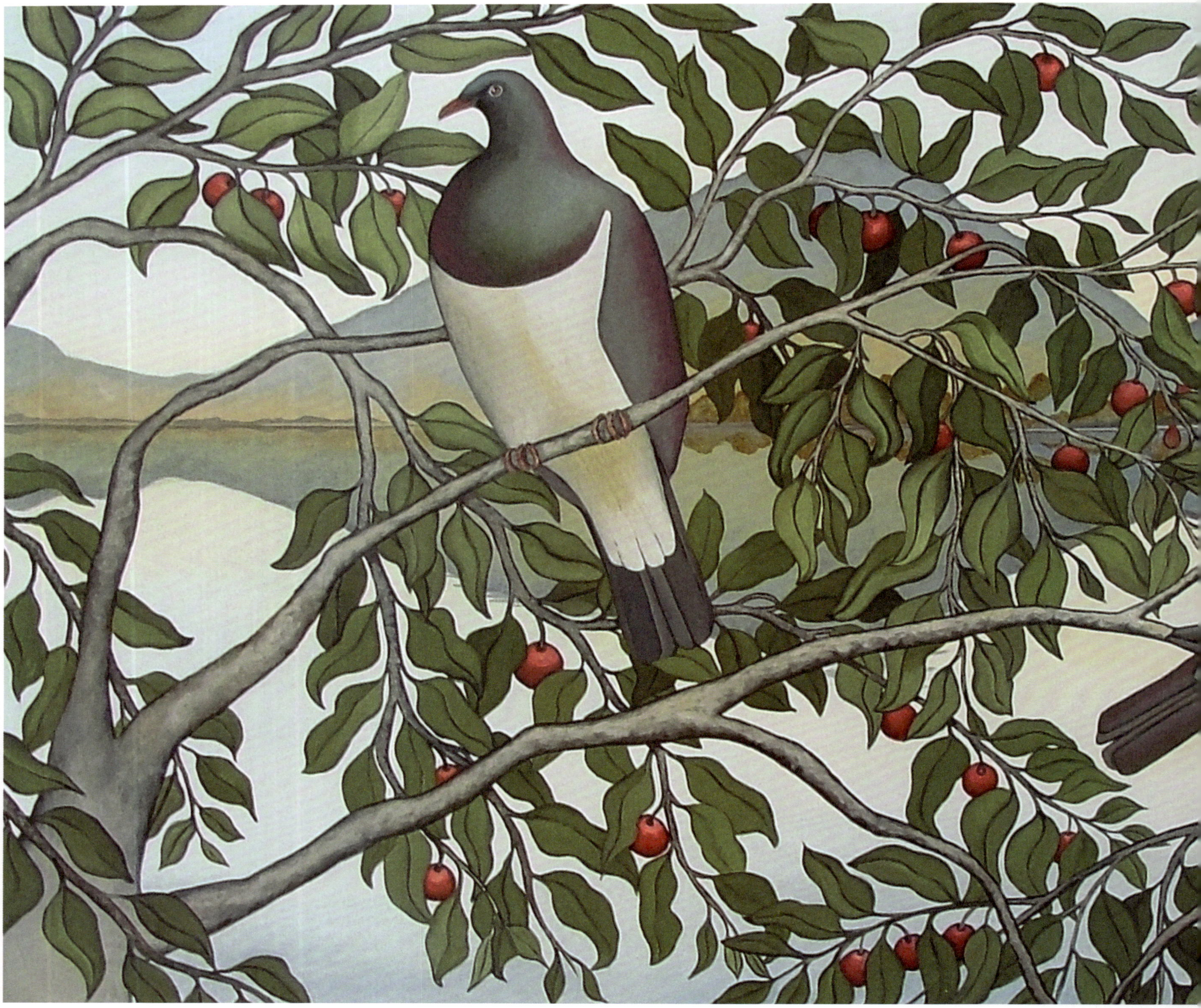

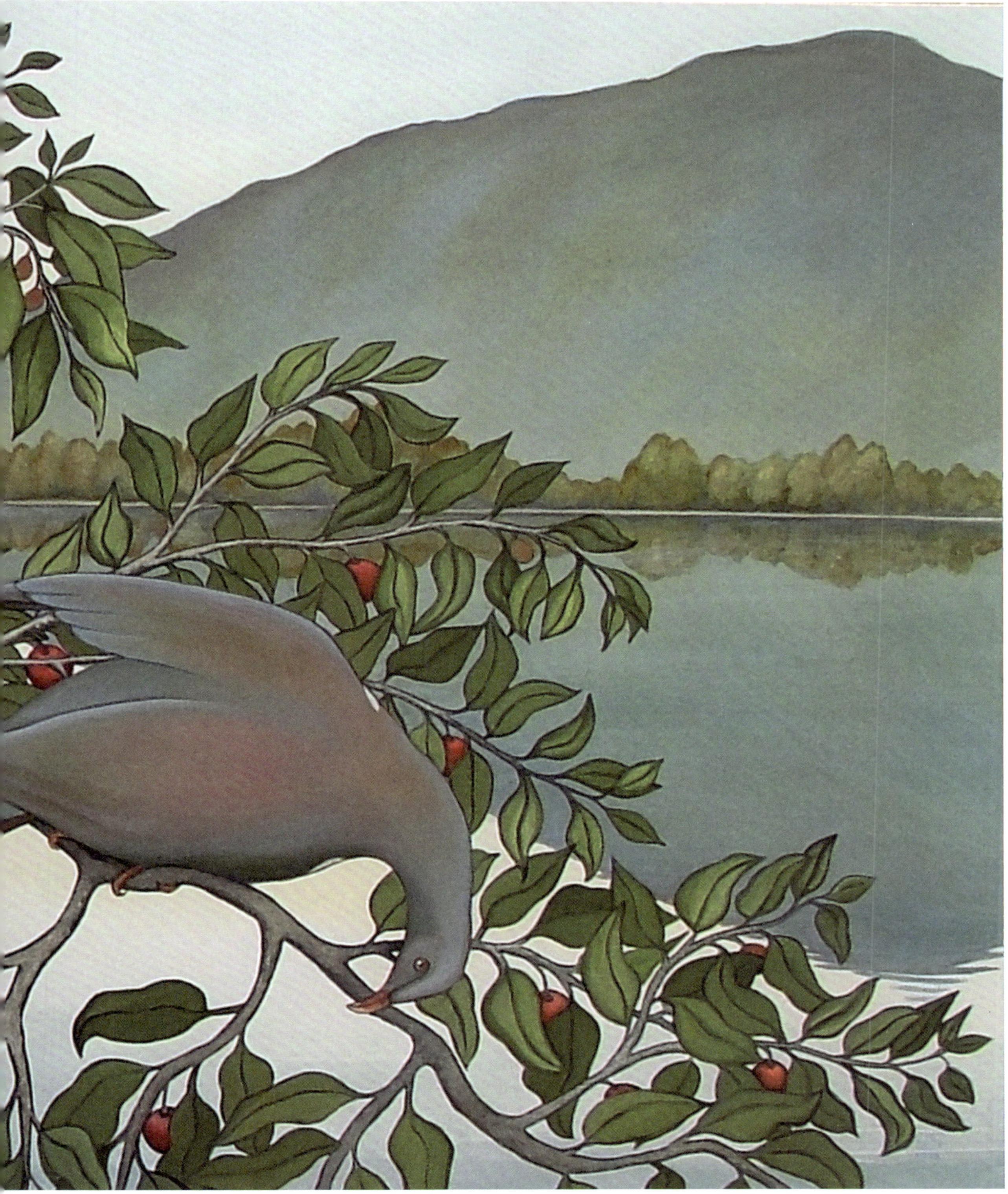

The Wild Plums 2007
600 x 1220 mm/23½ x 48 in

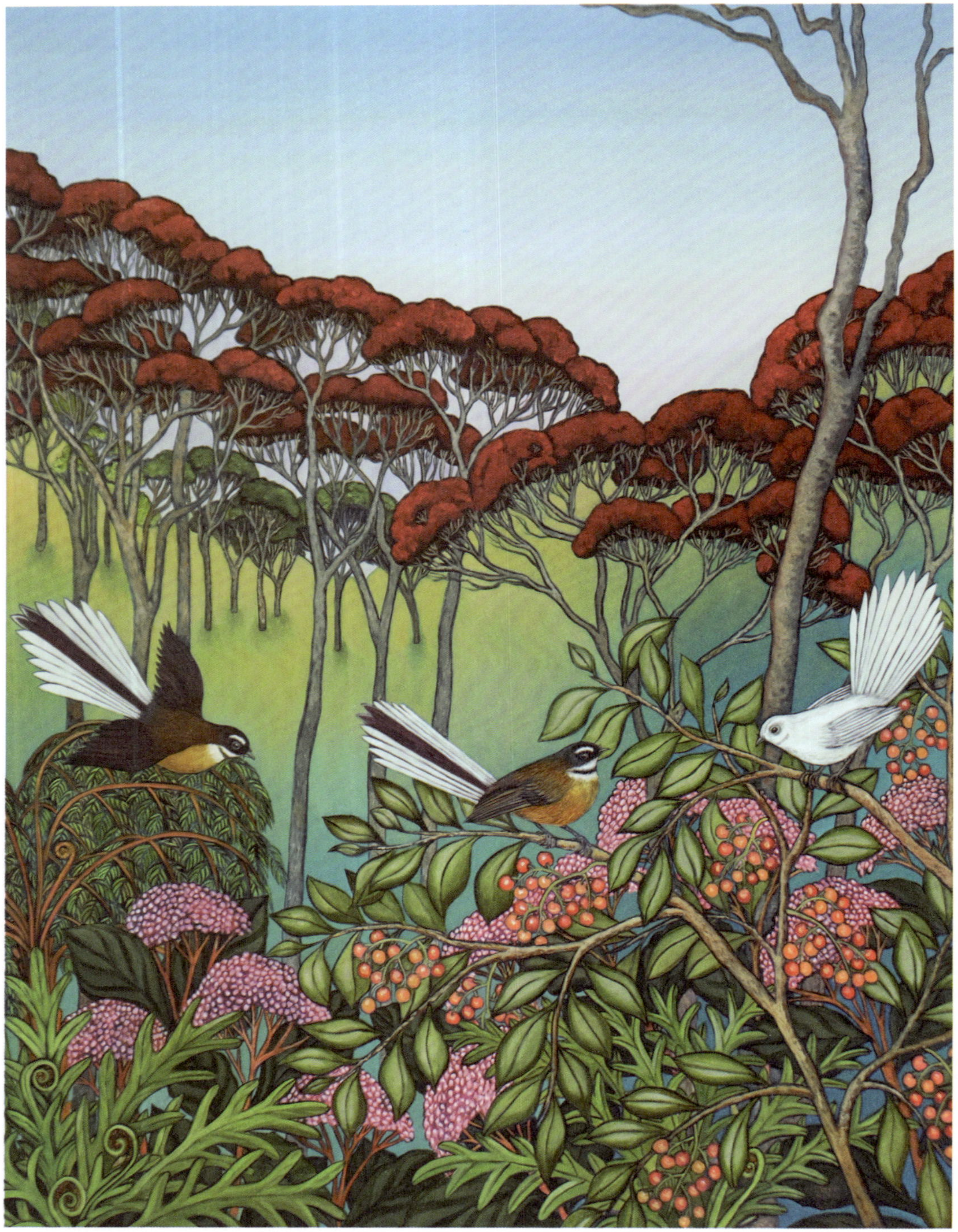

Glad Tidings from the Inner Land 2020
1000 x 800 mm/39¼ x 31½ in

Opposite

The Path Forward 2009
1000 x 800 mm/39¼ x 31½ in

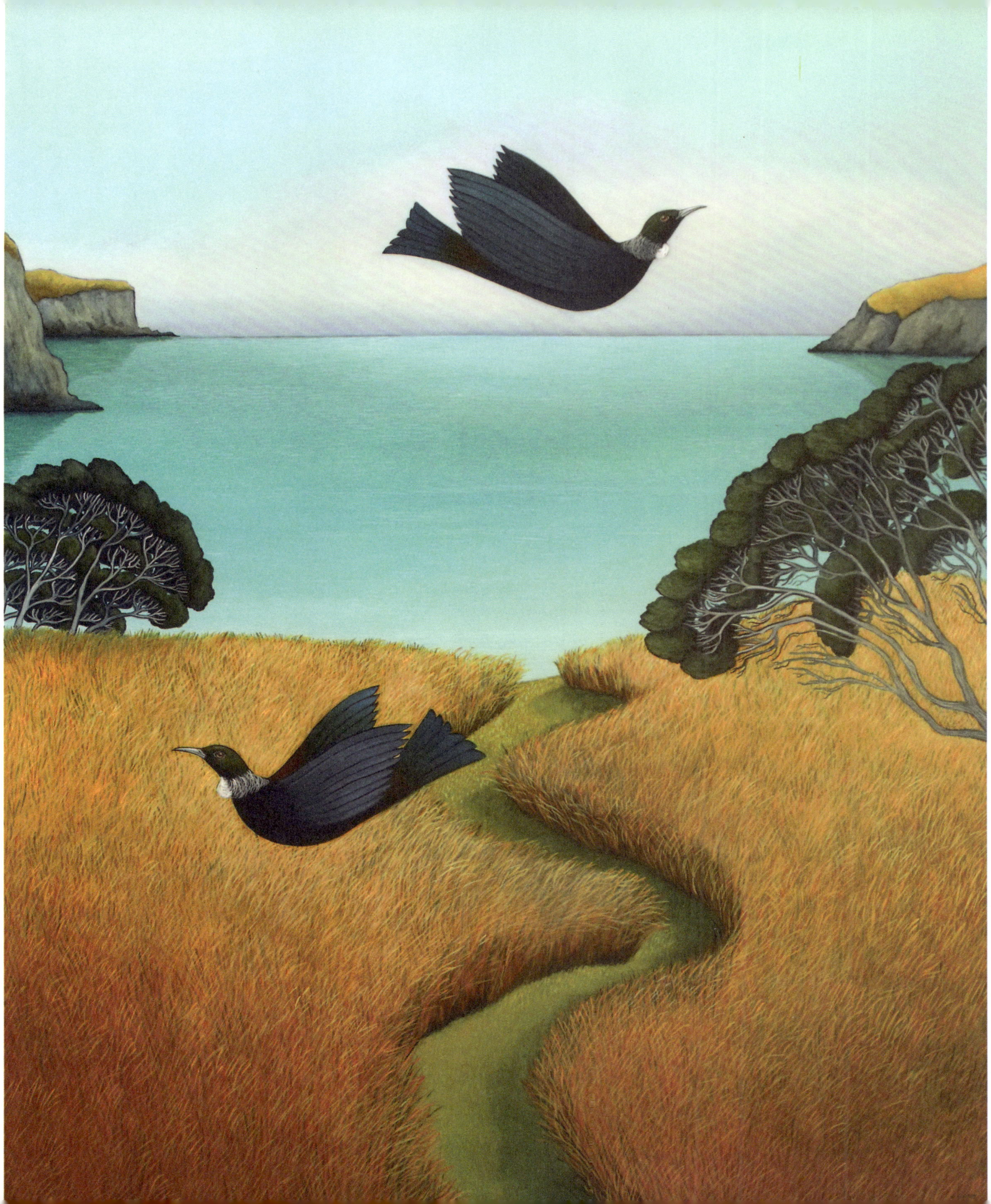

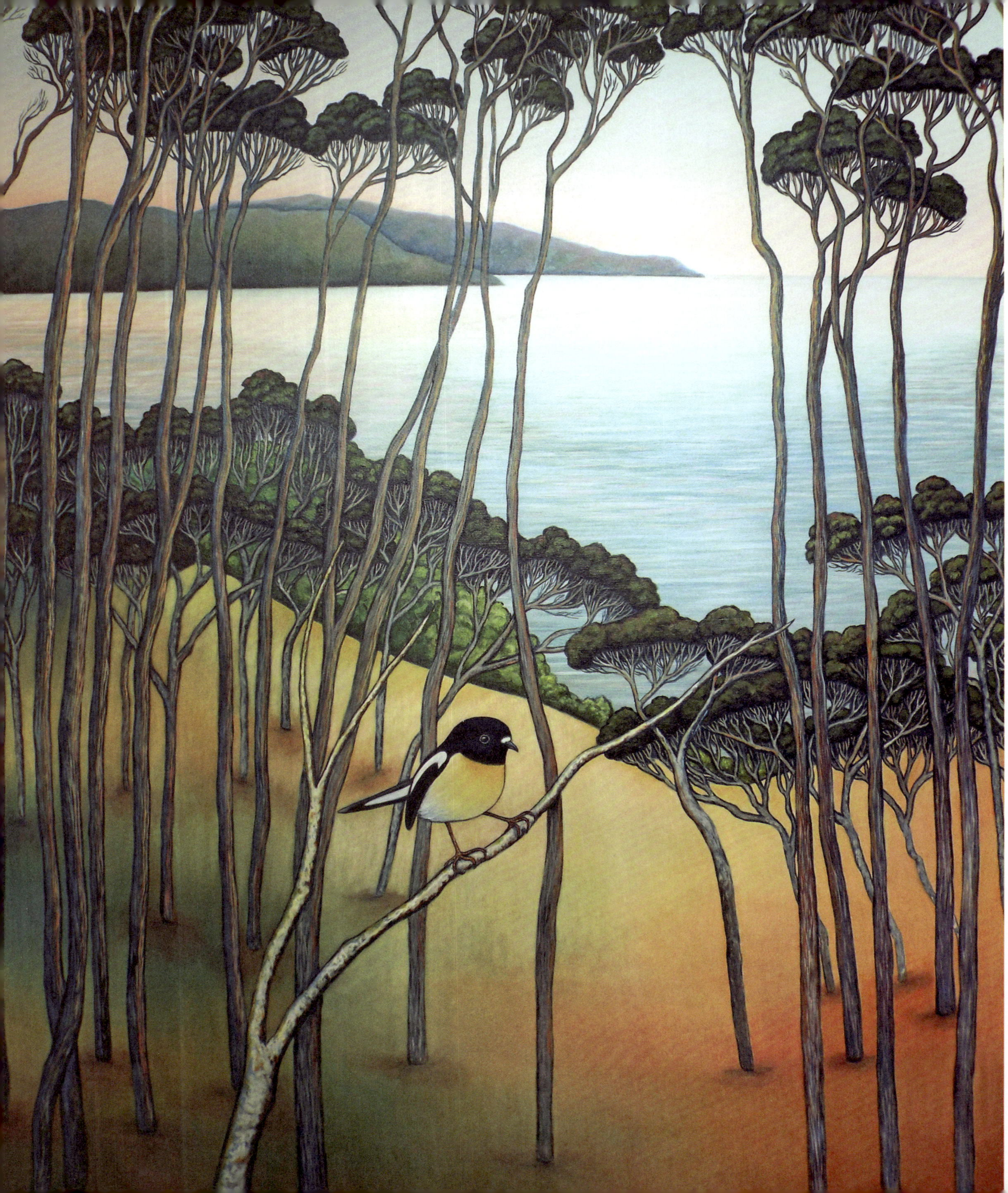

Dance Me into a New Dawn 2019
1000 x 1000 mm/39¼ x 39¼ in

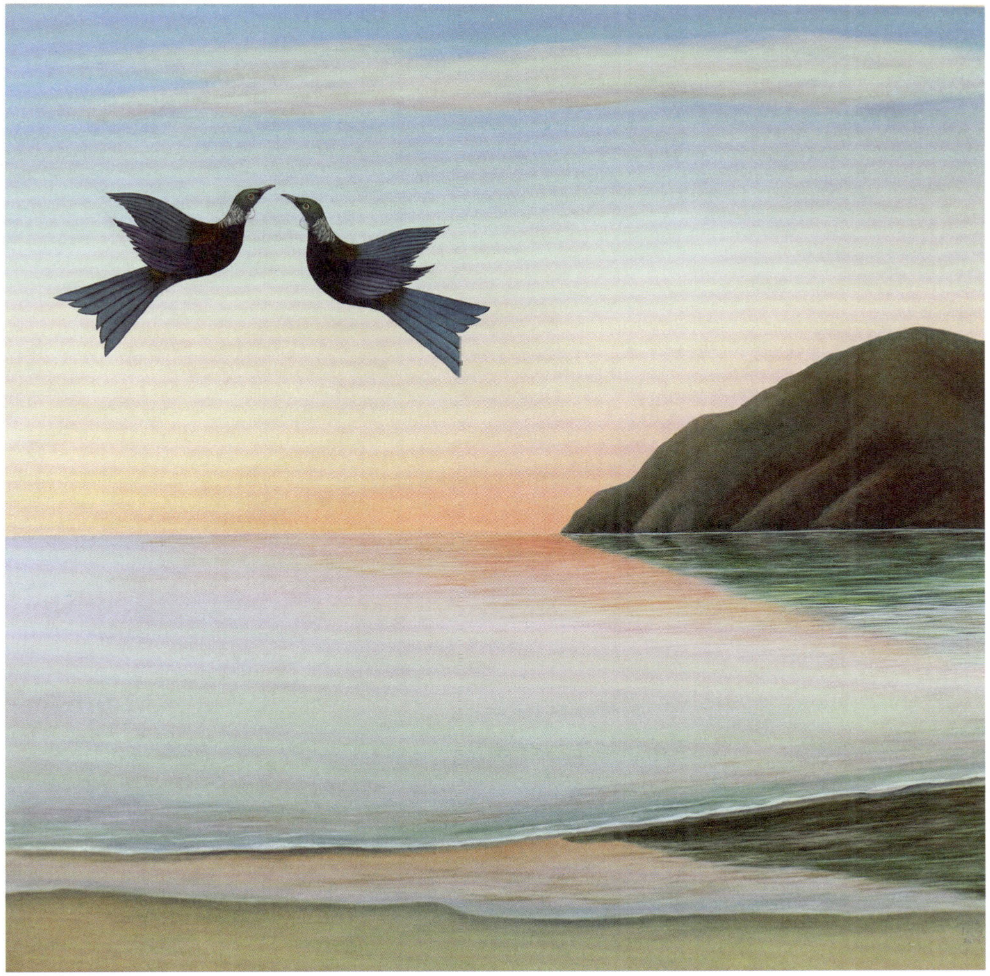

Dance Me into a New Dawn

The pristine freshness of a new dawn
Holds endless possibilities for the day ahead
I am open to the horizon and new experiences
Not wanting the heavy weight of loss to enclose me
Dance with me into this day.

Opposite
Tomtit in the Kānuka 2018
1000 x 800 mm/39¼ x 31½ in

Kōkako at Dawn 2014
1000 x 840 mm/39¼ x 33 in

Places of Sanctuary: Islands

New Zealand had been an ark of forest and birds, sailing adrift in the Southern Ocean. Much has been lost since human habitation and especially over the last 150 years. To see scraps and tiny pockets of bush and wetlands in places where the land used to be cloaked from skyline to shore in dense forest that sustained a vast array of birds is sobering. It is amazing that some offshore islands have been made safe havens for some of our rarest bird species, which have been tenuously nurtured back from the brink of extinction.

In this body of work, partly inspired by my time on Maud Island, Marlborough Sounds, and visits to Tiritiri Matangi, Hauraki Gulf, and Ulva Island, Stewart Island, I explored the dream of rich lands ringing with birdsong. It is heartening to see some rare birds thriving on these lifeboats of habitat; if they had remained on mainland New Zealand these species would also have been lost.

I am very grateful for the work carried out by conservationists, ornithologists and many local communities to maintain and preserve these habitats.

Some Enchanted Island

Floating into the margin
between sleeping and waking
come the haunting bell notes
of kōkako at dawn.

The gentle lap of silvery water
fizzing into the soft damp sand of the cove
accompanies the tūī and saddlebacks,
as they join in with the chant,
each cadence rising and falling
into the liquid cool air.

Pīwakawaka dance over a singing stream,
while kererū feed on the fruits of the forest,
kākāriki are calling in the creamy cabbage tree flowers.
miromiro sings of white rata above
the blazing pōhutukawa bay.

This enchanted Island
with its fragrant musty bush of
māhoe, tree fern, and nīkau grove,
of kānuka, pigeonwood and mighty kauri,
an Ark, a treasure trove,
sails on over the oceans of time.

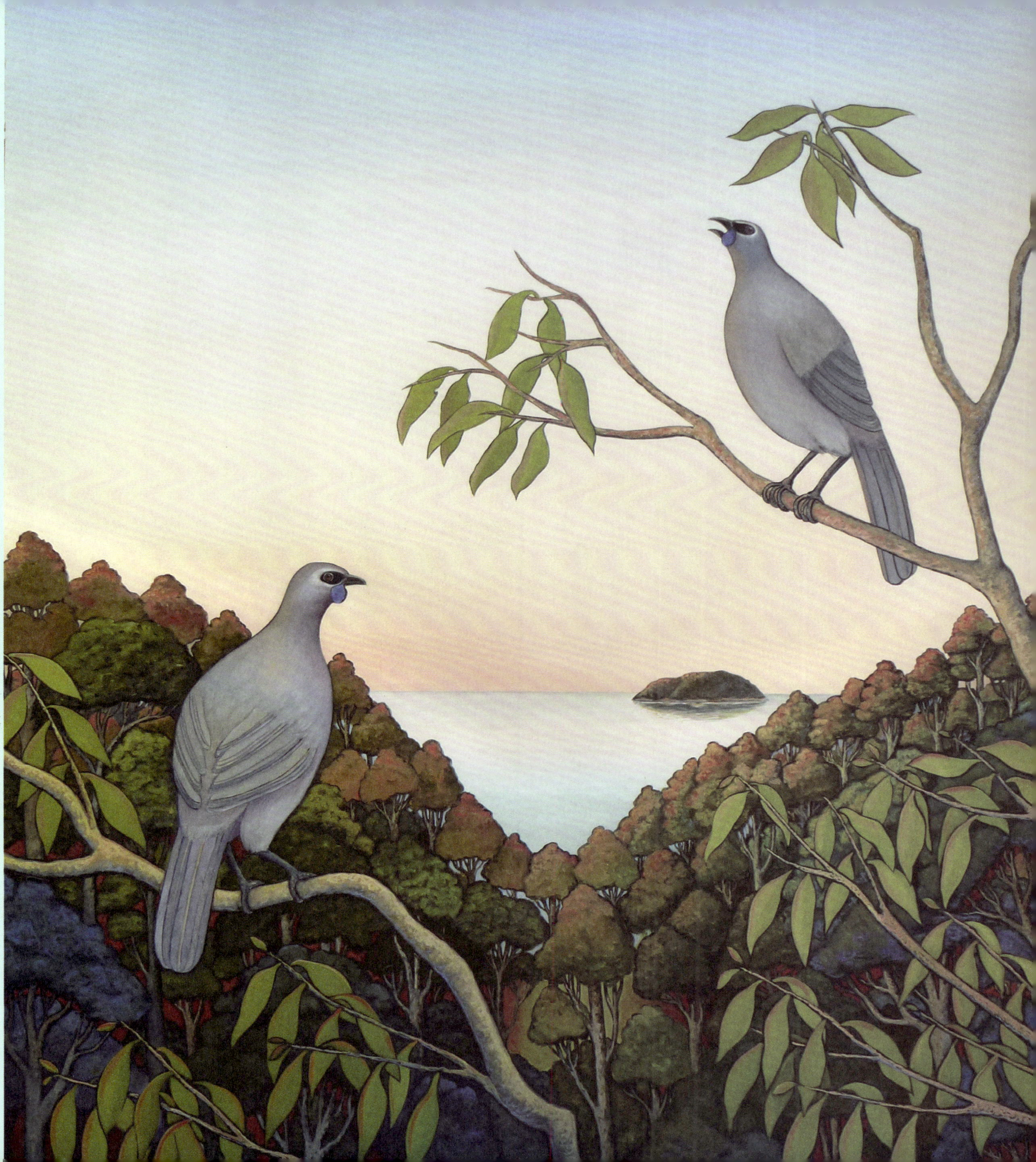

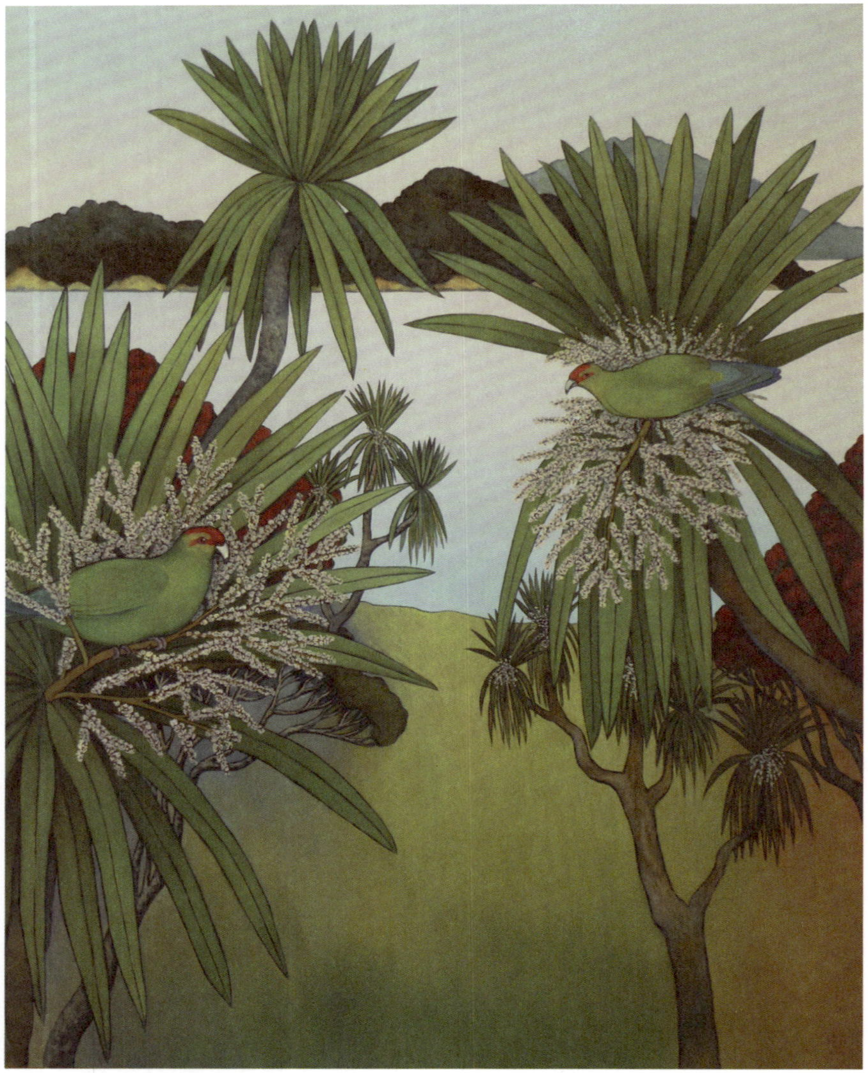

Kākāriki Are Calling 2014
1000 x 800 mm/39¼ x 31½ in

Opposite
Saddlebacks Sacred Clearing 2014
800 x 1220 mm/31½ x 48 in

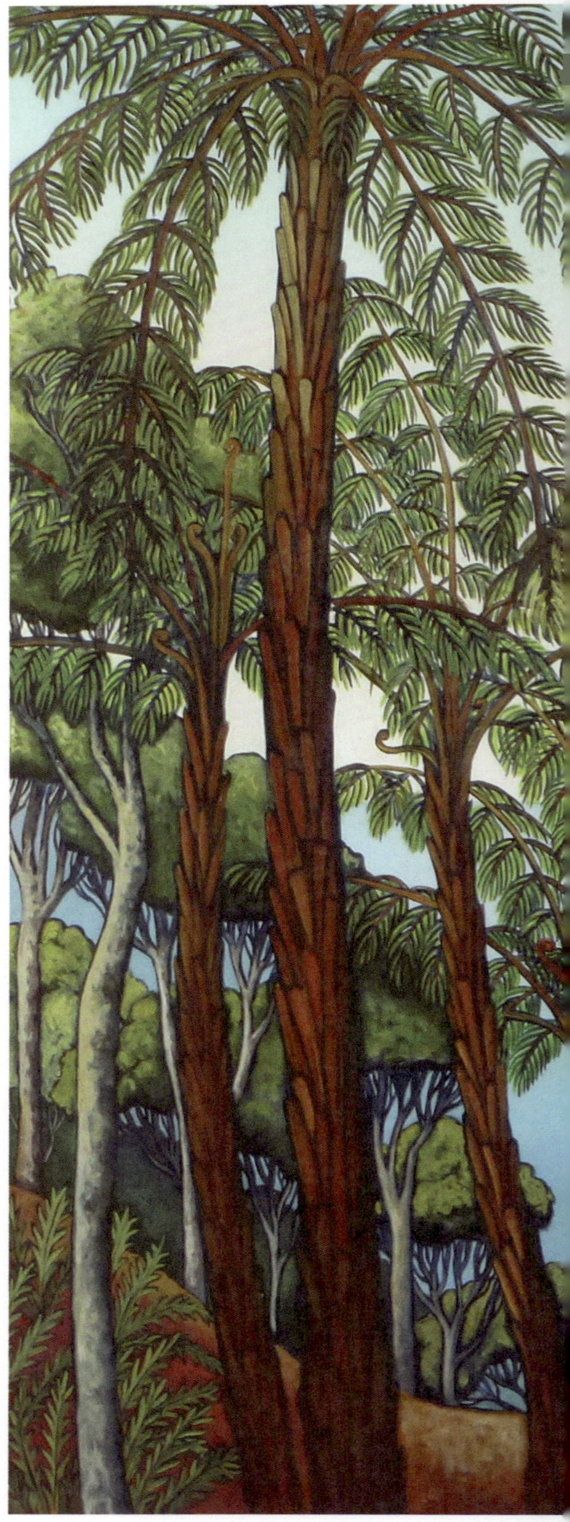

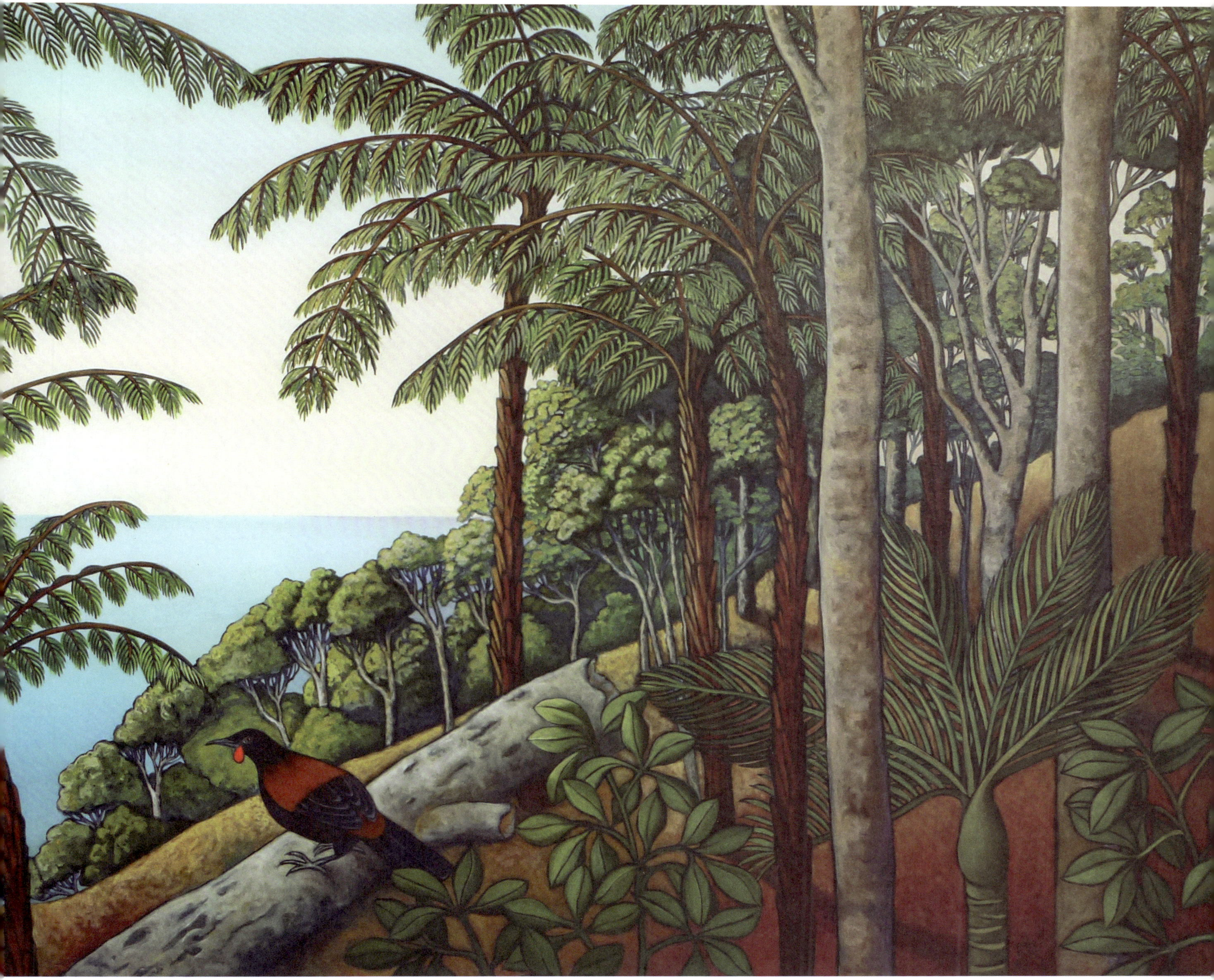

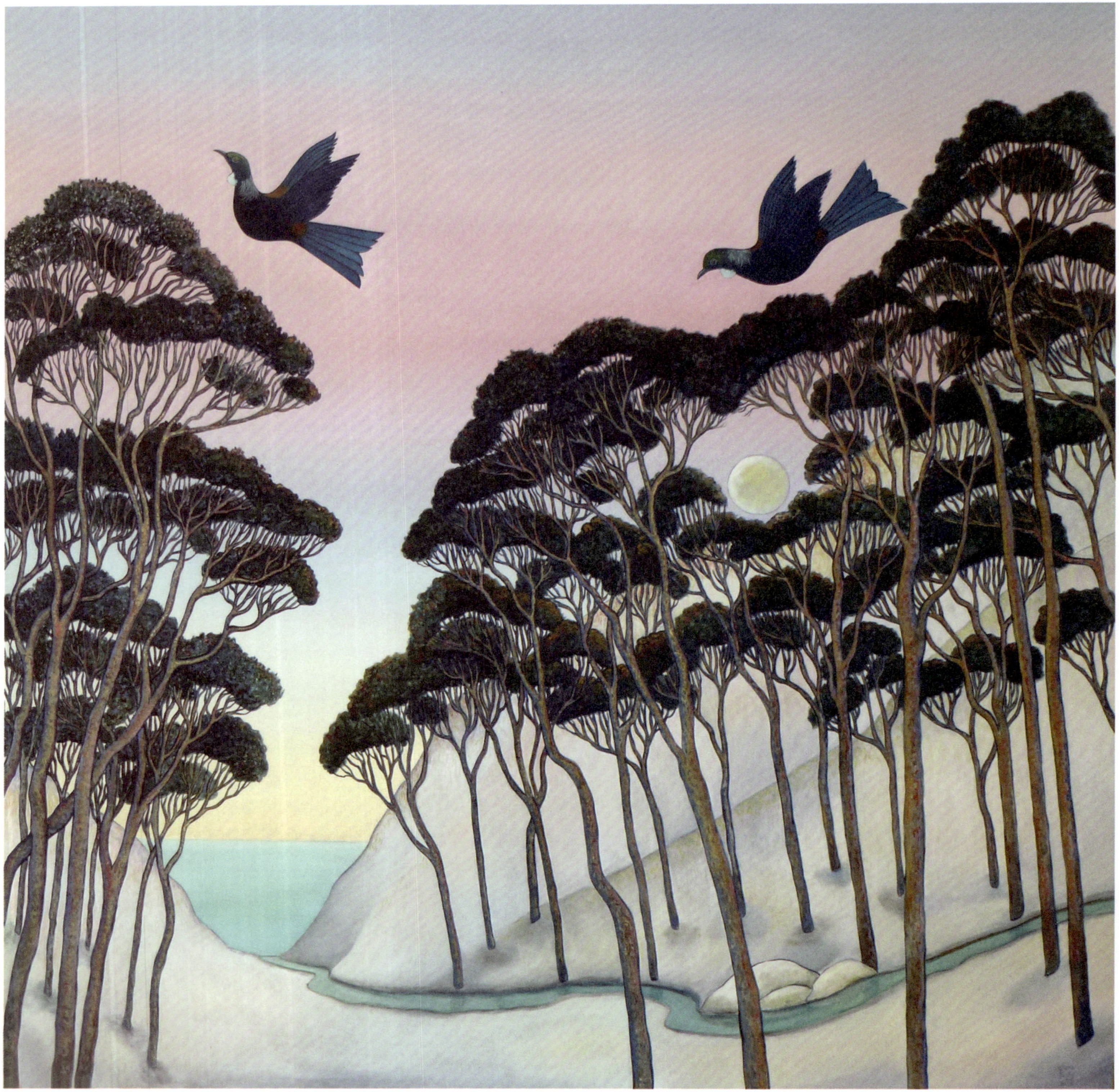

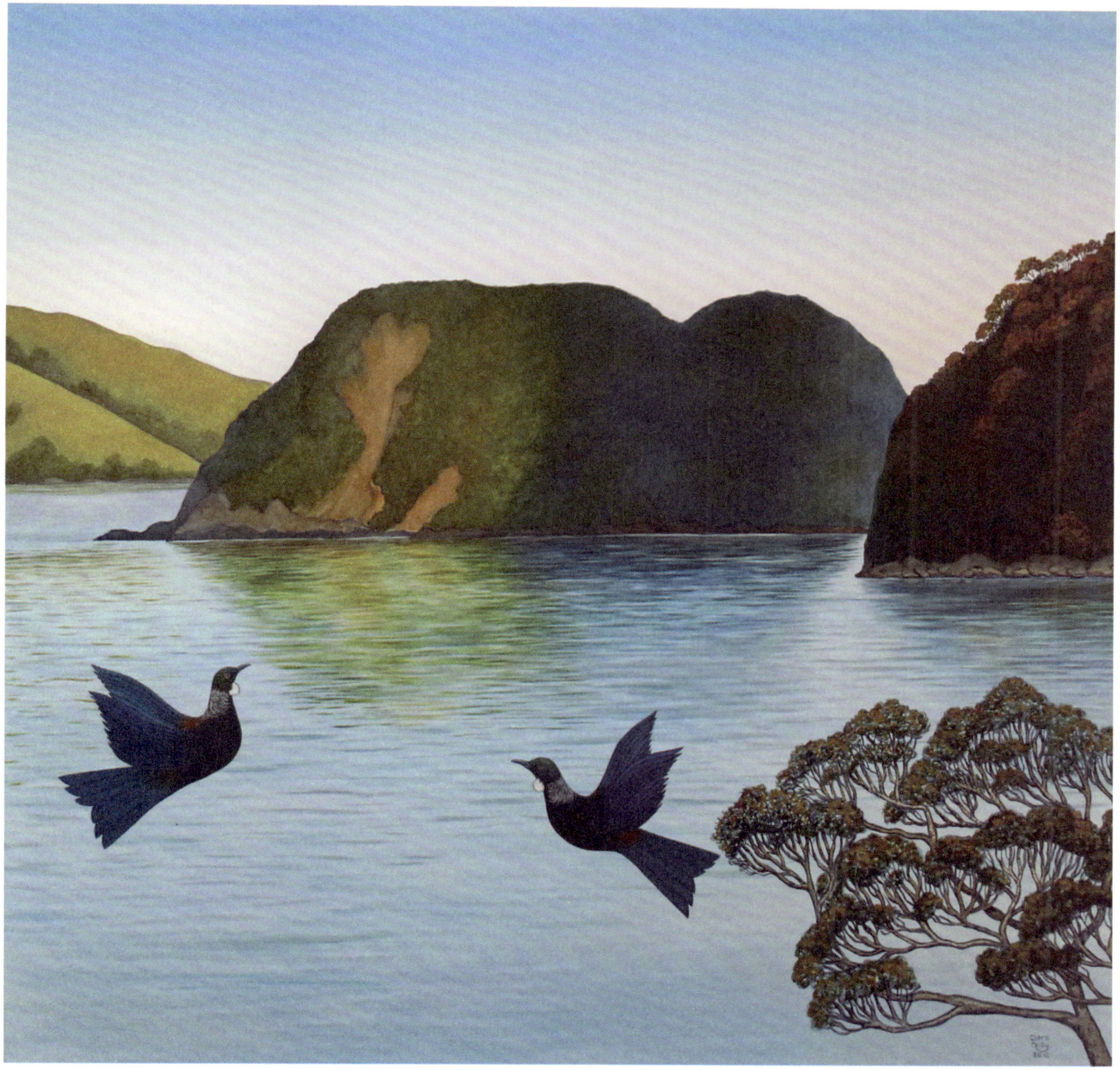

Dancing Round the Island of Life 2017
1000 x 1000 mm/39¼ x 39¼ in

Opposite
The Winter Solstice 2015
1000 x 1000 mm/39¼ x 39¼ in

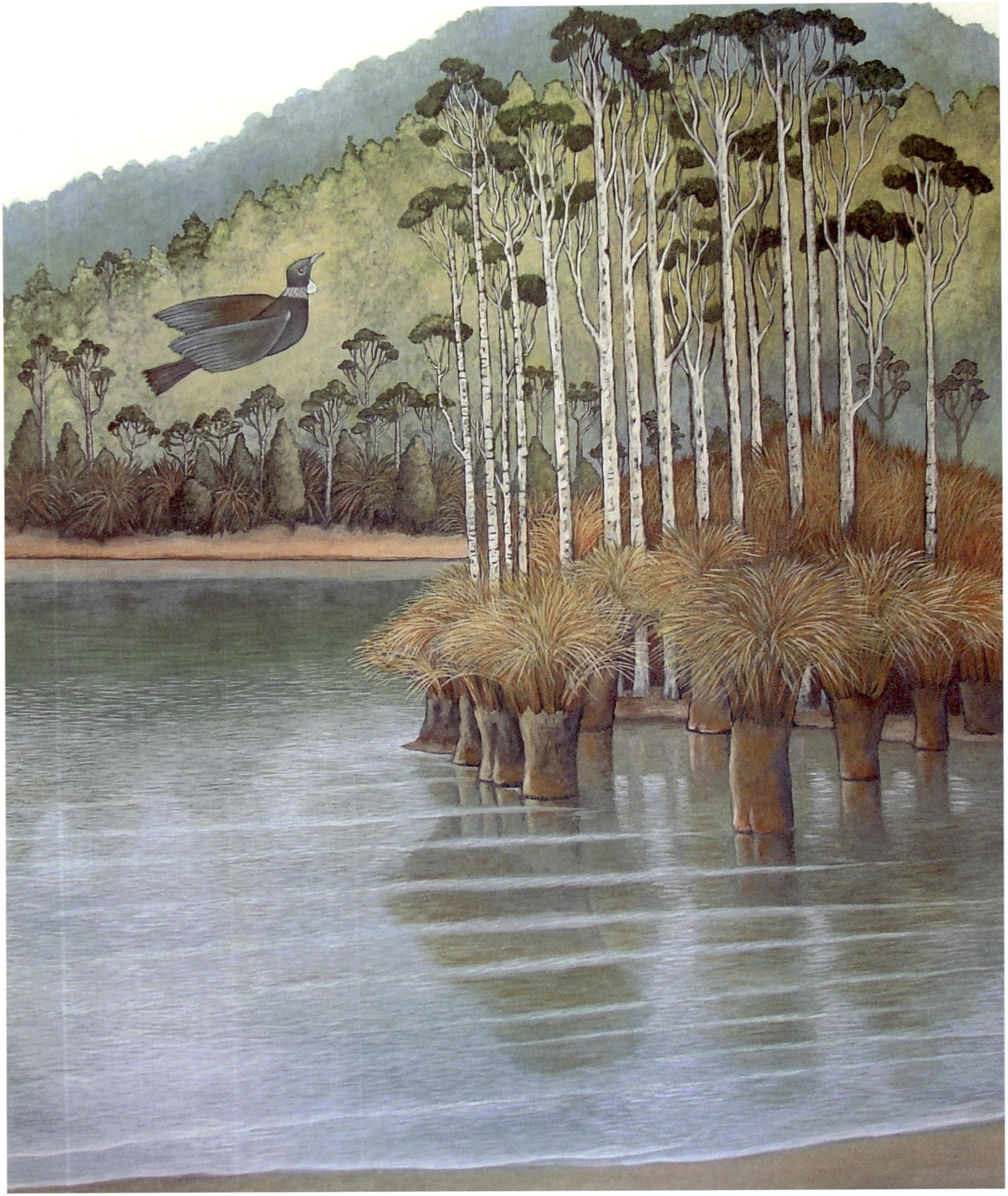

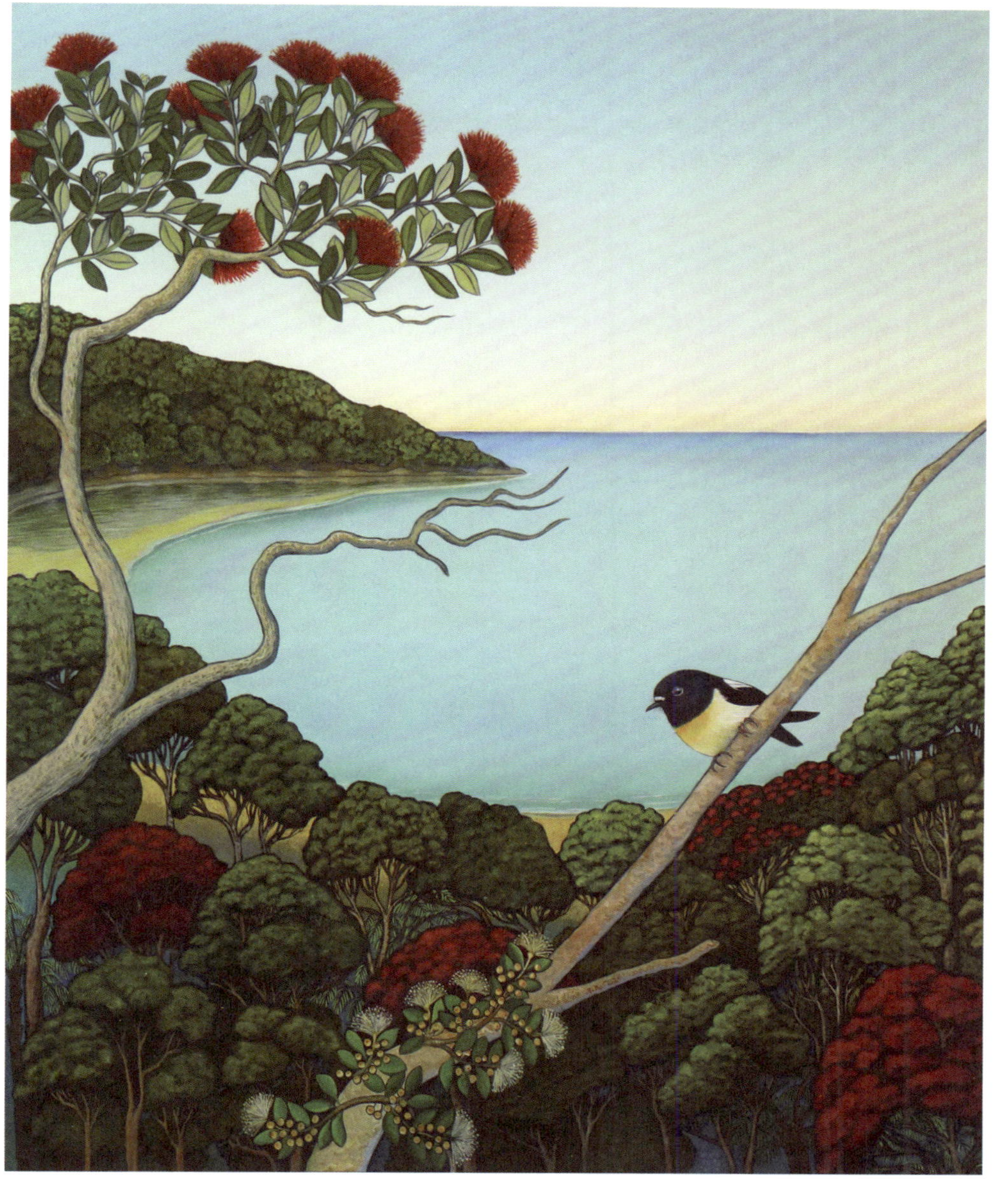

MiroMiro Sings of White Rata 2014
1000 x 840 mm/39¼ x 33 in

Opposite
Tiny Islands II 2008
1000 x 800 mm/39¼ x 31½ in

Death of My Muse

Somehow, I had managed to paint in the margins of the days during the ten prior months of Max's illness. He found sleeping at night very difficult and was constantly up throughout the night, so I got very little sleep, but during the day there were periods where he slept for several hours and I would take refuge in my studio and paint. The solace of doing something normal was grounding.

I managed to pull together a collection of works for my Little River Show titled *The Dance of Life* in late September 2017, just two months after Max's death. There was a sense of unreality that I could still function on this level in amongst such huge changes in my life, but once that show had opened I needed time and space to grieve and try to find my way forward in a new life, in a new house, and a new community. The paintings that then flowed out of me, explored the sense of departure of a soul, not to some dark place, but into the sublime. A journey into the wide blue yonder.

As soon as Max's vibrant paintings went up on the walls of the new house, I felt energised; that even though my muse had departed, he had left me a legacy of his work to inspire and accompany me. I started teaching Nia Dance in my local community, and I found an inner strength again, with my later works continuing to express the joyful vitality of nature. Now I am filled with a sense of resilience and renewal.

Til Death Do Us Part

Oh, my darling,
Here you lie, cooling
In the gritty light of dawn

Your beautiful golden skin
Is waxing and waning in
The flickering candlelight

Your utter stillness and silence
In this small room is
An absence so profound
and unmistakable

I am torn asunder
Shredded like a paper doll
Teetering and tumbling
On the precipice of
Grief and longing

Just as well I had
No real idea just
How hard life is
Without you.

Opposite
Into the Sublime 2017
1000 x 800 mm/39¼ x 31½ in

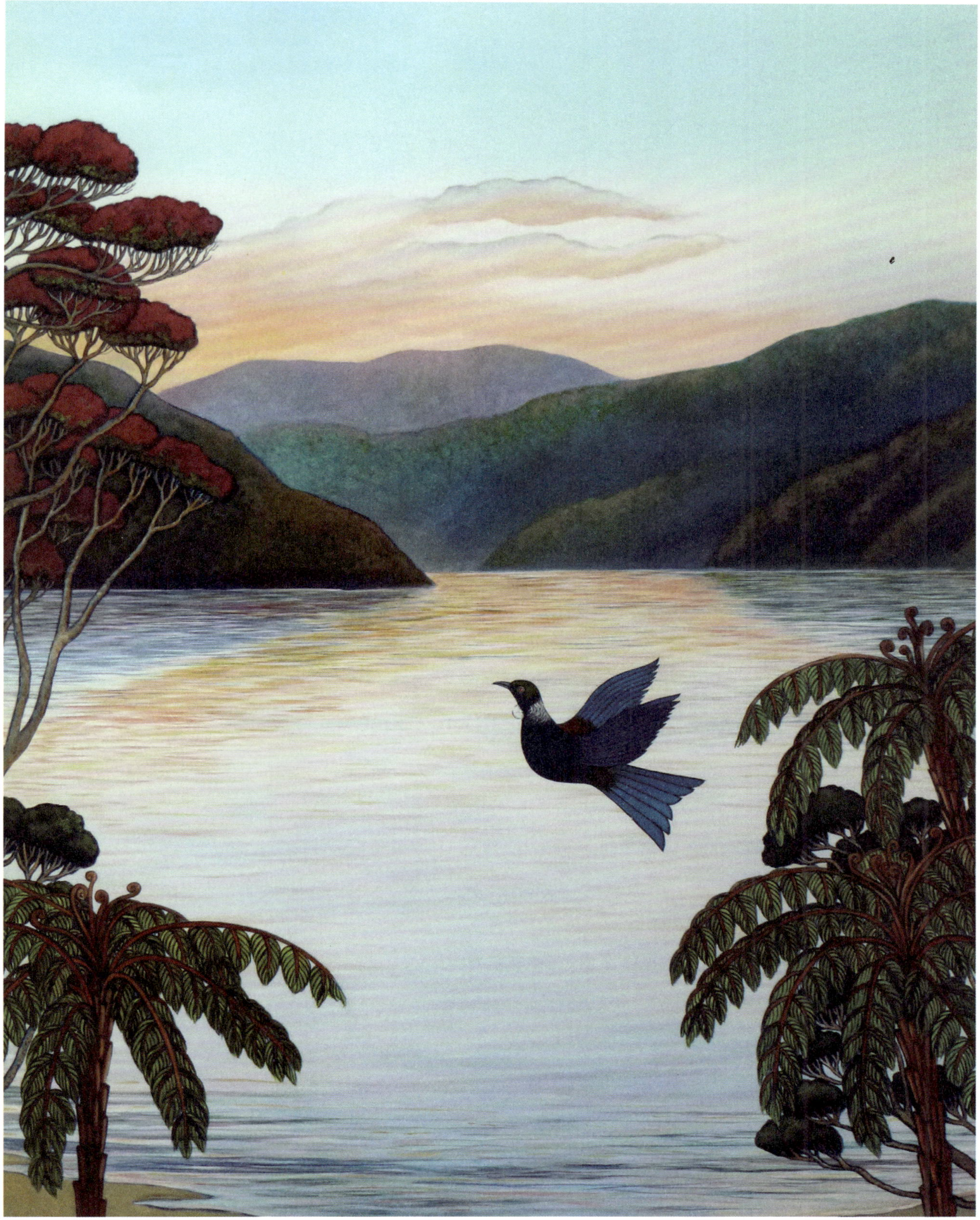

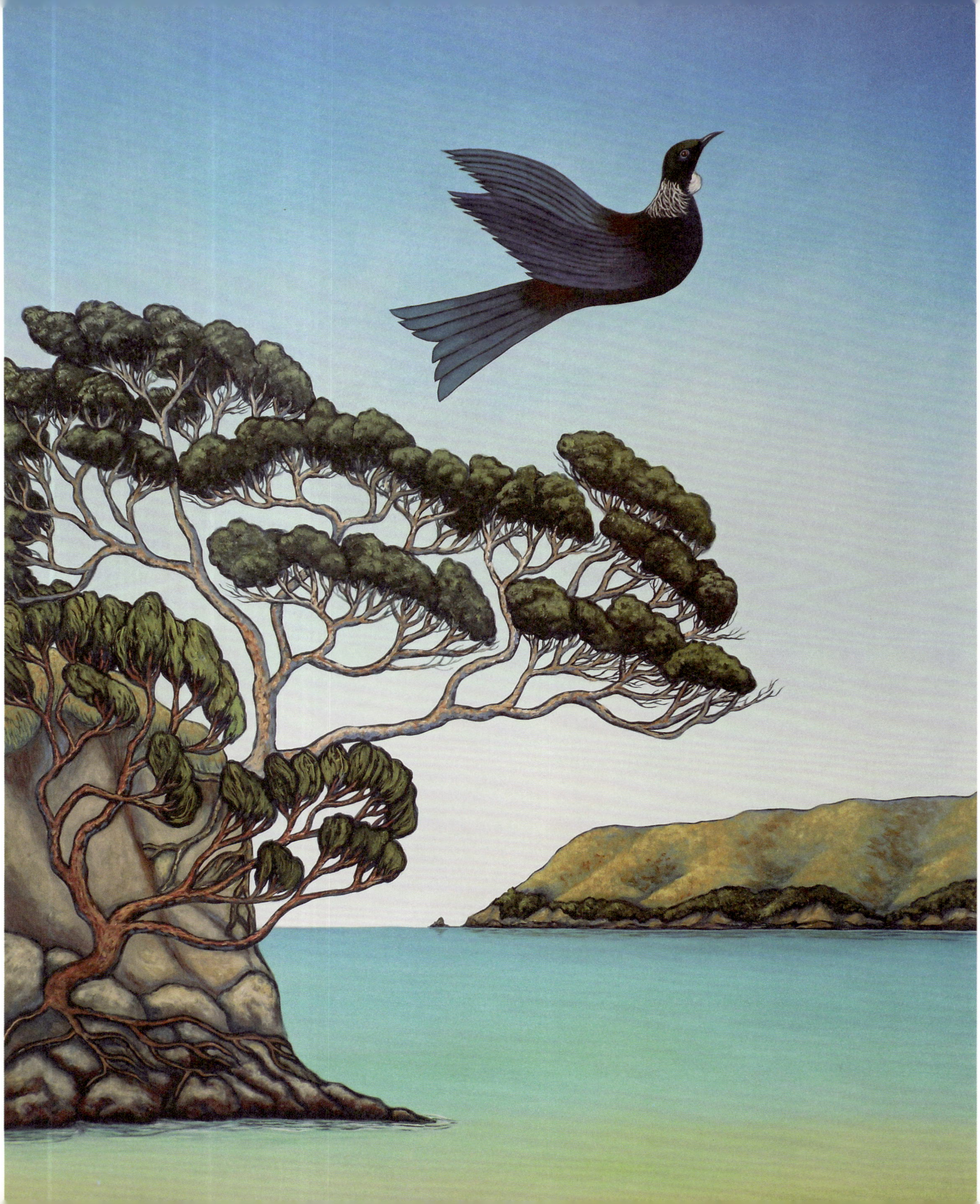

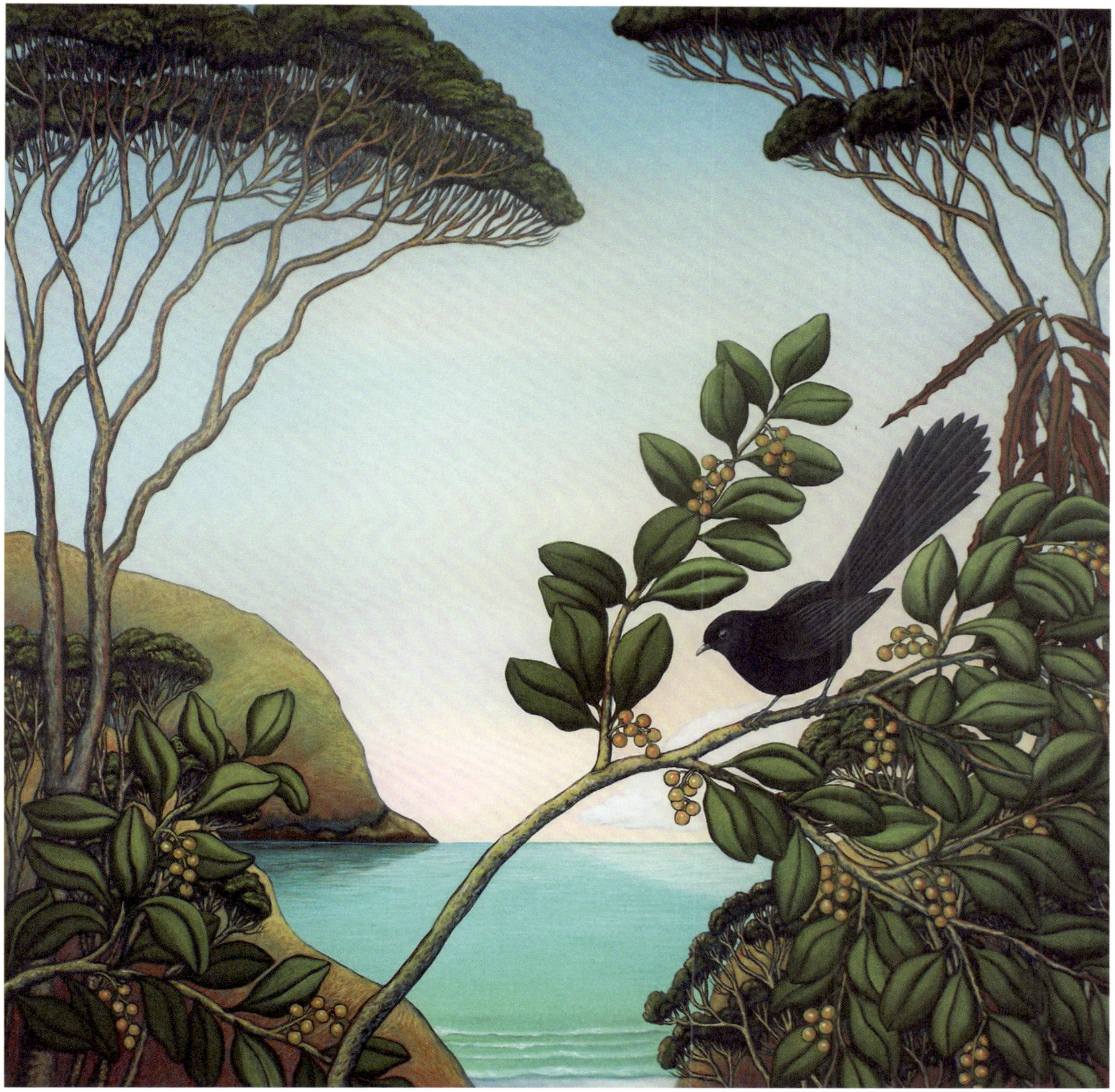

The Constant Companion 2017
1000 x 1000 mm/39¼ x 39¼ in

Opposite
Into the Wide Blue Yonder 2017
800 x 600 mm/31½ x 23½ in

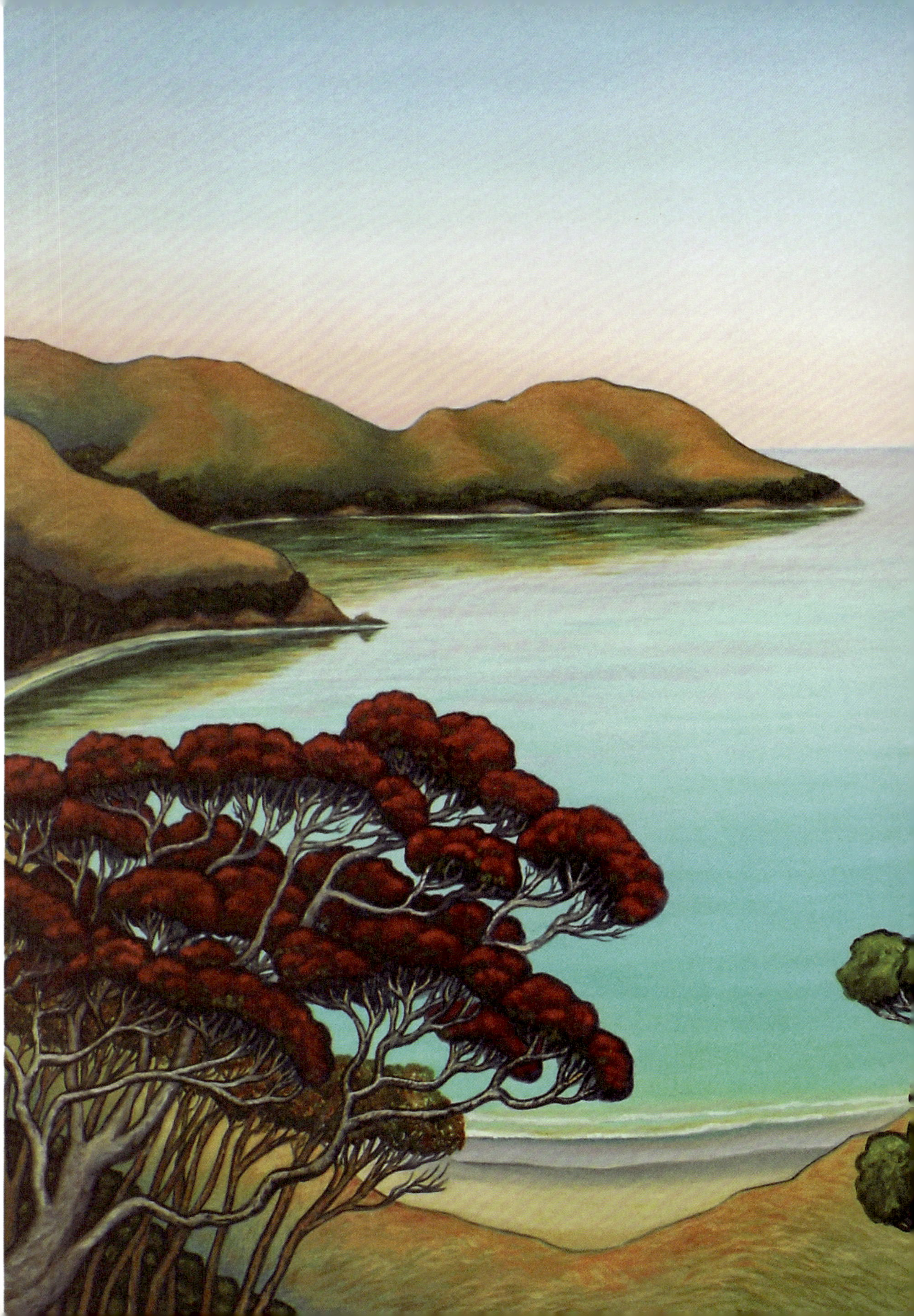

Dance of Ascension 2017
1220 x 800 mm/48 x 31½ in

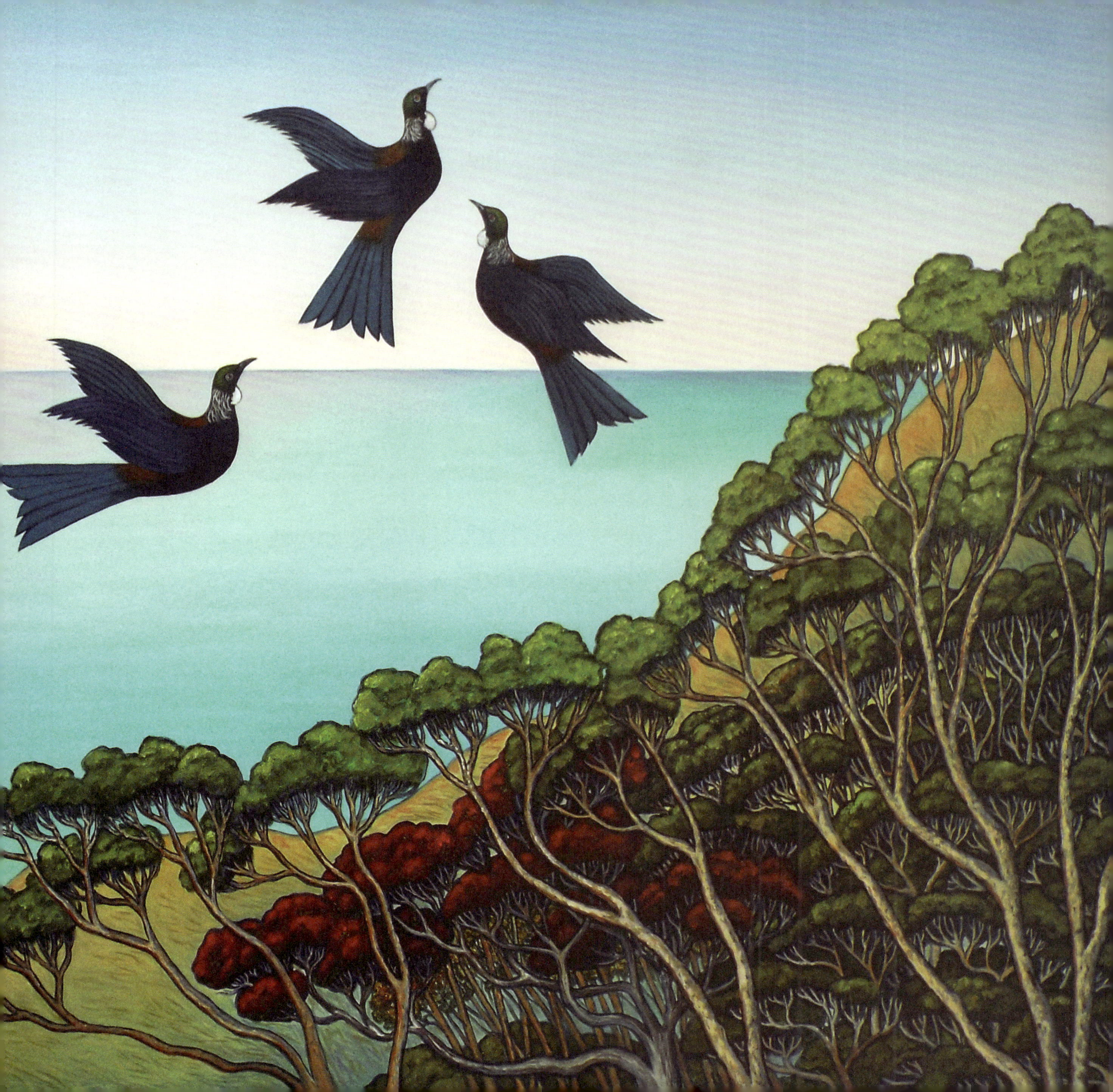

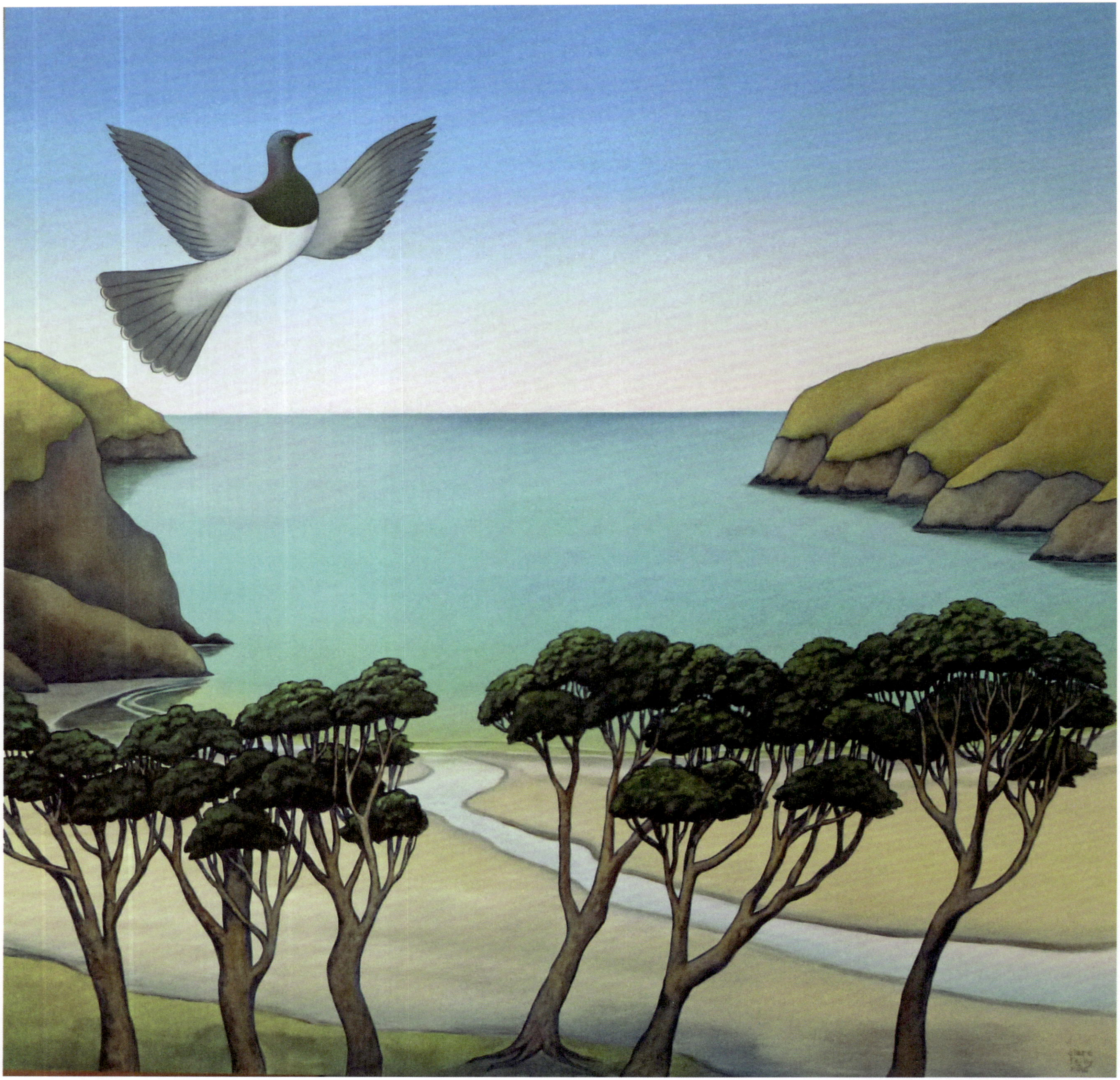

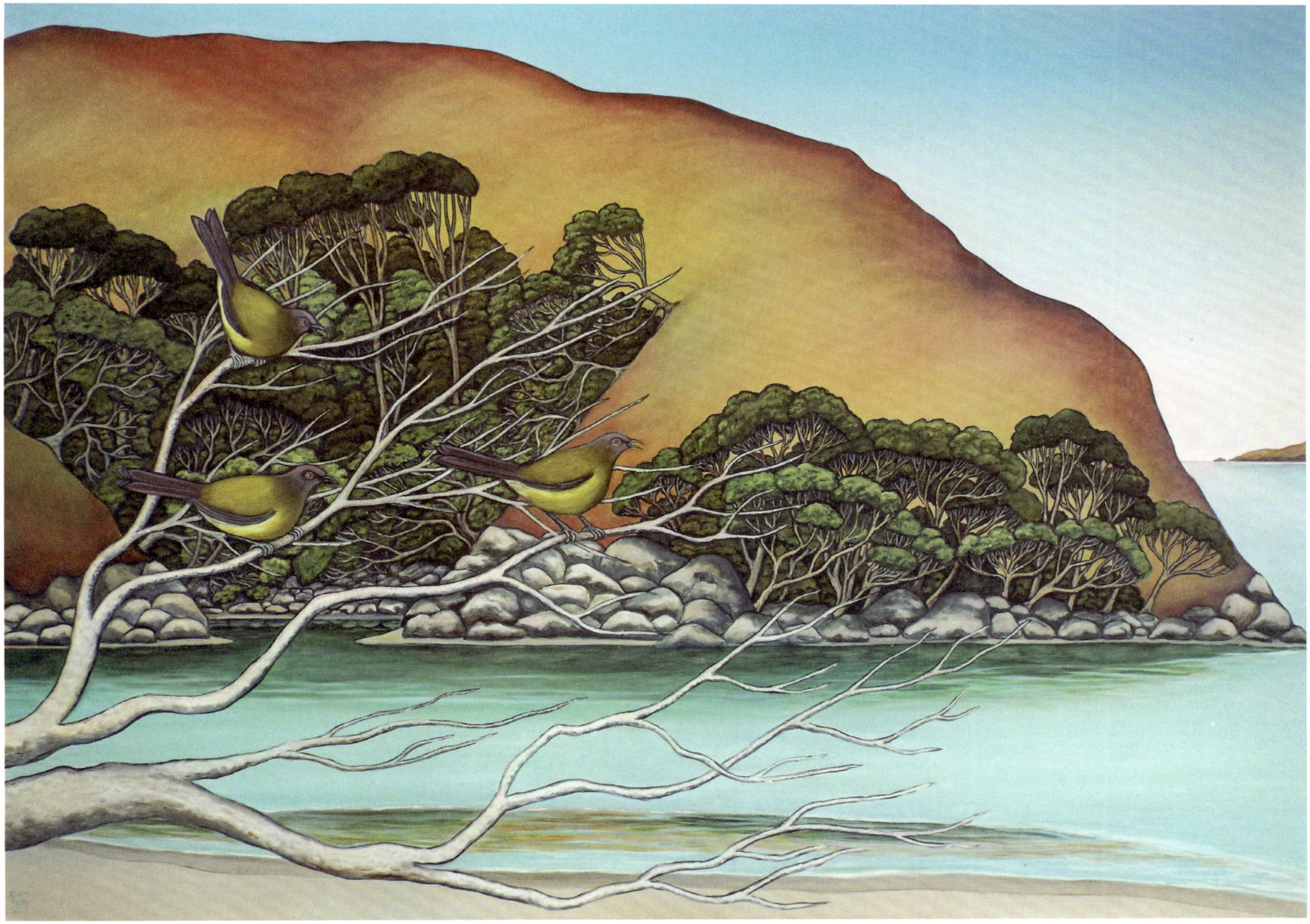

Calling You Home 2017
1270 x 890 mm/50 x 35 in

Opposite
Joie de Vivre 2019
1000 x 1000 mm/39¼ x 39¼ in

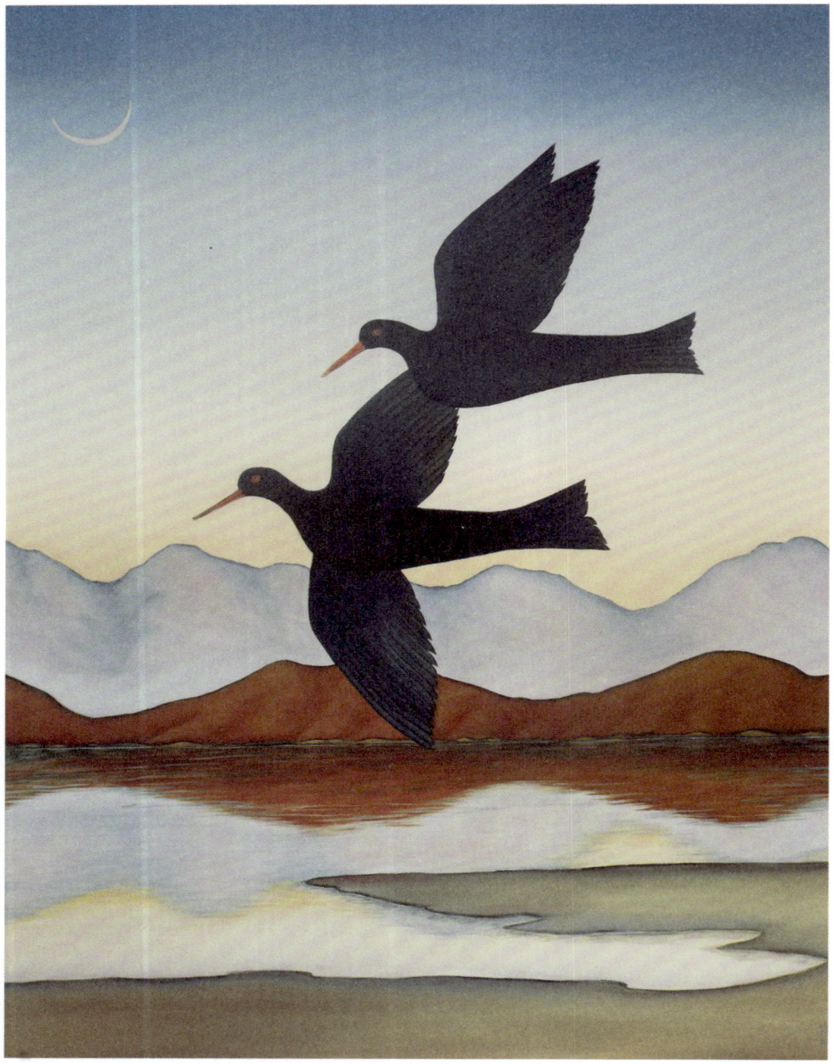

Pas de Deux 2018
1000 x 840 mm/39¼ x 33 in

Anchor Me 2017
1270 x 790 mm/50 x 31 in

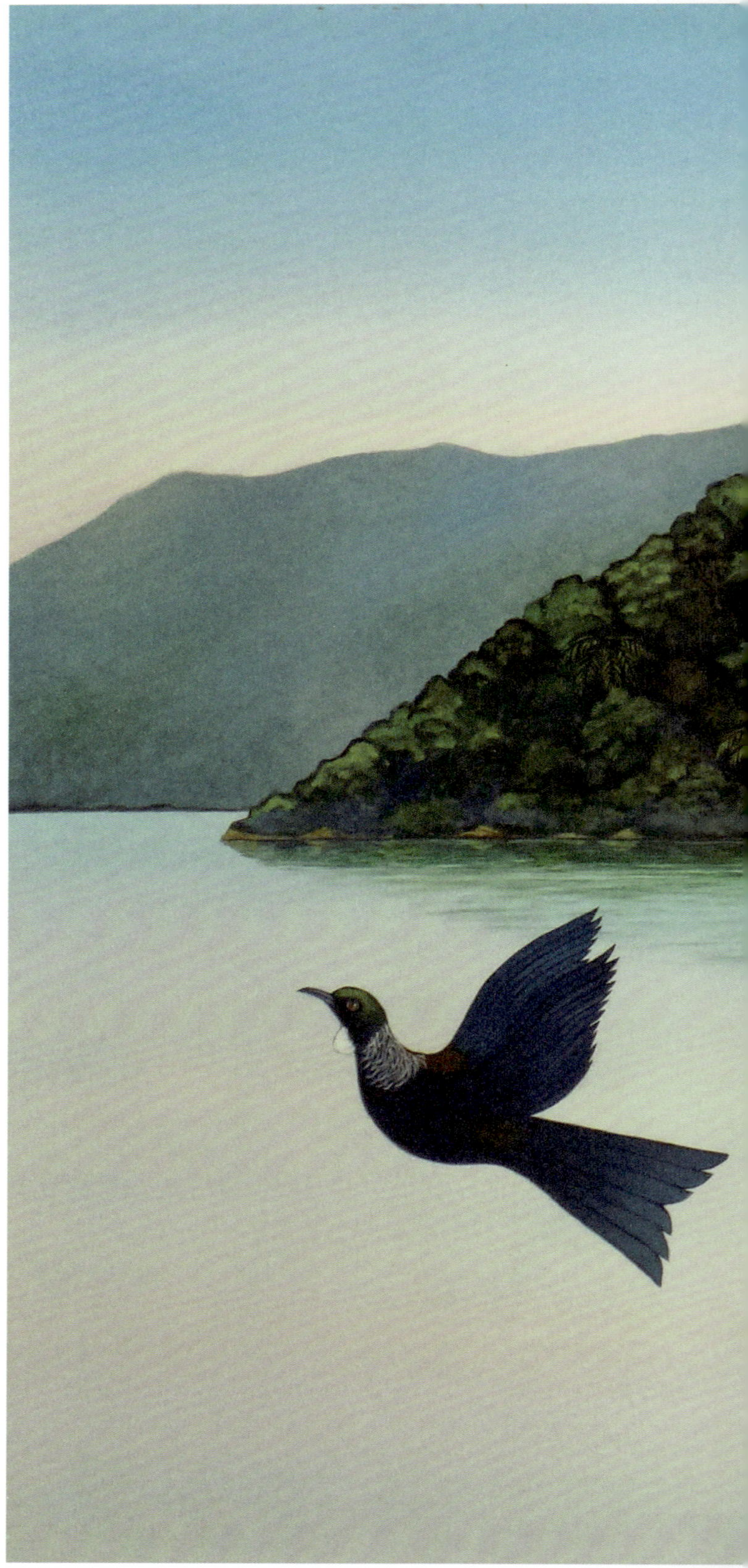

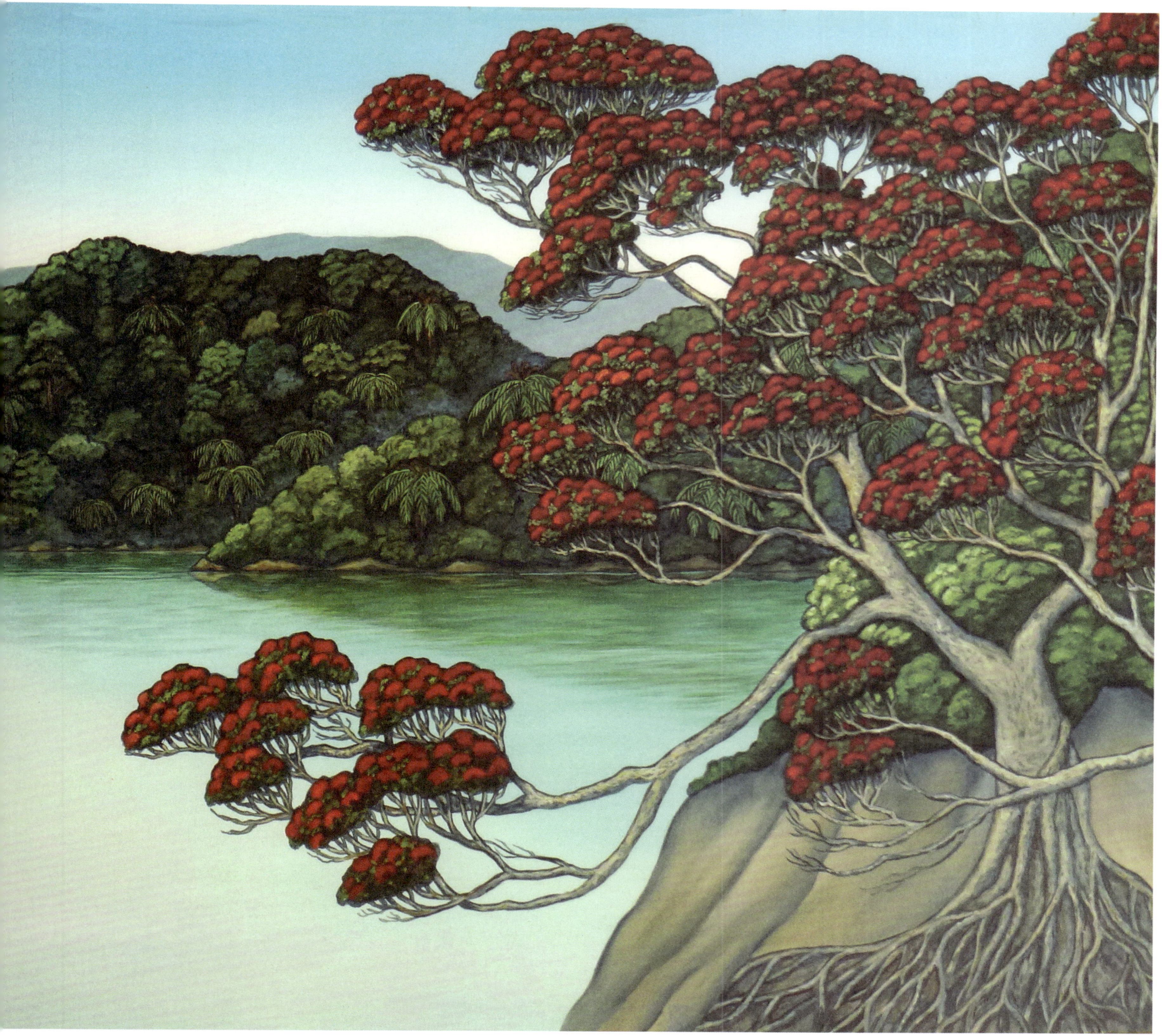

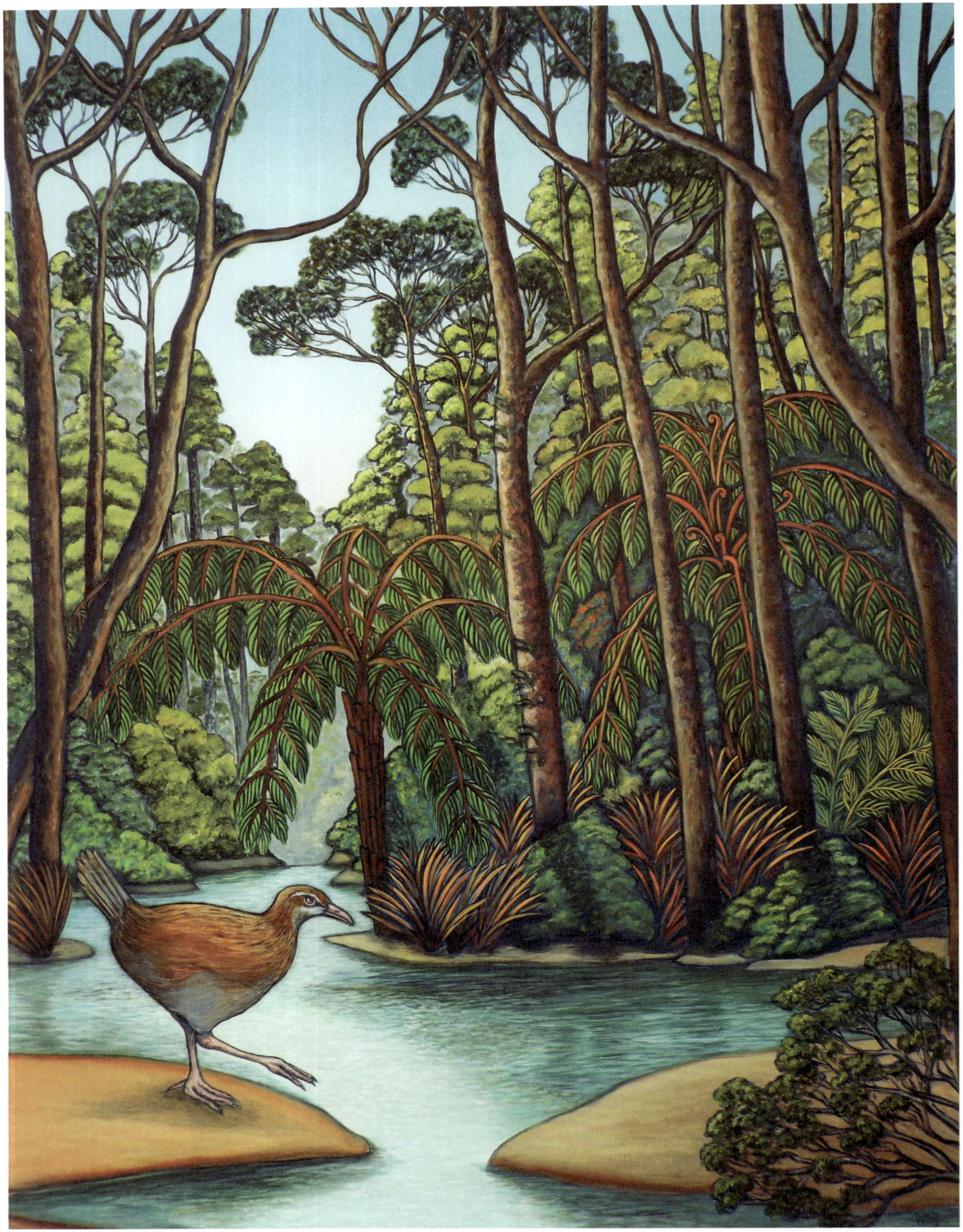

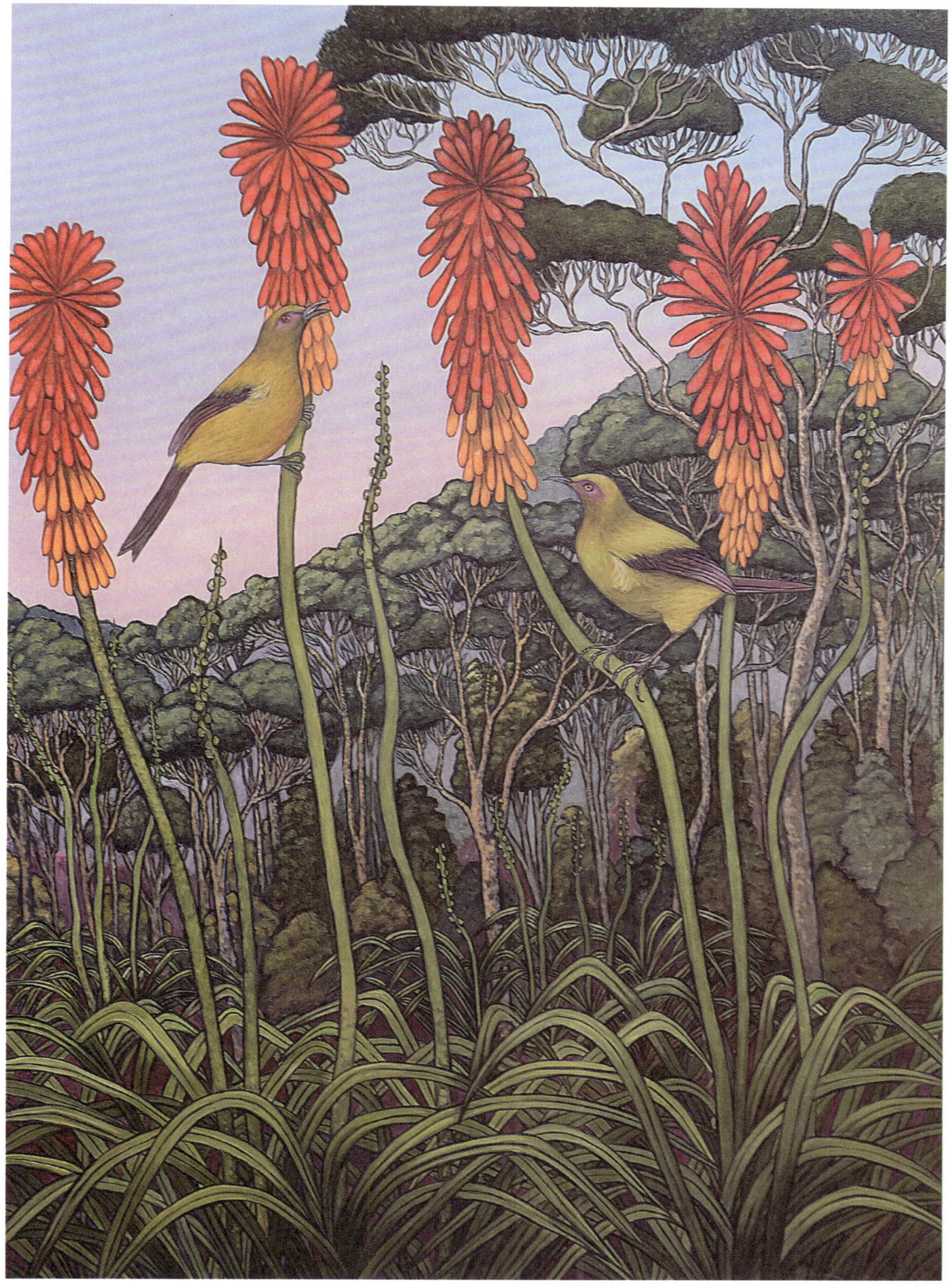

Sing Me The Path Forward 2019
800 x 600 mm/31½ x 23½ in

Opposite
Stepping on Out 2017
800 x 600 mm/31½ x 23½ in

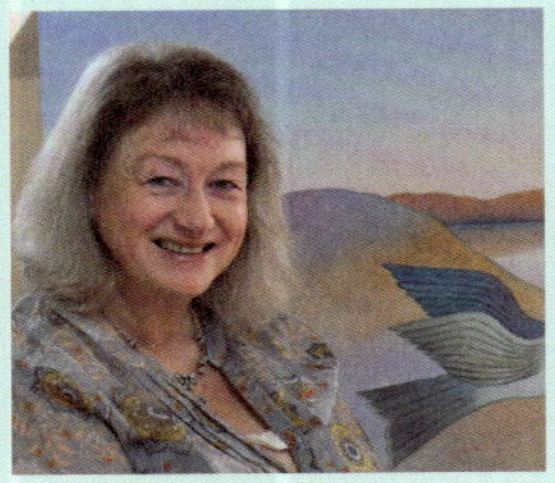

Exhibitions History

2021

Ode to Fiordland, solo show, Little River Gallery, Banks Peninsula, 30 October–23 November

2020

Wider Horizons, solo show, Kereru Gallery, Mapua, 29 February–30 March

Inner Lands, solo show, Little River Gallery, Banks Peninsula, 26 September–28 October

2019

Going Native, group show, Orion Powerhouse Gallery, Akaroa, 26 January–17 February

Journeys of the Heart, solo show, Little River Gallery, Banks Peninsula, 19 October–19 November

2017

Dance of Life, solo show, Little River Gallery, Banks Peninsula, 28 September–25 October

2016

Hinewai, group show, Orion Powerhouse Gallery, Akaroa, 16–31 January

Birds of a Feather, group show, Kereru Gallery, Mapua, 11 March–6 April

Coast, solo show, Little River Gallery, Banks Peninsula, 1–28 October

2015

Nest, group show, Kereru Gallery, Mapua, February

Earthsong, solo show, Little River Gallery, 3–28 October

Summer Collection, group show, Monterey Gallery, Howick , 7–19 December

2014

Group show, Orion Powerhouse Gallery, Akaroa, April

Bird Call, group show, Bryce Gallery, Christchurch, July

Water Song Cycle, solo show, Little River Gallery, Banks Peninsula, 4–29 October

Some Enchanted Island, solo show, Monterey Gallery, Howick 4–20 December

2013

Over This Singing Land, Little River Gallery, Banks Peninsula, October

2012

Guardians of the Song, Monterey Art Gallery, Howick, November

The Bringer of Gifts, Little River Gallery, Banks Peninsula, September

Group exhibition, Orion Powerhouse Gallery (temporary), 5–24 May

Seeking Sanctuary, Gallery on Blueskin, Waitati, Dunedin, February–March

2011

Sanctuary, group exhibition, Reflection Gallery, Nelson, December 2011–March

Out of the Blue, Monterey Art Gallery, Howick, November

Dancing Island to Island, Orion Powerhouse Gallery, Akaroa, December 2010–January

2010

Dancing Island to Island, Monterey Gallery, Auckland, November

Old and New Dreams, Tamarillo Gallery, Wellington, October–November

Return of the Tūī — a celebration, Gallery O, The Arts Centre, Christchurch, January–February

2009

Eye of the Calm, Monterey Art Gallery, Auckland, November

Flight into Spring, Catchment Gallery, September–October

Our Land, Our People, group exhibition, Taupo Museum, Taupo, May–June

Flora and Fauna, group exhibition, Catchment Gallery, Nelson, May

Eye of the Calm, solo exhibition, Orion Powerhouse Gallery, Akaroa, December 2008–January

2008
Terrain, group exhibition, Catchment Gallery, Nelson, May

Landscope, group exhibition, Palette Gallery, Auckland, March

Rima — Five, group exhibition celebrating Catchment Gallery's fifth year, Nelson, February–March

2007
Solo exhibition, Orion Powerhouse Gallery, Akaroa, December 2006–January

2006
The Primitive Bird Group, joint exhibition with Max Podstolski, Catchment Gallery, Nelson, September

2005
Songs and Silence, Selwyn Gallery, Darfield, October–November

Ornithology, Primitive Bird Group exhibition with Max Podstolski, Salamander Gallery, Christchurch, March–April

Birds from the Outside and Inside, Primitive Bird Group exhibition with Max Podstolski, Orion Powerhouse Gallery, Akaroa, December 2004–January

2004
Reilly, Podstolski, Ball, with Derek Ball, Catchment Gallery, Nelson, October

West to East, Primitive Bird Group exhibition with Max Podstolski, Aigantighe Art Gallery, Timaru, May

Aotearoa Flora & Fauna, group exhibition, Catchment Gallery, Nelson, February–March

Tahi: the First Exhibition, group show, Catchment Gallery, Nelson, January–February

West to East, Gallery Lavaud, Akaroa, December 2003–January

2003
Tūīs at Te Kinga, Primitive Bird Group exhibition with Max Podstolski, Left Bank Art Gallery, Greymouth, October–November

Enchanted Wilderness, Primitive Bird Group exhibition with Max Podstolski, Salamander Gallery, Christchurch, May

Scratching the Surface, Primitive Bird Group exhibition with Max Podstolski, Akaroa Gallery, Akaroa, December 2002–January

2002
Austral Paintings, Primitive Bird Group exhibition with Max Podstolski, Left Bank Art Gallery, Greymouth, April

2001
Te Omanga Hospice Art Auction, group exhibition, Government House, Wellington, September

1996
Te Omanga Hospice Art Auction, group exhibition, Government House, Wellington, October

1993
Joint exhibition with Max Podstolski, Merilyn Savill Gallery, Wellington, August–September

Solo exhibition, Picturesque Gallery, Akaroa

1992
Joint exhibition with Max Podstolski, Merilyn Savill Gallery, Wellington

1991
Solo exhibition, CSA Gallery, Christchurch, September

1990
Solo exhibition, The Villas Gallery, Kelburn, Wellington, October

BP Now and Tomorrow, NZ Academy of Fine Arts, Wellington

National Bank Contemporary Painting '90, NZ Academy of Fine Arts, Wellington

Solo exhibition, CSA Gallery, Christchurch, March

1989
Caltex Art Award, NZ Academy of Fine Arts, Wellington

National Bank Contemporary Painting '89, NZ Academy of Fine Arts, Wellington

IBM Urban Images, NZ Academy of Fine Arts, Wellington

New Zealand Modern Primitives, CSA Gallery, Christchurch

BP On the Move, NZ Academy of Fine Arts, Wellington

1986
Private View, joint exhibition with Max Podstolski, 357 Gloucester Street, Christchurch

1981
Three Christchurch Artists and a Wellington Poet, group exhibition with Max Podstolski, Julie Podstolski and Jeannie Beauchamp, Antipodes Gallery, Wellington

Solo exhibition, CSA Gallery, Christchurch

1980
Solo exhibition, Antipodes Gallery, Wellington

Solo exhibition, CSA Gallery, Christchurch, January

1979
Joint exhibition with Max Podstolski, Antipodes Gallery, Wellington

1978
Joint exhibition with Max Podstolski, Antipodes Gallery, Wellington

1976
Seven Young Wellington Artists, including Max Podstolski, Stuart Porter, Peter Baker, Prue Donald, Peter Bennett, Antipodes Gallery, Wellington

Index of Artworks

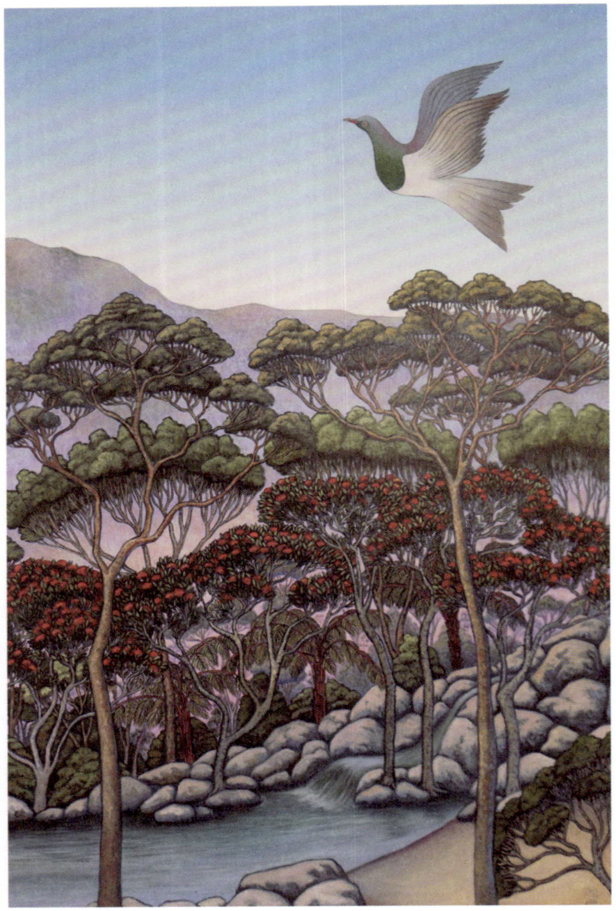

Uplift My Singing Heart 2019
1220 x 800 mm/48 x 31½ in

Journeys of the Heart

Uplift my singing heart,
as once it was torn asunder.
The wound, now papered over,
is not forgotten, but pulsing with
a tenderness for a further chance of life.
With every beat it grows
a little stronger,
a little lighter.

The cycle of returning
to old places,
empty now without you,
gives me a knowing that
each movement forward, when
facing the storm of solitude,
is a healing.

The call of the light
reveals an illuminating path.
Not merely to survive but truly thrive.
Now dance me into a fresh dawn
of hope and possibilities on
these Journeys of the Heart.
I'm over the moon to be alive.